JEWS AND CHRISTIANS

JEWS AND CHRISTIANS

People of God

Edited by

Carl E. Braaten *&* Robert W. Jenson

WILLIAM B. EERDMANS PUBLISHING COMPANY
GRAND RAPIDS, MICHIGAN / CAMBRIDGE, U.K.

Wm. B. Eerdmans Publishing Co.
255 Jefferson Ave. S.E., Grand Rapids, Michigan 49503 /
P.O. Box 163, Cambridge CB3 9PU U.K.

Printed in the United States of America

08 07 06 05 04 03   7 6 5 4 3 2 1

Library of Congress Cataloging-in-Publication Data

Jew and Christians: people of God / edited by
Carl E. Braaten & Robert W. Jenson.
p.   cm.
"Most chapters of this book originated as addresses presented at a
conference on 'Jews and Christians: People of God,' held at Augsburg College,
Minneapolis, Minnesota, June 10-12, 2001" — Introd.
Includes bibliographical references and index.
ISBN 0-8028-0507-8
1. Christianity and other religions — Judaism — 1945 — Congresses.
2. Judaism — Relations — Christianity — 1945 — Congresses.
3. Judaism (Christian theology) — Congresses.
I. Braaten, Carl E., 1929- II. Jenson, Robert W.
BM535.J494   2003
261.2'6 — dc21

2003049060

www.eerdmans.com

Contents

CONTENTS

Introduction

CARL E. BRAATEN AND ROBERT W. JENSON

Theologians and scholars of both Judaism and Christianity are today radically rethinking the relation between their two covenant communities. While Christians and Jews have always been aware of the connection established by their shared and disputed claim to continue the history of Israel and by their shared Scripture of the Tanakh or Old Testament, that awareness has until recently not given rise to a coherent Jewish theology of Christianity or a Christian theology of Judaism. This volume presents the work of Christian and Jewish thinkers who have engaged in extensive conversation and take each other's work seriously, precisely as theology.

Current discussions between Jews and Christians are conditioned by two decisive events of the twentieth century: the Holocaust and the founding of the modern state of Israel. We can scarcely exaggerate their combined impact on contemporary Christian and Jewish minds. Christian thinkers, for their part, have been moved to identify the roots of anti-Judaism and to eradicate its lingering effects within the church.

Founding theologians of modern Protestantism, such as Friedrich Schleiermacher, G. W. F. Hegel, and Adolf von Harnack, regarded Judaism as an obsolete religion. They regarded Jews as fit candidates for absorption into the modern enlightened religion they called "Christianity." Schleiermacher wrote in his *The Christian Faith:* "Christianity does indeed stand in a special historical connection with Judaism, but so far as concerns its historical existence and its aim, its relations to Judaism and

Heathenism are the same."[1] Similarly Harnack wrote: "To repudiate the Old Testament in the second century was an error, which the great church was right to reject; to retain it in the sixteenth century was a fate from which the Reformation was not able to free itself. But to conserve it in the nineteenth century as a canonical source is the result of religious paralysis in the church."[2] And in Hegel's dialectical interpretation of history, Judaism represents a primitive stage in the history of religions, superseded by Christianity as the absolute religion. In such a climate of opinion, contempt for things Jewish could readily flourish.

The Christian scholars represented in this volume all repudiate supersessionist theory, which holds that in the providence of God the church is a "new Israel" in such fashion that there can be no other, thus removing Judaism from God's saving plan. On the basis of rereading Romans 9–11, anti-supersessionists now affirm the abiding force of God's election of Abraham and Sarah's descendants, until the end of time. Then the theological question for Christians is: How do we understand *ourselves* as the "people of God," and what does the answer to this question mean for future relations between Judaism and the church?

Leading Jewish scholars have responded to new Christian theology of Judaism with new Jewish understanding of Christianity. In 2000 they issued two publications: a manifesto and a book. The manifesto, *Dabru Emet: A Jewish Statement on Christians and Christianity*, is printed at the end of this volume, with a symposium of responses. The book is entitled *Christianity in Jewish Terms;*[3] among its editors are two contributors to this volume, David Novak and Peter Ochs. These publications are not merely political but intensely theological, asking how Jews and Christians can together speak about God and their shared and distinctive beliefs, in ways that are faithful to their sacred texts.

Both partners in this conversation have avoided the pitfalls so common in "dialogue," of watering down distinctive beliefs to accommodate their partners. Jewish theologians, for example, are not asking Christian

1. Friedrich Schleiermacher, *The Christian Faith*, trans. H. R. Mackintosh and J. S. Stewart (Edinburgh: T. & T. Clark, 1928), p. 60.

2. From Harnack's famous book on Marcion, here quoted from Helmut Gollwitzer, *An Introduction to Protestant Theology*, trans. David Cairns (Philadelphia: Westminster Press, 1982), p. 126.

3. *Christianity in Jewish Terms*, edited by Tikva Frymer-Kensky, David Novak, Peter Ochs, David Fox Sandmel, and Michael A. Signer (Boulder, CO: Westview Press, 2000).

theologians to compromise their trinitarian interpretation of God or their incarnational belief in Jesus' Messiahship. Readers will indeed find much reflection on these pillars of Christian identity precisely in this volume. They will see that the new theological exchange goes to the roots of that "olive tree" of which both Judaism and Christianity are somehow branches (Rom. 11:17).

Most chapters of this book originated as addresses presented at a conference on "Jews and Christians: People of God," held at Augsburg College, Minneapolis, Minnesota, June 10-12, 2001. The conference was sponsored by the Center for Catholic and Evangelical Theology.

Toward a Christian Theology of Judaism

ROBERT W. JENSON

The subtitle of the conference for which this essay was prepared, "Toward a Christian Theology of Judaism," is perhaps too presumptuous. The conference was organized by an ecumenical *Christian* foundation, and inevitably its conception reflects Christian fears and hopes. The foundation, moreover, is one that greatly cherishes its independence from other structures, which in this case turns out, of course, to include the existing structures of Jewish/Christian conversation. The board of the foundation generally approved a conference on the matter, and the directors created a title and a purpose statement and invited the speakers we thought would have the most to say.

But the planners did not abandon *all* caution. And the combination of just going ahead and doing it, with the remnants of caution, created a certain asymmetry in the program. The planners were convinced that Christianity indeed urgently needs precisely a new theology of Judaism. But as Christians, they did not have quite enough nerve to say flat out that Judaism needs a theology of Christianity; therefore they did not specifically ask anyone to speak under that rubric. On that score, we could only wait to see what would develop.

My assignment is to attempt some bits of a *Christian theology of Judaism*. All three main words of the phrase should be taken very strictly.

In the first place, the following is recommended to the self-understanding of the Christian community. No word of it should be taken as instructing Jews in anything other than Christianity's problems and possibilities — except indeed insofar as Jews may find their own sort of profit from my remarks.

Thus in the following I am doing the Christian theologian's normal thing, proposing theologoumena to the Christian church. But on this occasion I am venturing on questions about which it might well be thought that we need some help, and thus I am laying my proposals before both Jews and Christians for joint discussion.

Second, I am indeed proposing *theology* of Judaism. Whether the sorts of conversation usually called "interreligious dialogue" are at all appropriate between Judaism and Christianity, I much doubt. For Christianity, Judaism cannot be an "other religion," and this is true whether or not Judaism can say anything reciprocal about Christianity. Conversations aimed at increasing mutual understanding or improving relations between the communities, however vital and hopeful precisely in our time, are not in the first instance those to which I hope in this instance to contribute. What I hope to do is to strike up a conversation with Jews and Christians about a topic of Christian thinking, and that topic is the Jews themselves.

Christian theology is the thinking internal to the life of the church. Every vital community lives in part by reflective converse about its "self-understanding," about the special character of its own continuity through time, about what we are likely now to call its "mission." The present essay is offered as a piece of such reflection, where the Christian church is the community in question.

Finally, it is precisely *Judaism* that is my concern, as distinct from what I will call "canonical Israel." In the usage of this essay, "canonical Israel" denotes the national political and cultic entity that was established through Moses and David and endured, in one recognizable form or another, for something like a millennium. *This* Israel came to an end when Rome terminated temple-worship and made the land of promise foreign territory, this time apparently for good.

With other nations or peoples about which such a judgment must be made, one might go on to talk about lasting achievements and inheritances and influences living on today, but that would be the end of it. In the case of Israel, however, there is a remarkable phenomenon: subsequent communities appeared that to the eye of a secular historian little resemble canonical Israel and must seem connected to it at most genetically, but which nevertheless claim to *be* Israel. Canonical Israel came to an end, but is claimed not to be ended, in that its *identity* is claimed by subsequent and outwardly very different historical entities. This is a remarkable claim, of a sort that perhaps can be made only theologically.

It is not clear whether we should include the modern state of Israel among such claimants, though we must acknowledge its great importance for Judaism itself. The claimants with which we are directly concerned are the two represented in the conference: the ethnic-religious community created by the great rabbis in succession of the Pharisees, which to avoid endless descriptive phrases I will simply call Judaism, and the Christian church.

As has often been noted, the religious life of Israel in the time just before the Roman destruction was a sort of capacious denominational system, united by temple-worship, by Torah — but this quite variously interpreted — and by allegiance to the land. When land and temple were gone, two denominations survived that could if need be do without land and temple, and it is vital to remember that both were indeed denominations *within* what is often called late second-temple Judaism.

First, there was and is the Judaism of the sages, which is adaptable to the absence of the temple and to exile from the land, in that it finds the identity of Israel in familial descent from Abraham and Sarah and in Torah-study and obedience, which latter can be done anywhere. Second, the Christian ecclesia, in close parallel, has its identity around one in whom it believes Torah "became flesh and dwelt among us" and who is risen above the limitations of space so that, like the written Torah, he can be found anywhere. Rabbinic Judaism and the church have each added a second volume to canonical Israel's Scriptures, to create a double canon — in the one case, the double Torah, and in the other, the two Testaments. And the synagogue and the church have throughout their histories lived in remarkably paired, if sometimes horrific, lock-step.

Both of these historical consequents to canonical Israel raise the theological claim to *be* Israel. It is of course the compatibility or incompatibility of these claims that agitates us. A Christian theology of Judaism will be at its center an attempt to understand Judaism's claim and in so doing to understand its own better.

That there should be any difficulty in understanding Judaism's claim to be Israel may, of course, seem preposterous to Jews. But for Christian theology it is not merely a difficulty but a torment. Christian faith is the conviction that the God of Israel has raised his servant Jesus

3

from the dead and installed him, if hiddenly and proleptically, as the Messiah of Israel, and that by this prolepsis he has opened the ingathering of the gentiles to Zion. That the vast majority of Abraham and Sarah's descendents have rejected and do reject this claim, and maintain a claim to be faithful Israel without acknowledging Jesus' resurrection, must indeed give the church furiously to think, and has done so since at least the time when Paul wrote his letter to the Romans. From a certain angle of vision, the mere existence of Judaism looks much like a refutation of Christianity — and may indeed be just that.

Only consider Paul in those famous three chapters of his letter to Rome (Rom. 9–11). We see in them a man who is not in control of either his problem or his warrants. What *ought* to have been happening, as Paul is bound to think, is that the Jewish diaspora received his news of resurrection, of the beginning of that great day, with thanksgiving. But that is *not* what is happening. How is Paul to understand this? He cannot shrug it off: his whole mission is to gather gentiles precisely to Israel. Is it then a sign that God has rejected his people, or that God is confirming their rejection of him? He cannot think that either: for to his "kinsmen" belong — and only ponder his list — "the sonship, the glory, the covenants, the giving of the law, the worship and the promises; to them belong the patriarchs, and of their race, according to the flesh, is the Christ" (9:4-5).

To be sure, that "according to the flesh" may be a momentary thought about a way out of the problem, but Paul of all people cannot finally take it, he cannot devalue what is "according to the flesh," not when he proclaims so fleshly an event as a crucifixion as the central saving fact — the Roman troops did not, after all, hang Jesus' spirit. Nor can he possibly think that God's "promises" will not be fulfilled — and it is of course the Israel of his "kinsmen" whose participation in the promises is at issue; if it were simply some invisible Israel he again would have no problem.

Paul takes such refuge as he can find in Isaiah, in the notion of a "remnant" and in the mystery of God's absolute will. But *who* is the remnant? Who is predestined? Are these the same? Is the remnant and/or the predestined only those minority Jews like himself who do accept the gospel? Or the church, plainly soon to be predominantly gentile? Or "all Israel" after all? It has gone like that ever since.

A theology of Judaism has of course been propounded, which we label "supersessionism." It was never dogmatized, but its hold on the church was long considerable. "Supersessionism," in the current semi-technical sense, is not the church's claim to be Israel. It is the theological opinion that the church owns the identity of Israel in such fashion as to exclude any other divinely willed Israel-after-Israel. It is perhaps worth noting that typically Judaism has equivalently denied the legitimacy of the church's claim — so that had Constantine become a God-fearer instead of a catechumen, "supersessionism" might again be a problem, but in mirror-image. Supersessionism is — to say the least of it — not now much in favor, a point to which I shall return.

It will have been noted that my starting point is thus a mere historical *observation:* that rabbinic Judaism and Christianity are parallel claimants to be Israel after canonical Israel. This is obviously an observation from a viewpoint outside both communities — or at least from as far outside as historical observations ever get. It deliberately abstracts from each community's own conception of its continuity with Israel. Each community has practices of continuity with canonical Israel, and interpretations of those practices and so of itself, that display a continuity with Israel not displayed in the life or reflection of the other. From inside either community, therefore, so blunt a paralleling with the other may appear improper.

Thus, for example, rabbinic Judaism defines Jewishness in part by descent from Abraham and Sarah. This is a palpable continuity with canonical Israel that the church obviously lacks — and would lack even if Jews so defined were a majority within her. On the other hand, for instance, the second volume of the church's canon is a narrative, in part of her own history, that simply carries straight on from the end of canonical Israel's Scripture, in a fashion in which rabbinic Judaism has little interest.

My paralleling of the two communities is purely formal, and no one, I think, should be alarmed by it. Whatever balance of continuity and discontinuity each community claims or acknowledges for itself, and whatever balance an omniscient historian might make between them, the observed parallel remains, and I will regularly return to it, as a sort of cleared ground for theological reflection.

There are now few Christian theologians willing to be called supersessionist. There are doubtless several reasons for this.

Guilt is surely one. As most Christians and many Jews have insisted, Nazi anti-Semitism can hardly be laid directly at the door of Christian theology, not even at the door of supersessionism. Nevertheless, there have been centuries of anti-Jewish Christian polemics — that is, of Paul's anguish or John's resentment on the lips of those who unlike Paul or John were not Jews themselves — and these must surely have shaped the culture in which anti-Semitism is possible. Moreover, it is easily documented that anti-Semitism — however itself occasioned or grounded — has sometimes quite directly shaped Christian theology. Thus establishment of "historical-critical" method as *the* way to appropriate the Old Testament was driven in considerable part by (sometimes explicit) desire to distance Christianity from a despised Judaism.

But perhaps more decisive in the church's present attention to Judaism, and so in its sharper eye for the falsity of supersessionism, is a possibly terminal time of troubles in Christian theology's always stormy affair with Hellenic religious wisdom. As Christian theology sees ever more clearly what different wisdom Isaiah and, say, Plato offer, in the same way we see ever more clearly how Jewish the Christian claims and fundamental patterns of understanding are, indeed how very much the predominant gentile part of the church is indeed grafted onto someone else's tree. And just so, Judaism looks less and less alien to us. My gloss, "The Torah became flesh and dwelt among us," may have been surprising, but only a few years ago it would have been incomprehensible.

Christianity needs a theological interpretation of Judaism, and not a supersessionist one. How do we do that? My proposals will not be very systematic, except insofar as there is a step that seems to me the necessary first one. In describing this first step I must repeat contentions earlier published and can only ask patience from any readers who may have come upon the earlier work.

Christianity simply *is* the claim that by raising Jesus of Nazareth from the dead, the God of Israel has marked him as Messiah and therefore in his own person the fulfillment of the promises to Israel — and this in a comprehensive way that was not typical of all strands of Jewish expectation and still is not. This claim can be understood in a way that leaves no remainder of expectation, that takes Israel's mission as *concluded* with the life, death, and resurrection of this one Israelite. If one then further tacitly identifies Judaism with canonical Israel — an odd thing for Christians to do, of course — supersessionist conclusions must follow: if Judaism is a direct continuation of canonical Israel and if canonical Israel's mission is concluded, Judaism can have no further divine purpose.

Some projects of non-supersessionist Christian theology have supposed that in order to avoid this, the minor premise of that supersessionist syllogism must be rejected; that is, the church's high claims about Messiah Jesus must be attenuated. But all this depends on a rather careless reading of what in fact appears in the New Testament.

Messiah's advent as the Galilean rabbi and prophet, and as the crucified and even as the risen Lord, is plainly *not* such an advent as can simply conclude Israel's history, and it is not so regarded in the New Testament. As the rabbis have insisted, had the Messiah simply arrived, things would have to look rather more fulfilled than they do. And the church has, at least when that was directly the question, in fact made the same judgment. Early and paradigmatically, Paul vehemently rejected the enthusiasm that acts as if the Last Day had already come. Until he comes, as we sometimes say, "in glory," the Messiah is not yet come in such a way as to end history or, therefore, to conclude the promises.

Christians thus often speak of Messiah's "second coming," and that can perhaps serve as a quick slogan. But strictly speaking there can be — precisely in the context of the New Testament's comprehensive interpretation of Messiahship — only one advent of Messiah. Therefore the time of the church, the time of the ascension, is not the time between two advents; it must be understood as a time *within* the one advent.

In Luke's account of the risen Jesus' final appearance, the disciples ask, "Lord, is this the time when you will restore the Kingdom to Israel?" (Acts 1:6). The question was reasonable and comes from what had to be the straightforward expectation of anyone who believed that Jesus was in fact risen as Messiah. But Jesus bypasses the question, and it is important to note that this is *all* he does. He does not say, "Yes, but remember my kingdom is an invisible kingdom" or anything along that line. In place of an answer, he promises the gift of the Spirit as the power to conduct a mission to Jews and gentiles. And then a beginning and an end are set for this mission, by Jesus' departure and the angelic promise of his return.

The church is not the kingdom; it is what the disciples are sent to be *instead* of rejoicing in the kingdom as they expected. It is what God ordains in the time of Jesus' ascension, the time — as I suggest — accommodated *within* the coming of Messiah. The church is a *detour* from the expected straight path of the Lord's intentions, a detour to accommodate the mission to Jews and gentiles.

But why should we think of this as a detour? Because even as a way through a time unexpectedly opened within the one advent to accommodate the bringing in of the gentiles, the church does not turn out to be the straight path of what might have been expected, and was in fact expected by missionaries like Paul. Had God willed what Paul evidently first expected, the descendents of Abraham and Sarah, with Torah indeed at the center of their lives, would have acknowledged Jesus as the risen Messiah and would have somehow opened to accommodate gentiles, as gentiles, within the community. But that is not what happened. The church is very decidedly a detour on God's way.

If the church can understand its own time in this way, as detour encompassed within the one extended event of Messiah's advent, then the church's question about the other community, gathered by descent from Abraham and Sarah and by Torah, acquires a precise context. For Judaism then appears to the church as a paired phenomenon in the time opened within Messiah's advent, and then the church may see Judaism as another detour taken by God on his way to the final fulfillment.

Why would God ordain two parallel detours? Within Christian understanding, we must say that what *should* have happened was familial and Torah-observant Judaism's allegiance to the risen Jesus and the accommodation of the gentiles in *this* new Israel. But that did not happen, and we cannot think that events at this point escaped God's providence.

Perhaps the whole Christian claim is thereby discredited. If it is not, two things follow. First, the mysterious will of God here, as elsewhere, encompasses what *we* — in this case the church — can only say is not what should have happened. What the church cannot but think should have happened is a Judaism living by faith in Messiah Jesus, with room for gentiles in the gentiles' own character. Second, if the church accepts what for her must remain the mystery that this did not and will not happen, we have to ask about God's will in the situation thereby created, that is, about God's ordination of the community shaped by the great rabbis.

What the new Jerusalem is to be, of which the church should have been an anticipation, is described in the Revelation of John: "on the gates the names of the twelve tribes of the sons of Israel were inscribed. . . . And the walls of the city had twelve foundations, and on them the twelve names of the twelve apostles of the Lamb" (21:12-14).

My central thesis is this: given what the church *in fact* quickly became and is, had the church been the only Israel in the time of its detour, the promises would have been not merely "fulfilled and not yet fulfilled," would not have displayed the famous "already but not yet"; they would have been simply in abeyance. I have three proposals under that rubric.

First, supposing that Jews in the gentile-dominated church had been the only descendents of Abraham and Sarah who gathered explicitly to worship Abraham and Sarah's God — that is, supposing that there were no synagogue — how long would that lineage have identifiably endured? Let us suppose the best case: that antiquity's anti-Semitism was overcome, that Christianity did not become identified with a gentile empire, etc.

The famous clash between Paul and Peter at Antioch is suggestive. Table-fellowship, central to the life of the church, became so difficult between Torah-observant Jewish believers and gentile converts that Peter actually withdrew. Paul rebuked Peter for that, and rightly, but what did Paul have to propose? And insofar as he may have envisaged a table-fellowship in which all yielded to all, was this vision an actual possibility?

Perhaps Jewish thinkers must view the baptism of Jews as apostasy, but the church must — even if she does not conduct any sort of "mission" to achieve this — greet those that do occur as gifts of God. But identifiable Jewishness does not long survive within the gentile-dominated church. To be sure, identifiable continuing descent from Abraham and Sarah is perhaps more likely within the church than among those assimilated into the secular world. But even so, if God is to have a people identified by descent from Abraham and Sarah, the church as it is will not provide it. I propose to my fellow Christians that God wills the Judaism of Torah-obedience as that which alone can and does hold the lineage of Abraham and Sarah together during the time of detour.

And that lineage must continue, until the day when lineages shall end. For the promises, as St. Paul insists to himself and his gentile readers, are the property of that lineage. Israel is *not* yet vindicated; you and I are *not* yet raised; the promises are still promises. And as long as they remain promises, hope for their fulfillment belongs to a people descended from Abraham and Sarah.

This leads to my second proposal. By this time, the world is surely full of biological descendents of Abraham and Sarah who are not jointly part of any recognizable people. What holds some descendents of Abraham and Sarah together as a people is the religion of Torah-observance, and this is true also of the many who do not themselves pay much attention to *mitzvoth*.

Now the Torah can have this function only, of course, if at least some of the commandments it lays on Jews are different from those observed by other nations. And that brings us to the matter of "the Law," controverted between rabbinic Judaism and Christianity from the first.

The second volume of Judaism's double canon is a predominantly legal compilation, and just as the church's second volume leads the church to read the Old Testament as a narrative that is given moral structure by Torah, so the Mishnah leads Judaism to read the Tanakh as Torah that is given context by the narrative. How should the church regard this other appropriation? (We might also ask how Judaism should regard the church's mode of appropriation, but I of course have no standing to propose any answer.)

Christian theology generally thinks of God's "Law" as doubly directed. On the one hand, it reveals the conditions for any community's existence and perdurance; no community can perdure in which familial bonds are flouted, vendetta is the means of justice, etc. On the other hand, the Law is the charter of God's particular people. Some individual commands can be sorted out between the two roles of the Law, some play both roles. Moreover, some individual commands seem to have no point *except* to mark out God's people as particular, though in Christian theology this point is not often emphasized. Why, after all — as David Novak once put it to me — can't Jews eat shrimp? Just to be marked off as different? Shrimp indeed lack properly fishy fins, but then fish lack proper exoskeletons. The seeming arbitrariness is much of the point. In Martin Luther's exegesis of the paradise story in Genesis, the tree of the knowledge of good and evil is so called only after the fact, in view of the consequences of disobeying God's command. In itself, the tree was just a particular tree, and the command not to eat of it gave humankind a first opportunity of obedience — the arbitrary choice of a particular tree was part of the point.

In its time between the times, the church sees herself as Israel called to the promised gathering in of the gentiles and, following the victory of Paul's understanding, precisely *as* gentiles. But as played out in that scene between Paul and Peter, this inevitably entails the church's inability to enforce — or, if one prefers, the church's liberation from — the Law in its role as charter of a people that is just *different*. The church is essentially an *ekklesia* of Jews and gentiles, but the Jews within it constantly tend to vanish from sight as Jews. Thus the church has sidestepped this question from the beginning: Can the Law simply cease in its role of creating *difference?* Can God's purpose in calling Israel be sustained if before the final advent there is not a people of his calling who are simply peculiar among the peoples?

The church, too, is of course called to be different. Sometimes and in some places life in the church is so different from life outside the church that lengthy preparation is required if converts are morally to survive baptism. But there is something *quantitative* about the church's difference from surrounding culture: it properly waxes and wanes, and the differences appear at different points in different places and at different times. The second-century church could identify itself as a "way" different from the "way" of the world around it by noting that "we do not abort our children," but then there came to be centuries in which the culture, too, regarded abortion as a crime, however much it may nevertheless have been practiced. As the *Epistle to Diognetus* famously noted, with the church's own brand of peculiar self-awareness, Christians do not stand out from the cities they inhabit, except by their righteousness — which is of course often a great exposure indeed. There is the church of the martyrs, also today, but there is also the church of the American main street, which has its own sort of authenticity.

Thus my second proposal is this: the church should acknowledge that God, in the time between the times and when there is no temple, wants a community that studies and obeys Torah as Judaism does, so that he may have an unavoidably special people also in that time.

As the church reads its Old Testament in its narrative way, it should also strive to overhear that other reading of the same documents, conducted over there by other folk, some of whom even dress and act in particular ways as they do it: a rehearsal of Torah as God's revelation of his will for his particular people, including his will that it be particular. In her time between the times, the church is not able herself to bear such exegesis, and this is not a failing. But she should attend to it, in preparation for that day when the one hundred and forty-four thousand will lead the multitude from all nations in praise of the Lord and his righteousness.

Christian theology cannot, however (and so I come to my third suggestion), regard such proposals as true, unless they can be christologically founded — unless, that is, their truth is upheld by the truth about who and what the risen Christ is. Undoubtedly a foundational text of Christology, of teaching about who and what the risen Jesus is, must be the first chapter of St. John's Gospel. We may summarize its teaching in this way:

"The Word, that was in the beginning with God, became flesh, so as to dwell among us."

In centuries of analysis and speculation about the nature and provenience of that "Word," it has not so often been asked what its *content* might be. God eternally speaks, and it is this speech that occurs in fleshy fashion with Jesus. Very well — but what does he *say?* So soon as the question is asked, it is quickly answered, for John is plainly playing off the first chapter of Genesis. There God creates by saying "Let there be . . . , and let it be good." The word that God eternally speaks is moral command. Thus the word that is "in the beginning" is one discourse with the word he speaks to his people. The parallelisms of Psalm 147 display this: "He sends out his command to the earth, and his word runs very swiftly. . . . He makes his wind blow, and the waters flow. . . . He declares his word to Jacob, his statutes and his judgments to Israel." Though Jewish theology may not typically regard the word of Genesis 1 as Torah, in a general sense it is clear: the Word that became flesh as Jesus, according to John, is the word "from the mouth of the Lord" by which God's people live, as do all his creatures; it is the Word called "Torah."

Or, more directly, we may listen to what Jesus says in Luke 18: "You know the commandments; do them and you shall live." Even the final twist, "Sell all and follow me," is in simple continuity with the Old Testament, which is, in a way, one long command to "Leave . . . and follow. . . ."

By whom is Torah heard, in this time of detour? And by whom is Jesus, the enfleshed Torah, actually *believed* in this time of detour? As we have seen, the church hears Torah only — and necessarily — very selectively. When the Son of Man finally comes, "will he find faith on the earth?" (Luke 18:8). Not, I suggest, unless he finds *both* those who "have believed" in his coming in the flesh and those who hang on every syllable of that Word that he is. The church is bound to think these should have been the same community, but evidently God does not, and the church can only affirm the mystery of his will.

And then there is that flesh, which Torah became and is. The risen Jesus is also flesh, in that he is risen bodily, for to be an embodied creature is to be flesh. Now, flesh is never an individual possession; that we are flesh means among other things that we have parents and ancestors, who — at least until we get to Adam — are not everyone's parents and ancestors. The Word who has come in the flesh belongs to the lineage of Abraham and Sarah, and this fact belongs to his identity, to what traditional Christology calls the "one hypostasis" of the Word who is Jesus.

Paul teaches, and the church follows his teaching, that the church is the body of the risen Christ, and Paul does not initially mean that as a trope. As my body is myself as I am present and available to you, so the church is Christ's presence to the world, in the time of detour. But what sort of flesh is this body?

Can there be a present body of the risen Jew, Jesus of Nazareth, in which the lineage of Abraham and Sarah so vanishes into a congregation of gentiles as it does in the church? My final — and perhaps most radical — suggestion to Christian theology (*not,* let me say again, to Jewish self-understanding) is that, so long as the time of detour lasts, the embodiment of the risen Christ is whole only in the form of the church *and* an identifiable community of Abraham and Sarah's descendents. The church and the synagogue are together and only together the present availability to the world of the risen Jesus Christ.

Hallowed Be Thy Name!
The Tetragrammaton and the Name of the Trinity

R. KENDALL SOULEN

Introduction

Few issues are at once so central to biblical faith and yet so perplexing as the name of God. When the LORD accosted Moses at the burning bush and commissioned him to deliver the Israelites from bondage, Moses had the presence of mind to ask, "Who shall I say sent me?" (Exod. 3:13, paraphrased). While some gods might have slain Moses on the spot, the LORD evidently thought Moses asked a sensible question, and so he answered it. Ever since, the people whom Moses led from bondage, as well as those from among the nations who have learned to call upon the LORD as God, have treasured God's name as the incomparable token of God's character and power.

Still, the notion of God's name evokes our wonder, astonishment, and awe, not to mention our curiosity, puzzlement, and consternation. When Jacob begs the wrestling angel to declare his name, the angel rebuffs him: "Why do you ask my name?" (Gen. 32:29). Even God's reply to Moses at the bush is anything but straightforward, consisting not in one answer but in three: "I am who I am," "I am," and "YHWH" (Exod. 3:14-15). The world itself is scarcely big enough to contain all the rumination that this mysterious answer has provoked among Christians and Jews.

Of course, it is no accident that the name of God is both central and perplexing, for according to the biblical witness, God's name brings both God's identity and God's uncircumscribable mystery into our midst.

Please note: these two features of divine reality are not related in inverse proportion, like hot and cold, up and down, true and false. When God reveals God's identity, God's mystery is not *diminished* but *intensified*. Surely the Swiss theologian Emil Brunner was right when he said that the truly mysterious God is not the nameless One, but the One who has a name and makes it known.[1]

Two Questions and One Proposal

In this essay, I propose to approach the theme of this book indirectly, by focusing on a question that may initially seem to be far removed from a Christian theology of Judaism. The question I have in mind is this: What is the name of the Trinity? If I am not mistaken, the name of the Trinity is the point where the question of God's name becomes most pressing for Christians today. Many Christians today would agree that the doctrine of the Trinity embodies the distinctively Christian understanding of God's identity and God's mystery in the most succinct and comprehensive way. Nevertheless, the *name* of the Trinity raises deep-going difficulties about God's identity and God's mystery that quickly take us to the limits of this consensus. Let me mention two such difficulties.

A first difficulty, and one that does bear directly on the theme of this book, concerns the relation between the name of the Trinity and the tetragrammaton. What is the significance of the tetragrammaton, if any, for the Christian understanding of the name of the Trinity? Although the question may initially strike us as odd, it is important because it poses in a particularly pointed way the problem of how Israel's faith in the One God is related to the church's confession of God as triune. This ancient problem has acquired new urgency in recent decades as many Christian communions have sought to express Christian faith in non-supersessionistic ways, that is, in ways that do not claim or imply the abrogation, obsolescence, or nullity of God's covenant with the Jewish people.[2]

The tetragrammaton, of course, is the most common name for God

1. Emil Brunner, *The Christian Doctrine of God* (Philadelphia: Westminster, 1950), p. 119.

2. I attempt to give a more extended definition and analysis of supersessionism in the Christian tradition, and a proposal for countering it, in my book *The God of Israel and Christian Theology* (Minneapolis: Fortress Press, 1996).

in the Old Testament and the most sacred name for God in Judaism. Nevertheless, the tetragrammaton played little role in Christian thought during the patristic and early medieval periods, in large part because of linguistic obstacles. During the later medieval and post-Reformation period, Christian theologians used the term "Jehovah" to designate the one divine essence common to the three persons of the Holy Trinity.[3] Since the early modern period, however, Christian theologians and biblical scholars have portrayed the relation between the tetragrammaton and the Trinity in light of the progressive character of the economy of salvation. According to this view, the tetragrammaton belonged to the preparatory stage of God's self-revelation, while "the Father and the Son and the Holy Spirit" belongs to God's definitive self-revelation. This view was frequently accompanied by an explicitly supersessionistic construal of the relationship between the church and the Jewish people. In addition, modern biblical scholarship has further underscored the impression that the tetragrammaton is obsolete by its transliteration of the Name as *Yahweh,* a reconstruction of the divine name with no living basis in Christian worship.

Christians today who are heirs of this history are faced with the following problem. Can Christians understand the name of the Trinity, and in particular, the relation between the name of the Trinity and the tetragrammaton, in a manner that is faithful to the evangelical center of the church's faith, and yet that does not contribute to or imply a supersessionistic understanding of the church's relation to the Jewish people? If so, how might this be done?[4]

In addition to this primary question, let me briefly mention a secondary difficulty that also touches on the name of the Trinity. In North America today, there is a lively debate concerning whether or not the

3. This understanding of the divine name, formed in part by assimilating the tetragram to the exposition of God's name in Exod. 3:14 ("I am who I am," "I am"), seems to have fallen out of favor in the modern period to the same extent that the traditional "metaphysical" interpretation of Exod. 3:14 also fell out of favor. Wolfhart Pannenberg summarizes a whole epoch of biblical interpretation: "In the Bible the divine name is not a formula for the essence of deity but a pointer to experience of his working (Exod. 3:14)" (*Systematic Theology,* vol. 1, trans. Geoffrey W. Bromiley [Grand Rapids: Eerdmans, 1991], p. 360).

4. Christopher Seitz provides an overview of some key issues regarding the Christian posture toward the tetragrammaton in "Handing Over the Name: Christian Reflection on the Divine Name YHWH," in *Trinity, Time, and Church: A Response to the Theology of Robert W. Jenson,* ed. Colin Gunton (Grand Rapids: Eerdmans, 2000), pp. 23-41.

Trinity has a uniquely appropriate name at all. The immediate occasion of this debate is the vitality of feminist Christian theology in North America and the concern to distinguish between authentic Christian discourse and its patriarchal distortion. Many feminists, appealing to the apophatic and mystical traditions of Christian theology, hold that the triune God does not have a uniquely appropriate name at all. They emphasize the necessity of naming God in many ways as the token of God's uncircumscribable mystery.[5] Others hold that the Holy Trinity does have a uniquely appropriate name, namely, "the Father and the Son and the Holy Spirit."[6] They emphasize this name above all others as the unique token of God's reliable identity.

At first glance, the two difficulties that I have identified may seem to have little to do with one another. In fact, however, I believe that both difficulties illuminate a more basic weakness in the Christian doctrine of God's name. So far as I can see, Christian theology has generally lacked a fully *trinitarian* account of the name of the Trinity. Instead, Christian theologians have tended to discuss the name of the Trinity in *binary* terms. So, for example, pre-modern theologians framed the discussion of the tetragrammaton and the Trinity in terms of the binary contrast between the one essence and the three persons, while the modern church has framed the discussion in terms of the binary contrast between the Old and New Testaments. Similarly, feminist theologians and their interlocutors today frame the debate about "the name of the Father and the Son and the Holy Spirit" in terms of the binary contrast between apophatic

5. An important statement of this position can be found in Elizabeth A. Johnson, *She Who Is: The Mystery of God in Feminist Theological Discourse* (New York: Crossroad, 1993). See also Gail Ramshaw, *God beyond Gender* (Minneapolis: Fortress Press, 1995); and Ruth C. Duck, *Gender and the Name of God: The Trinitarian Baptismal Formula* (New York: The Pilgrim Press, 1991).

6. The thesis that "the Father and the Son and the Holy Spirit" is the proper name of the triune God was proposed by Robert W. Jenson, *The Triune Identity: God according to the Gospel* (Philadelphia: Fortress Press, 1982), pp. 1-20, and has since been taken up by others; cf. the essays in *Speaking the Christian God: The Holy Trinity and the Challenges of Feminism,* ed. Alvin F. Kimel Jr. (Grand Rapids: Eerdmans, 1991), pp. 188-208. The thesis that "Father" is the proper name of God was advanced earlier; see Claude Geffre, " 'Father' as the Proper Name of God," in *God as Father?* ed. Johannes-Baptist Metz and Edward Schillebeeckx, Concilium 143: Dogma (Edinburgh: T. & T. Clark; New York: Seabury Press, 1981), pp. 43-50; also Ralph Quere, " 'Naming' God 'Father,' " *Currents in Theology and Mission* 12 (February 1985): 5-12; Pannenberg, *Systematic Theology,* vol. 1, p. 262.

and kataphatic speech, or, alternatively, in terms of the contrast between natural and revealed knowledge of God, or between one name and no name, or one proper name and many metaphorical names.

In the remainder of this essay, I hope to persuade you of two things. First, I hope to persuade you that Christian thinking about the name of the Trinity can be more adequate to the texture of the church's Scriptures — as well as more adequate to the identity and mystery of God attested therein — by being more truly *trinitarian*. My thesis is that the name of the Holy Trinity is *one name in three inflections*. According to the *Oxford English Dictionary* (second edition), an inflection is "the modification of the form of a word" that expresses "the different grammatical relations into which it may enter"; it is also defined as "a modulation of the voice; in speaking or singing: a change in the pitch or tone of the voice." Bending and blending these definitions, I wish to suggest that the name of the Trinity exists in three modifications of form that correspond to the three persons of the Trinity. As we shall see, each inflection identifies all three persons of the Trinity. But each inflection does so in a distinctive way, in a "modulation of the voice" characteristic of one person of the Holy Trinity and of the personal relations in which that person stands. Thus, there is an inflection of the triune name that corresponds to the *first* person, an inflection that corresponds to the *second* person, and an inflection that corresponds to the *third* person. For convenience' sake, I will call these the *theological, christological,* and *pneumatological* inflections of the triune name.[7] By the end, I hope to have persuaded you that the name of the Trinity is a truly trinitarian name in a more radical sense

---

7. I have chosen to label the three inflections in a manner that follows the "economic" usage of the New Testament rather than that of formal trinitarian doctrine. My aim is to link each inflection to the appropriate person in a way that is clear but that avoids privileging or prejudging the content of the three inflections themselves. In an important sense, all three inflections are "theological," since all three concern persons who are equally eternal and divine. The New Testament, however, most commonly uses "theos" to designate the first person of the Trinity, and here I am following New Testament usage (see Karl Rahner, "Theos in the New Testament," in *Theological Investigations,* vol. 1 [London: Darton, Longman, and Todd, 1963], pp. 79-148). Similarly, "christological" is arguably not a trinitarian term at all in the strict sense, since it is usually thought not to apply to the eternal identity of the second person distinct from the economy of salvation. Nevertheless, I use it in this context because it clearly picks out the second person of the Trinity. The labels are terms of convenience only and are not intended to be pushed too hard.

than is ordinarily suspected: the triune name consists in the unity of three inflections that are irreducibly distinct yet inseparably interrelated.

In addition, I hope to persuade you of a second thing. Surprising though it may seem, the key to a properly trinitarian understanding of the triune name is a proper estimate of the centrality and abiding significance of the tetragrammaton for Christian faith. As we shall see, the affirmation of the tetragrammaton's centrality and abiding significance is not an obstacle to a trinitarian understanding of the name, but rather its enabling condition.

The import of these two claims, I hasten to add, will not be an account of God's name to which Christians can or should expect Jews to give their assent. Indeed, I expect that the proposal I make will in some respects serve to intensify awareness of abiding differences between Christians and Jews and of the humanly irreconcilable character of their respective truth claims. Nevertheless, it is my hope that my account of the triune name can make a contribution toward an understanding of the Trinity that recontextualizes the abiding differences between Christians and Jews, in such a way that Christians are less likely to understand their faith in supersessionistic ways. Furthermore, it is my hope that this account of the triune name will also serve to make more perspicuous a belief that Jews perhaps can accept — not, to be sure, that God is the Trinity, but rather that in "worshipping and believing in their Trinity Christians somehow touch, as it were, Israel's God."[8]

The Theological Inflection of the Triune Name

The name of the Holy Trinity is one name in three inflections. Let me begin with the theological inflection, the one appropriate to the first person of the Trinity. As we shall see, it belongs to the logic of this inflection to begin with the personal proper name of the One to whom Jesus prays, and to proceed from there to tell us who Jesus and the Spirit are.

At the heart of the theological inflection is the holy tetragrammaton, the four-lettered name that consists in the Hebrew consonants *yod,*

---

8. Bruce D. Marshall, "Israel: Do Christians Worship the God of Israel?" in *Knowing the Triune God: The Word of the Spirit in the Practices of the Church,* ed. James J. Buckley and David S. Yeago (Grand Rapids: Eerdmans, 2001), pp. 231-64.

heh, waw, and *heh.* As I noted at the start, this is the third and final name that God gave to Moses at the burning bush, the name that finally resolves Moses' question, that Moses takes back to the Israelites, and that appears thousands of times in the subsequent Scriptures.

Without a doubt, the tetragrammaton is a mysterious name, in part because it is surrounded by a host of unanswered — perhaps unanswerable — questions.[9] What are the historical origins of the name? How was it originally pronounced? What is its etymological meaning, if any? How is it related to the other names that God gave to Moses at the bush, "I am who I am" and "I am"? But these questions are not the genuine mystery of the name. At most they are signs that point to the mystery, just as in the Gospel narratives the sign of the empty tomb points to the mystery of the resurrection. The genuine mystery of the tetragrammaton is at once extremely simple and inexhaustibly deep: the tetragrammaton is a proper name, a personal proper name, like Moses, or Jeremiah, or Mary Magdalene. The Jewish theologian Michael Wyschogrod has written, "The God of Israel has a proper name. There is no fact in Jewish theology more significant than this."[10]

A personal proper name is a very humble thing. Unlike a metaphor, or a class term, or a concept, a personal name ordinarily has little or no conventional meaning of its own. The role of a personal name is not to define or describe, but to identify. If all you know about me is my name, you know very little indeed. This is the truth in the well-known expression, "What's in a name?" Yet the very humility of a personal name is the source of an unexpected strength. Because a personal name has little conventional meaning of its own, it acquires its sense wholly from the personal history of its bearer. Over time, a personal proper name can become saturated with an intensity of connotation and resonance that exceeds any other form of human speech. The songwriter asks, "How do you find a word that means Maria?" The point is, we can't. For those who know and love her, the name Maria conveys a fullness of meaning that cannot be circumscribed by any other word or description, no matter how apt. The

9. Martin Rose, *Yahwe: zum Streit um den alttestamentlichen Gottesnamen* (Zürich: Theologischer Verlag Zürich, 1978).

10. Michael Wyschogrod, *The Body of Faith: God in the People Israel* (San Francisco: Harper & Row, 1989), p. 91. Among Christian scholars, Walter Zimmerli in particular has drawn attention to the centrality of the personal name for Israel's faith; cf. Walter Zimmerli, *Old Testament Theology in Outline* (Atlanta: John Knox Press, 1978).

personal proper name is the linguistic token of the person in the fullness of his or her identity. That is why personal proper names have such astonishing power and dignity.

The tetragrammaton is the personal proper name of the God of Israel. That is its special mystery. Other names for God in the Scriptures of Israel are not personal proper names but common nouns, appellations, and epithets.[11] The tetragrammaton alone is the linguistic token by which the God of Israel distinguishes himself from all other gods, indeed, from everything else altogether. In Catherine M. LaCugna's words, it is God's "self-given name."[12] Regardless of the name's etymology or historical origins, the sense of the tetragrammaton in the Scriptures comes not from any conventional or generic meaning of the word itself, but solely from the incomparable uniqueness of God's personal identity. The psalmist shouts: "Who is like the LORD our God?" (Ps. 113:5). *That* is the sense of the tetragrammaton.

According to Maimonides, the tetragrammaton belongs on God's side of the distinction between eternity and time: it betokens God's *whoness* in a manner that transcends God's relation to what God has created (see *Guide for the Perplexed,* 1, 60-62). Yet we may say that there is also a singular relationship between the tetragrammaton and the people Israel. For it is in Israel that God makes himself known and available, not merely as the unnamed origin of all things, but according to his eternal identity and character. Indeed, we perhaps do not go too far astray of the biblical witness if we say that God's covenant with Israel is the outworking of God's desire to be known by name. For the sake of this name, God fashions a people out of the barren womb of Sarah and out of the chaos of bondage, so that by works of steadfast love and faithfulness, God might be glorified by name not only in the heavens but also by men and women on the earth. The biblical sense of the tetragrammaton is thus finally also eschatological in orientation. Under the pressure of God's great promise, "I will sanctify my great name" (Ezek. 36:23), the tetragrammaton points irresistibly forward to the consummation of God's universal rule, when there will be an end to the state in which "all day long my name is de-

---

11. On the special place of the name YHWH and its relation to other names of God, see T. N. D. Mettinger, *In Search of God* (Minneapolis: Fortress Press, 1987).

12. Catherine M. LaCugna, *God for Us: The Trinity and the Christian Life* (New York: HarperCollins, 1991), p. 302.

spised" (Isa. 52:5), and God's incomparable uniqueness will be fittingly honored by Israel, the nations, and all creation.

The tetragrammaton is thus the unique token of God's reliable identity and of God's uncircumscribable mystery. And Israel is the people uniquely marked out for service of this name, a service that it provides in part by the reserve that it practices in refusing to pronounce the name.

Now, for all of that, the Christian relationship to the tetragrammaton has long been a conflicted one. On the one hand, Christians can scarcely deny its importance for the Old Testament and for Judaism. On the other hand, Christian theologians and biblical scholars, especially in the modern period, have regularly disputed the idea that the tetragrammaton continues to be important for the New Testament and for Christian faith. Christians readily concede that the tetragram is essential to Christian faith as a mark of who God was, but are much slower to concede that it remains relevant for who God is and will be. Two arguments are often given, one historical and one theological.

The historical argument begins from a well-known fact to which I have already briefly alluded. Sometime after their return from exile in Babylon, the Jews gradually restricted the circumstances in which the tetragrammaton might licitly be pronounced. Out of reverence for God's name, they used reverential circumlocutions in place of the name itself, such as *adonai* in Judea or *kyrios* among Greek-speaking Jews. Eventually, so the argument goes, knowledge of the name was eclipsed by the circumlocutions themselves. By the time of the New Testament, the tetragrammaton no longer served as the personal name of the God of Israel, certainly not among Greek-speaking Jews. The theological argument simply adds that this development is a necessary condition for the growth of monotheism and a useful preparation for the Christian understanding of God. As Bruce Metzger, one of America's senior biblical scholars, wrote in his preface to the *New Revised Standard Version* of the Bible, "The use of any proper name for the one and only God, as though there were other gods from whom the true God had to be distinguished, began to be discontinued in Judaism before the Christian era and is inappropriate for the universal faith of the Christian Church."[13]

---

13. Bruce M. Metzger, "To the Reader," *The New Revised Standard Version*, Division of Christian Education of the National Council of the Churches of Christ in the United States of America (Nashville: Thomas Nelson, Inc., 1990).

The idea that the tetragrammaton has become obsolete in the New Testament and for Christian faith generally is ripe for debunking. The idea rests not on a sound reading of the New Testament but rather on a theology that interprets the nature of God, the Scriptures, and the historical evidence in a supersessionistic way. Far from being moribund, the personal name of the God of Israel is alive and well in the New Testament. It has not been buried beneath periphrastic speech, any more than it is buried today among reverent Jews who intentionally refrain from pronouncing it. On the contrary, the tetragrammaton directs the logic of the New Testament's identification of God the way magnetic north directs the needle of a compass. For those with ears to hear, the unspoken tetragrammaton speaks on every page.[14]

Let us begin by considering how the Gospels portray Jesus' own identification of God. We know, of course, that Jesus taught his followers to pray — first and before all else — for God's name to be hallowed. Still, we do not often consider what the first petition implies for the typical way in which Jesus *identifies* God. Still less do we notice how this petition models a reverence for God's name that saturates every aspect of Jesus' public teaching.

To understand the first petition of the Lord's Prayer, we must notice that Jesus formulates it in the passive voice: "hallowed be thy name." The same is true of the third petition, "thy will be done." Even the second petition avoids directly referring to the agent of the desired action: "Thy kingdom come." Jesus' use of the passive is to be understood in the context of Jesus' very Jewish reverence for God and God's

14. I borrow the metaphor from Sean M. McDonough, *YHWH at Patmos: Rev. 1:4 in Its Hellenistic and Early Jewish Setting* (Tübingen: J. C. B. Mohr, 1999), p. 116. McDonough demonstrates the vitality of the tetragrammaton in the Second Temple period and its importance for understanding Rev. 1:4 and other New Testament texts, including Revelation, Philippians, and John. A page-by-page inventory of all the New Testament's forms of piety for the name can be found in Julius Boehmer, *Die neutestamentliche Gottesscheu und die ersten drei Bitten des Vaterunsers* (Halle, 1917). Boehmer wrote, "The New Testament is saturated with Jewish piety for the Name and identity of God, though the exegetes have scarcely ever taken notice of it." Interestingly, while Boehmer drew attention to the phenomenon, he assigned it only negative significance for modern Christian practice. For him it was the eggshell of ancient Jewish piety that Christians should become aware of in order to relinquish. Besides McDonough, contemporary scholars drawing attention to the importance of a theology of the divine name for the New Testament witness include Richard Bauckham, Christopher Seitz, and C. Kavin Rowe.

name.[15] Jesus employs what is sometimes called the "divine passive" in order to call reverentially upon God in a manner that avoids the direct mention of God. Here the passive voice does not imply any ambiguity regarding *who* is being called upon to act. Quite the contrary. In the context of Israel's piety for God's name, Jesus' reverential use of the passive voice actually serves to specify — indirectly but unmistakably — the exact identity of the first petition's logical agent: the God whose name is the tetragrammaton.[16] The form of the first petition thus corresponds to and underscores its content. The petition amounts to a plea that *YHWH* now act to glorify the name that Israel honors and loves, in accord with God's own ancient promise, "Then you shall know that I am the LORD!" (Exod. 16:2; Jer. 24:7; Ezek. 36:11; etc.). The promise means: "The day will come when I, the LORD, will display the incomparable glory of who I am in the works that I have done, my works of covenant fidelity to Israel and of mercy toward the nations." When Jesus instructs his followers to pray, "Hallowed be thy name!" he is teaching them to say, "LORD, let this be so now! Make your name great!"

Once we have learned to recognize Jesus' use of the passive voice, we see that it runs through Jesus' speech like a golden thread, linking together every aspect of his teaching and ministry, and setting them all in relation to the God whose name is the tetragrammaton:

"Blessed are those who mourn, for they will *be comforted*" (Matt. 5:4)

"Blessed are the peacemakers, for they will *be called* children of God" (Matt. 5:9)

"Do not judge, so that you may not *be judged*" (Matt. 7:1)

"Do not fear. Only believe, and she will *be saved*" (Luke 8:50)

"Take heart, son; your sins *are forgiven*" (Matt. 9:2)

---

15. On the "divine passive," see Gustaf Dalman, *The Words of Jesus* (Edinburgh: T. & T. Clark, 1909), p. 224; Joachim Jeremias, *New Testament Theology: The Proclamation of Jesus* (New York: Scribner's, 1971), pp. 10-14. Jeremias considers that the "'divine passive' occurs round about 100 times in the sayings of Jesus" alone.

16. See McDonough, *YHWH at Patmos,* chap. 2; C. Seitz, "The Divine Name in Christian Scripture," in *Word without End* (Grand Rapids: Eerdmans, 1997); Scot McKnight, *A New Vision for Israel: The Teachings of Jesus in National Context* (Grand Rapids: Eerdmans, 1999), chap. 1.

"all who exalt themselves will *be humbled,* but all who humble themselves will *be exalted*" (Luke 18:14)

"I must proclaim the good news of the kingdom of God to the other cities also; for I *was sent* for this purpose" (Luke 4:43)

"But after *I am raised up,* I will go ahead of you to Galilee" (Matt. 26:32).

Finally, consider what is perhaps the most astonishing divine passive of them all:

And Jesus came and said to them, "All authority in heaven and on earth *has been given* to me" (Matt. 28:18).

It is difficult to know wherein lies the greater provocation: in the claim that the Ancient of Days has vested all authority in a human slain and risen, or that the one so vested continues to employ the idiom of reverential deference for the Ancient of Days.

Ignatius of Antioch once wrote, "Whoever has the word of Jesus for a true possession can also hear his silence."[17] The silence of Jesus is the room he opens for God's name to be glorified in him. The countless divine passives that trace the contours of Jesus' ministry — from his sending to his glorification — are the audible tokens of the great divine passive at the heart of Jesus' prayer: "Hallowed be thy name!"

So, the unspoken tetragrammaton speaks. It speaks through periphrastic language to identify by name the One to whom Jesus prays: tetragrammaton, the Holy One of Israel. Perhaps the most staggering instance of this comes from John the Seer, who knows that Christians expect a Christian letter to begin, "Grace and peace to you from God *our Father.* . . ." John wants to remind his listeners just who this Father is, so he writes, "Grace and peace to you from he who is and who was and who is to come" (Rev. 1:4). This formula alludes to the tetragrammaton down to the details of its aberrant grammar and is the periphrastic equivalent of a slap in the face.[18]

But notice: the New Testament writers take these very forms of periphrastic speech that serve uniquely to identify the one to whom Jesus prays, and they use them — they exploit their linguistic volatility — to identify Jesus and the Spirit. That is the theological inflection of the tri-

17. Ignatius, *Epistle to the Ephesians* 15.2.
18. See McDonough, *YHWH at Patmos,* chap. 4.

une name. The inflection begins with the personal proper name of the one to whom Jesus prays, and it proceeds from there to tell us who Jesus and the Spirit are.

The New Testament provides many clues that identify the Holy Spirit with reference to the tetragrammaton. Some of these are relatively well known: the very phrase "Holy Spirit" derives from a reverential circumlocution, "the Spirit of holiness," an echo of which can still be heard in Paul's salutation in Romans: Jesus Christ, "designated Son of God in power according to the Spirit of holiness by his resurrection from the dead" (Rom. 1:4). But other clues are often hidden from us by translation. Consider the story in which Peter remonstrates Sapphira and Ananias for deceitfully withholding money from the saints. Peter asks, "How is it that you have agreed together to put the *Spirit of Lord* to the test?" (Acts 5:9). The Greek makes clear, by omitting the definite article, that "Lord" is not just an honorific title for God but a veiled reference to God's personal proper name, the holy tetragrammaton.[19] Sapphira falls down dead on the spot.

Most of all, the New Testament writers exploit the volatility of periphrastic speech in order to convey the mind-boggling truth about Jesus. They do so in an astonishing variety of creative and sophisticated ways. Sometimes they put familiar forms of periphrastic speech to startling new uses, as in Philippians 2:5-11, which uses the conventional surrogate *kyrios* to make the utterly unconventional point that "the name above every name" now resides in the humiliated and exalted Jesus.[20]

---

19. Carl Judson Davis points out that in a number of instances New Testament writers use *kyrios* (lord) in a manner that is grammatically explicable only if the word functions as a proper name. According to the grammatical rule known as the Canon of Apollonius, two nouns in regimen should both have the definite article or both lack it. An exception occurs, however, when the second noun is a proper name, in which case the second article may be omitted. Davis convincingly demonstrates that when Luke, for example, speaks of "the way of lord," he is using a convention that indicates that *kyrios* is a surrogate for God's name. C. J. Davis, *The Name and Way of the Lord* (Sheffield: Sheffield Academic Press, 1996), p. 93.

20. According to Richard Bauckham, it is "inconceivable" that a Jewish writer could use this phrase for a name other than God's own unique name, YHWH. See R. Bauckham, "The Worship of Jesus in Philippians 2:9-11," in *Where Christology Began: Essays on Philippians 2*, ed. R. P. Martin and Brian J. Dodd (Louisville: Westminster/John Knox Press, 1998). For a survey of views, see Ralph P. Martin, *Carmen Christi: Philippians 2:5-11 in Recent Interpretation and in the Setting of Early Christian Worship*, rev. ed. (Grand Rapids: Eerdmans, 1983).

Sometimes they create entirely new but unmistakable forms of peri-phrastic speech. I have already mentioned the unique way in which John the Seer replaces the ordinary "God the Father" with an elaborate allusion to the tetragrammaton (Rev. 1:4). Just as strikingly, John over the course of the letter breaks apart the elements of this and other similar allusions and uses the resulting elements to refer to Jesus Christ. The greeting thereby sets the stage for Revelation's extremely high Christology, accord-ing to which the coming of the Ancient of Days takes place in the advent of Jesus.[21] Jesus is quite literally the one who comes "in the name of the Lord!"[22]

We could look at many other examples, but the point is this: the New Testament uses an astonishing array of periphrastic language to identify the one to whom Jesus prays as YHWH, the God of Israel, and in order to include Jesus and the Spirit in the identity of this one God.[23] As Richard Bauckham shows, New Testament writers use this pattern of inclusion in order to articulate the highest conceivable Christology and pneumatology. What bears emphasizing is that this pattern does not re-sult in the obliteration of the distinctions among the persons. On the contrary, the pattern of inclusion we have described represents a distinc-tive New Testament idiom that expresses the distinctiveness of the per-sons in terms of the giving, receiving, and illumination of the sacred name. Time and again, it is precisely by differentiating himself from the one who bears the divine name that Jesus allows himself to be included in the event of its glorification. That is the theological inflection of the triune name. In passing, it is worth emphasizing that the theological in-flection of the triune name requires Christians to cultivate the capacity to hear between the lines. For this reason, Christians should give up the misguided custom of calling God "Yahweh." The term is a scholarly con-jecture that is offensive to reverent Jews and antithetical to the texture of

---

21. See McDonough, *YHWH at Patmos,* chap. 4.

22. See the splendid discussion in Richard Bauckham, *The Theology of the Book of Revelation* (Cambridge: Cambridge University Press, 1993).

23. I borrow the language from Richard Bauckham, *God Crucified: Monotheism and Christology in the New Testament* (Grand Rapids: Eerdmans, 1998), p. 27 and passim. In this significant work, Bauckham advances the thesis "that the highest possible Christology, the inclusion of Jesus in the unique divine identity, was central to the faith of the early church even before any of the NT writings were written, since it appears in all of them" (p. 27).

the New Testament's own witness. Like Jews, like Jesus, and like the writers of the New Testament, Christians need to "lift up" the unspoken tetragrammaton in a manner that allows it to speak in its own distinctive voice.[24]

The Christological Inflection of the Triune Name

The second inflection of the triune name is the familiar formula "The Father and the Son and the Holy Spirit." This is what I will call the christological inflection, the inflection most naturally appropriated to the second person of the Trinity, Jesus Christ. The christological inflection names or identifies all three persons of the Trinity, but from a perspective that accords centrality to the second person of the Trinity. A token of the Son-centered character of this inflection is the simple but impressive fact that according to Matthew's Gospel it is the risen Lord himself who utters this name when commissioning the disciples, now apostles (Matt. 28:19).

As I noted, discussion of "the name of the Father and the Son and the Holy Spirit" is divided today between those who regard the name as one among many possible metaphors for the triune God for which equivalent substitutes can and should be found, and those who argue that it is *the* proper name of the triune God, standing alone in a class by itself. Proponents of the proper name position undoubtedly have the better half of the argument, and we are much in the debt of Robert Jenson. Nevertheless, it is my view that neither position is quite sufficiently attentive to the full trinitarian texture of the baptismal formula, which entails elements of both *irreducible distinctiveness* and *inseparable relatedness*. Feminist proponents of the first position go badly astray because they overlook the fact that the christological inflection is irreducibly distinct in itself, having no equivalent substitute. Yet even proponents of the second position — who recognize the irreducible distinctiveness of the baptismal name — have hitherto overlooked the fact that the christological inflection is also insep-

24. Franz Rosenzweig, the great Jewish theologian and philosopher, hated the Protestant "scientific" use of "Yahweh," which he objected to on both scientific and religious grounds. See Rosenzweig, "The Eternal: Mendelssohn and the Name of God," in Martin Buber and Franz Rosenzweig, *Scripture and Translation* (Bloomington: Indiana University Press, 1994). For a similar viewpoint, see Jon Levenson, *The Hebrew Bible, the Old Testament, and Historical Criticism* (Nashville: Westminster/John Knox Press, 1993).

arably related to other, equally basic, inflections of the triune name. Let us examine both aspects of the christological inflection.

The christological inflection of the triune name is irreducibly distinct in itself, incapable of equivalent substitution by any other form of expression. How so? Let me briefly mention two points.

First, "the Father and the Son and the Holy Spirit" is irreducibly distinct by virtue of the simple but inescapable fact that Christians are commanded to baptize in this name by the risen Lord. Furthermore, and as befits a formula intended for liturgical use, the phrase identifies the persons of the Trinity in a simple, fixed, and pronounceable form. Note that this latter characteristic in particular distinguishes the christological inflection from the theological inflection that we just discussed. As we saw, the theological inflection is fecund, generative. It has a fixed center but not a fixed form of expression: the unspoken tetragrammaton speaks through a variety of pious circumlocutions. In contrast, the baptismal inflection is synthetic: it gathers together many forms of Jesus' speech — my Father, our Father, Son of Man, Son of God, Spirit of the Father, etc. — and stabilizes them in a single, coordinated phrase. If the theological inflection glows like a hidden fire through the billowing clouds of the ever-changing coverings, the christological inflection shines like Jesus' brilliant raiment on the Mount of Transfiguration, bringing the church's fragmentary knowledge of the mystery of Jesus, God, and the Spirit to brilliant, focused expression. Note, too, if you will, that one can detect a certain order or *taxis* between these two idioms. The theological inflection's sheer fecundity of periphrastic expression is the source — I am tempted to say the unoriginate origin — of much of the linguistic wealth (e.g., "my heavenly Father," "Holy Spirit") which the christological inflection brings to a delimited, unified focus.

Second, the christological inflection of the triune name is irreducibly distinct because it expresses the *distinction* and *mutuality* of the first two persons of the Trinity in terms of relationship of origin, and because it does so in language that according to the Gospels' witness is characteristic of Jesus' own self-designation and address to God. The terms "Father" and "Son" make the point that God and Christ are distinguishable identities by virtue of their essential relatedness to one another. Each is identified in terms of the other. In this case, to be is to be related.

Taken together, these two points amply justify the important place that the ecumenical church has accorded the baptismal name in its liturgical practice and dogmatic traditions. Yet now I wish to direct our attention to the other side of the equation, to the proposition that the christological inflection of the triune name is not only irreducibly distinct but also inseparably related to two other equally basic inflections of the triune name. In particular, I wish to explore the proposition that the christological inflection serves as a name that identifies the three persons of the triune God only by virtue of its inseparable connection to the theological inflection, which identifies the same three persons in a different idiom centered on the holy tetragrammaton.

Let me begin with an obvious point. "Father," "son," and "spirit" are all common nouns that can be predicated of many subjects. The christological inflection, however, particularizes these common nouns by the use of the definite article. It speaks not (as Christians often but misleadingly say) of "Father, Son, and Holy Spirit," but of "*the* Father and *the* Son and *the* Holy Spirit." The definite article serves to particularize the generic nouns, restricting their application from the many to the one. As a result, the phrase "the Father and the Son and the Holy Spirit" comes in practice to function like a personal proper name, as indeed the baptismal liturgy itself suggests: "I baptize you *in the name of* the Father and the Son and the Holy Spirit."[25]

In my view, this particularization is the key for deciding whether the use of the baptismal formula necessarily underwrites patriarchal ideas and social relations. Granted, Christians should want to distinguish between authentic evangelical discourse and its patriarchal distortion. But to speak of "*the* Father" is to pick out a particular identity within a given context, so that the disputed question properly turns on the relationship of this *particular* Father to patriarchy, not on the generic meaning of the word "father." When Jesus in prayer calls out "Father!" the sense of the word is supplied by the character of the One who sent him and raised him from the dead. This is why Jesus can say, "If you have seen me, you have seen the Father" (John 14:9). But is it possible to find even a single instance in the entire New Testament where Jesus appeals to the authority of this Father to underwrite male privilege? Is not the opposite much rather the

25. One finds a similar phenomenon in the New Testament's use of "Christ," which appears frequently enough as a title or common noun (as in Peter's confession in Matt. 16:16), but which through its application to *Jesus* comes also to serve as a personal name (as frequently in Paul's letters).

case? Whatever may be the case with other fathers or fatherhood in general, *this* Father is implacably opposed to every diminution of women for the sake of male privilege.[26]

However, we must go on and consider a further peculiarity of the definite article. The power of the definite article to particularize a common noun is dependent on context, apart from which its reference remains ambiguous. If my wife says to me, "Please go get the mail," I understand that she means the mail in our mailbox, not our neighbors'. But if I overheard the same request on a crowded street, I would have no idea how to fulfill the request. In the case of common nouns that designate persons, such as "mother" or "prophet," the framework of identification usually terminates in a personal proper name, such as Hannah or Elijah or Muhammad. In an analogous way, I would argue, even "the Father and the Son and the Holy Spirit" depends ultimately for its identifying power on a more complete framework of identification that terminates finally in a personal proper name. But what is the personal proper name that backs up "the Father and the Son and the Holy Spirit," by virtue of which it is enabled to serve as a name in the context, for example, of the baptismal liturgy? Is it, as Christians are no doubt inclined to suggest, the name "Jesus Christ"? But the Marcionites also worshiped "the Father and the Son and the Holy Spirit" and backed up their worship by appeal to the name of Jesus Christ. Nevertheless, the church deemed their worship heretical. Moreover, the name "Jesus Christ" belongs to the second person of the Trinity by virtue of God's eternal decrees with respect to time, while the name of "the Father and the Son and the Holy Spirit" belongs to God even irrespective of those decrees. Hence there must be some other personal proper name that backs up the baptismal name of the Trinity. And that name, it seems to me, can only be the holy tetragrammaton.

Consider the texture of the New Testament witness. When we look carefully, we discover time and time again that the terms "Father" or "Son" or "Spirit" or any combination of these regularly appear intertwined and side-by-side with language that orbits around the tetragrammaton. Moreover, we see that these two idioms serve mutually to interpret the identity

26. For a further development of this point, see Roberta C. Bondi, "Praying 'Our Father' and Formation in Love," in *Trinity, Community, and Power*, ed. M. Douglas Meeks (Nashville: Kingswood Books, 2000). The biblical data pertaining to the New Testament's use of "Father" for God is ably set forth by Marianne Meye Thompson, *The Promise of the Father* (Louisville: Westminster/John Knox Press, 2000).

of the trinitarian persons with respect to all three vectors of time — past, present, and future. "Our *Father* in heaven, hallowed be thy *name*" is not a redundant expression, as though "Father" were now the name of God *tout court*. Rather, the words point to *two* mutually interpreting and indispensable poles of Jesus' identification of God.[27] A similar pattern of intertwining is found in Philippians 2, where — in a dramatic double movement — Christ has received "the name that is above every name," so that he might receive the acclamation of all creation *"to the glory of God the Father."*[28] The logic of Philippians 2 is mirrored in a strikingly exact way throughout the Gospel of John, where the Son's mission from and unity with the Father are interpreted at the climax of the Gospel in terms of the Son's revelation of the Father's *name* (John 17), a revelation that Raymond Brown — rightly in my view — associates with Jesus' "I am" statements, which allude unmistakably to the unspoken tetragrammaton. But whereas the intertwining idioms of Philippians 2 direct our gaze to the ultimate future, those of the Gospel of John direct our gaze to the ultimate origin: "Before Abraham was, I am" (8:58). Or recall again the book of Revelation's improvisation on a typical Christian letter, where instead of the expected "God the Father" we are met by "He who is and who was and who is to come," again an allusion to the sacred tetragrammaton (by way of Exod. 3:14) that pounds now on all three keyboards of time. Finally, Dale C. Allison sug-

27. As Adelheid Ruck-Schröder notes, "The address to God as Father is immediately followed by the petition for the hallowing of God's name. This shows that the one who prays this prayer *practices* a hallowing of God's name, in that he or she addresses God with "Father" rather than with God's unspoken Name. For Jesus such reserve before the Tetragrammaton may be presupposed." Cf. Adelheid Ruck-Schröder, *Der Name Gottes und der Name Jesu: eine neutestamentliche Studie* (Neukirchen-Vluyn: Neukirchener Verlag, 1999), pp. 149-50. The author goes on to observe that Christian scholarship tends to be too preoccupied with Jesus' use of "Father" while neglecting his reverence for the name.

28. In my view, Phil. 2 is not most naturally read to imply that the Father gives the name away in such a fashion as to *dispossess* himself of it, as Christopher Seitz seems to imply when he speaks of "the loss of the divine name" ("Handing Over the Name," pp. 39-40). As the nineteenth-century Christian novelist George MacDonald wrote, "A name is one of those things one can give away and keep all the same" (*The Princess and the Goblin* [1871; New York: Everyman's Library Children's Classics, Alfred A. Knopf, 1993]). Rather, in Phil. 2 the Father gives away the sacred name so that it may be glorified *as his* in another (cf. John 17:11: "protect them in your name that you have given me"). Jesus does not gain the name by impoverishing another ("a robbery"), but receives it for the glory of another. Indeed, this deference is what makes him Son and Lord.

gests that even the baptismal formula of Matthew 28:19 includes an allusion to the tetragrammaton, inasmuch as *"the name of the Father and the Son and the Holy Spirit"* refers not epexegetically to "the Father and the Son and the Holy Spirit," but allusively and reverentially to the unspoken tetragrammaton, that is, the name which belongs to the Father and which the Father gives to the Son and whose praise is evoked by the Holy Spirit.[29]

My claim, then, is that "the Father and the Son and the Holy Spirit" stands in inseparable relation with another, equally basic inflection of the triune name, an inflection centered in the giving, the receiving, and the illumination of the holy tetragrammaton. To cast further light on this claim, permit me a brief digression on the topic of informative identity statements. An informative identity statement is a statement that creates new insight by conjoining two proper names for the same referent. The textbook example is "the evening star is the morning star," but more familiar examples include "Clark Kent is Superman," "Mark Twain is Samuel Longhorn Clemens," or "Mt. McKinley is Denali." The puzzle about informative identity statements is that they contradict the standard philosophical theory about proper names, according to which proper names differ from other forms of speech because they serve simply to *point to* or *pick out* that which they name. Beyond this, so the standard theory goes, a proper name has no other *meaning* at all. To put it technically, a proper name has denotation but not connotation, reference but not sense. The difficulty is that if the standard theory were correct, then it would seem that informative identity statements could never be informative. That is, "Clark Kent is Superman" would tell us no more than "Clark Kent is Clark Kent," since both names serve merely to pick out one and the same person. Yet we can easily imagine circumstances in which a person might be astonished to discover that Clark Kent is Superman. How can this be?

The philosopher Gottlob Frege addressed this puzzle by suggesting that proper names do after all have sense *(Sinn)* in addition to reference. According to Frege, the primary role of proper names is to pick out the object they name, but in doing so they also determine the object from a given perspective.

In the statement, "The evening star is the morning star," the two names have the same referent but different senses. The sense provides the

---

29. Dale C. Allison, *The Sermon on the Mount* (New York: Crossroad, 1999).

mode of presentation *(die Art des Gegebenseins)* of the object; the object is, as it were, illuminated from one side *(einseitig beleuchtet)* by the sense of the expression; and it is because the two expressions have different senses that the statement can convey factual information to us.[30]

For Frege, statements that join two proper names for the same object are not necessarily trivial or tautologous. Indeed, according to Frege, "the existence of different names for the same content is *the very heart of the matter* if each is associated with a different way of determining the content."[31]

Frege's analysis helps us understand why it is important for Christians to recognize that — according to the texture of the biblical witness — the name of the triune God exists in two different but equally basic inflections. The two inflections *identify the same triune reality, but from different perspectives.*[32] The theological inflection, centered in the tetragram-

---

30. John Searle, "Proper Names and Description," in *The Encyclopedia of Philosophy,* vol. 6 (New York: Macmillan, 1967).

31. Gottlob Frege, *Begriffschrift* (1879), para. 8; italics added. Frege's analysis is widely thought to have been fatally critiqued by Saul Kripke, who reaffirms a version of the traditional view according to which proper names are "rigid signifiers," that is, pointers that have reference but not sense. But so far as I can see, Kripke's analysis does not finally refute the notion that proper names have sense, but only a particular account of how this is so. According to Kripke, proper names cannot have *any particular* sense as an essential property, nor even a loose bundle of senses (Searle, "Proper Names and Description"). Rather, proper names can acquire sense only as a historical, contingent accretion that one can imagine possibly being otherwise. This view is sometimes called the "baptism" theory of proper names. Yet, even on this view, to have a sense of some kind, however minimal, appears to be an essential property of proper names, even if this sense extends no further than to allow one to recognize it as a proper name, even in total ignorance of its referent. Moreover, this view allows that proper names in ordinary usage do indeed have sense; so, to this degree at least, Frege's analysis seems to stand. In any case, informative identity statements are a reality, and any theory of proper names that cannot account for this fact will not do.

32. Consider two further analogies to the phenomenon of the informative identity statement, one drawn from the Bible, the other from rabbinic interpretation.

Paul M. van Buren observes, "In scriptural parallelism, the second half of the verse is no mere subordinate commentary on the first half, but is constructed to say the same thing in other words" (*According to the Scriptures* [Grand Rapids: Eerdmans, 1998], p. 66). Van Buren develops this point in a way that demonstrates how the church's reflection is impoverished when it fails to read the New Testament in light of the Old. Christians, van Buren points out, typically read John 1:14 so: "And the word became flesh." Thus they omit the second half of the phrase, "and pitched his tent among us." The second half of the phrase says "the same thing in other words" and should lead to the insight that "the

maton, serves to identify Jesus with respect to the God of Israel. The christological inflection, centered in the Son, serves to identify the God of Israel with reference to Jesus.[33] The two inflections together, in their difference and mutual relation, identify the One to whom Jesus prays, and, by extension, Jesus himself, and the Spirit by whom he lives and which he shares. This mutuality, I hasten to add, has suggestive implications for how Christians understand the economy of salvation with respect to God's election of the people Israel. The tetragrammaton enters the New Testament as a name that is already saturated, drenched with sense, and at the center of this sense, so to speak, is *Adoshem's* covenant with Israel. Hence it is all but impossible to evoke this name without also evoking this covenant and this people, whether implicitly or explicitly. To identify Jesus with respect to *this* name is also inevitably to identify him with respect to this people and their promised future. Consider this example. A striking feature of Paul's letters is that he often ascribes Septuagint passages containing the tetragrammaton to Christ (cf. Rom. 14:11; 1 Cor. 1:31; 10:26, etc.). Nevertheless, David B. Capes observes that when Paul comes to discuss the relationship of Jews and Gentiles, he frequently ascribes the relevant Septuagint passages to God (Rom. 9:26, 29; 15:9, 11).[34] If the first

---

Johannine story of the incarnation of the Word in Jesus is to be read in conjunction with the story of God's presence with his people in the tent of meeting, where 'the LORD used to speak to Moses face to face, as a man speaks to his friend'" (Exod. 33:11). When the scriptural parallelism is ignored, we fail to see that even "the 'highest' christological themes . . . are formulated 'according to the scriptures.'"

Another analogy: "For the rabbis no statement of scripture was haphazard or superfluous. They taught that even the two Hebrew words for God — Elohim and YHWH — were not synonyms but symbolized the different aspects of God's providence. Wherever the tetragrammaton appeared, God should be viewed as acting mercifully; where Elohim appeared, God's judgment should be understood. *Between them, the two names expressed the totality of God's providence* or, as they expressed it, His two Middoth or measures" (N. A. Dahl and F. Segal, "Philo and the Rabbis on the Names of God," *Journal for the Study of Judaism* 9, no. 1 [1978]: 1; italics added).

33. Luke/Acts provides a striking example of the fact that the sense of "Father" in the New Testament's narratives stems from Jesus: once Jesus has ascended, the term ceases to be used! The sole exception is found in Peter's Pentecost speech, in which he confirms that the gift of the Spirit was the Father's "promise" to which Jesus referred in Luke 24:49 and Acts 1:4. See Robert L. Mowery, "The Disappearance of the Father: References to God the Father in Luke/Acts," *Encounter* 55, no. 4 (Autumn 1994): 353-58.

34. David B. Capes, *Old Testament Yahweh Texts in Paul's Christology* (Tübingen: J. C. B. Mohr, 1992), pp. 114-15.

practice indicates Paul's conviction that the Scripture's promises about the Lord are now coming to pass in Christ (cf. Rom. 10:13!), the second practice indicates that this coming-to-pass still transpires within the context of God's still unfolding covenant with Israel (cf. especially Rom. 15:9, 11). It is the two practices together that enact "the heart of the matter."

Conversely, Frege's analysis helps us to understand what goes wrong when Christians read the biblical witness in a manner that permits the theological inflection of the triune name to drop out of consideration or awareness. In that case, God's identity is illuminated in a one-sided way *(einseitig beleuchtet)*. We have already touched on the most extreme example of this, namely, the Marcionites who worshiped the Father and the Son and the Holy Spirit, but refused to worship the God of Israel. More commonly, however, Christians read the New Testament as though God's identity as *Adoshem* were merely a preliminary stage of God's self-revelation on the way to God's self-revelation as "Father." Consider two examples:

> The name "Father" is the best calculated to manifest the novelty of the God of Jesus, as compared not only with the God of the Greeks but with the God of the Jews. Compared with the God of Israel the God of Jesus represents a revolution in so far as God is the God of grace before being the God of the law.[35]

Again:

> Everything that Christ taught, everything that makes the NT new, and better than the Old, everything that is distinctively Christian as opposed to merely Jewish, is summed up in the knowledge of the Fatherhood of God. "Father" is the Christian name of God.[36]

In 1933 Gerhard Kittel argued along such lines when he wrote that Jesus' use of *abba* "far surpasses any possibilities of intimacy assumed in Judaism" and introduces "something which is wholly new."[37] Kittel's

---

35. Claude Geffre, "Father as the Proper Name of God," in *God as Father?* ed. Metz and Schillebeeckx, p. 44. Cited in Thompson, *The Promise of the Father*, p. 11.

36. J. I. Packer, *Knowing God* (Downers Grove, IL: InterVarsity, 1973), pp. 182-83. Cited in Thompson, *The Promise of the Father*, p. 11.

37. Gerhard Kittel, "abba," in *Theological Dictionary of the New Testament* (Grand Rapids: Eerdmans, 1964-76), vol. 1, pp. 5-6.

claim was partly taken up by Joachim Jeremias, and subsequently many biblical scholars and theologians have sought to make Jesus' experience of God as *abba* the basis of his unique self-understanding, messianic vocation, and divine sonship.[38] Yet when Christians read the New Testament through this lens, the result is a systematic distortion of the biblical witness, in which what is perceived to be "distinctively Christian" is lifted up at the cost of what is "merely Jewish" in Christianity.

To summarize, "the Father and the Son and the Holy Spirit" is not merely one among many possible metaphors for God, but neither is it *the* proper name of the triune God. Rather, it is the second of three inflections of the triune name, one that is indispensable in its own right and yet must be held in balance with two other equally indispensable inflections of the triune name. The theological and christological inflections interpret each other mutually, with respect not only to who God *was* but also to who God *is* and *will be*. The illumination that arises from the conjunction of the two inflections in and through the medium of the evangelical history is not a passing stage of the Christian witness, but belongs permanently to "the heart of the matter."

The Pneumatological Inflection of the Triune Name

The third and final inflection of the triune name is what I will call the pneumatological inflection, the inflection most naturally appropriated to the third person of the Trinity. The pneumatological inflection also provides a way in which to designate all three persons of the Trinity, but it does so in a voice and idiom that are characteristic of the Holy Spirit.

In the biblical narratives, the Holy Spirit astonishes us by the uncanny way in which it unites constancy and variety. The Holy Spirit comes always from the living God, bearing the gift of new life, yet it does so in an endless variety of ways. It manifests its presence and power now as a dove descending, now as the sound of wind roaring, now as tongues of fire dancing, now as the gift of speech in ecstasy. So too the pneumato-

38. See Joachim Jeremias, *The Prayers of Jesus* (Naperville, IL: A. R. Allenson, 1967); Edward Schillebeeckx, *An Experiment in Christology* (New York: Seabury Press, 1979), pp. 256-71; Jürgen Moltmann, *The Trinity and the Kingdom* (Minneapolis: Fortress, 1993), pp. 61-96. For a valuable review of Jeremias's contribution and its subsequent history, see Thompson, *The Promise of the Father*, chap. 1.

logical inflection of the triune name unites constancy and variety in the church's naming of the triune God. It has no fixed vocabulary of its own but enlists general forms of speech and possibilities of speech present in the discourse of the peoples, tribes, and nations, and gives them a new and unique imprint in service of the gospel.

On the one hand, the pneumatological inflection has a constant theme: the mystery of God's eternal identity as manifested in God's covenant with Israel irrevocably confirmed in the gospel of Jesus Christ. It is important to stress that this inflection does not ignore or bypass the inflections we have already discussed but pours forth from them as their Great Expositor and Interpreter. In addition, the pneumatological inflection has a constant goal: to draw us ever more deeply into knowledge and vital piety, and thereby to make us more suitable vessels of the glory of God's name. Yet, on the other hand, the pneumatological inflection traces an unpredictable variety of paths from source to goal. The pneumatological inflection is not only the Great Expositor and Interpreter but also the Great Improviser.

The roots of the pneumatological inflection go deep into the Scriptures of Israel. Already the prophets of Israel sought to exposit or interpret God's unique identity by enlisting generic forms of speech. Consider one of Israel's most common refrains: "The LORD is God!" Here "LORD," of course, stands for the tetragrammaton, the personal name of the One who accosted Moses at the bush. But the word for God, *Elohim,* stems from a generic term for the divine that was common in the ancient Near East. It is a class term that could be and was applied to a variety of gods and goddesses, and not to Israel's God only. Thus when the prophets declared, "The LORD is God!" they staked a claim and took a risk. They staked the claim that the generic term *Elohim* receives its true and proper sense from the name, character, and promises of Israel's God, and Israel's God alone. But they also took the risk that the generic term was a suitable vessel for bringing the LORD's unique identity to the nations.

Over two millennia of Christian tradition, the pneumatological inflection has enlisted a staggering variety of words and forms of speech to designate the persons of the triune God. Some of these names have acquired a more or less permanent place in the language of the ecumenical church. Examples include the New Testament's own designations of Christ as "Word" and as "Wisdom," or the technical vocabulary that the ancient church devised in order to clarify its trinitarian faith, such as

"Trinity," "person," and "substance" in the West, and *hypostasis* and *ousia* in the East. These familiar examples of the pneumatological inflection are important, not because they exhaust the possibilities of pneumatological speech, but because they offer us paradigmatic examples of how such speech operates. They have the power to teach us again and again the amount of care and discernment that is needed in order to practice rightly the kind of expository improvisation that the pneumatological inflection requires. As any jazz musician can tell you, faithful improvisation is the greatest of all musical skills, a skill that for most requires years of apprenticeship in the school of the masters. Above all, the pneumatological inflection is not simply a license that says anything goes. The same prophets that dared to say, "The LORD is God!" refused to say, "The LORD is *Ba'al*," even though *Ba'al* was also a generic or class term meaning "Master." The prophets discerned that *Elohim* possessed possibilities that *Ba'al* could not, probably because the sense of the latter term had come to be determined too completely by the identity of a competing deity.

Yet, by the nature of the case, the pneumatological inflection of the triune name demands to be exercised afresh in every time and place. The theologian Abhishiktananda, writing as a Christian in a Hindu context, speaks of the persons of the Holy Trinity as *Sat, Cit,* and *Ananda,* which translates roughly as "Source and ground of all being," "the divine self-consciousness," and "expression of love within the godhead which brings being and consciousness into the bliss of love."[39] We find other examples of the pneumatological inflection in the writings of contemporary feminist theologians. The Roman Catholic feminist Elizabeth Johnson speaks of Unoriginate Love, Love from Love, and Mutual Love. While the church must test the adequacy of these and other proposals, I humbly submit that they cannot be ruled out of court. At the end of the day, the pneumatological inflection of the triune name cannot be fixed in a single form of speech, nor indeed in any fixed set of already existing names. Its specific task is to express the inexhaustible fullness of the mystery of the one God, a fullness for which no single fixed form of expression is the uniquely adequate token. This is the kernel of truth in the apophatic and mystical traditions of Christian thought, which affirm that the deity of God is nameless and that therefore God must be praised with many

39. Abhishiktananda, *Saccidananda: A Christian Approach to Advaitic Experience,* 2nd ed. (Delhi: ISPCK, 1984).

names. This statement summarizes a crucial aspect of the pneumatological inflection, even though it does not provide a sufficient account of the name of the triune God as a whole.

"These Three Are One"

The name of the triune God is one name in three inflections. Like the persons of the Holy Trinity, these three inflections of the triune name are interrelated but not interchangeable. None can be replaced by another without loss; none can be ignored without peril. Each inflection opens up an indispensable — but not independent — perspective on the whole mystery of Holy Trinity. Yet there is a real sense in which the church's trinitarian faith — in all its fullness and distinctiveness — neither adds nor subtracts one jot or tittle from the centrality and uniqueness of the personal proper name of the God of Israel, the sacred tetragrammaton. It simply unfolds that name in a threefold way, three different times, in a way that is mandated for the church by the gospel of Jesus Christ. In closing, I return to a claim I made at the start: the affirmation of the centrality and abiding significance of the tetragrammaton is not an *obstacle* to a trinitarian understanding of God's name, but rather its enabling condition.

Our Father Abraham: A Point of Theological Convergence and Divergence for Christians and Jews

MARVIN R. WILSON

Abraham may be deceased, but he is not dead. In agreement with these words is another Abraham, Abraham Joshua Heschel, an impressive scholar who has significantly impacted the thinking of Jews and Christians. In Heschel's view, Abraham is not a principle or idea to be comprehended but a life to be continued: "The life of him who joins the covenant of Abraham continues the life of Abraham. For the present is not apart from the past. . . . Abraham endures for ever. We are Abraham."[1] Karl-Josef Kuschel makes a similar observation regarding Abraham in relation to the apostle Paul: "Anyone who reads Paul will immediately note that for him, as for any Jew, Abraham is not a memorial to faith from distant, past times, but a living reality."[2] To be sure, the Abrahamic legacy has endured nearly four thousand years. Judaism and Christianity each look to Abraham as father.[3] The biblical phrase "our/your father Abraham" (Isa. 51:2; Luke 1:73; Jas. 2:21) expresses the family relationship that

---

1. Abraham J. Heschel, *God in Search of Man* (New York: Farrar, Straus & Giroux, 1955), p. 201.

2. Karl-Josef Kuschel, *Abraham: Sign of Hope for Jews, Christians and Muslims* (New York: Continuum, 1995), p. 82.

3. Islam considers Abraham (Ibhraim) to be father of Muslims. He is mentioned frequently in the Koran. However, the Koran states, "Abraham was neither Jew, nor Christian; But he was true in faith, and bowed his will to Allah" (3:67). Abraham is identified with the Kaaba, a cubical building in the courtyard of the mosque at Mecca containing a sacred black stone. A mosque in Hebron marks his place of burial.

every person of faith has with "the man of faith"; it also epitomizes the deep spiritual link every Christian has with the Jewish people (cf. Gal. 3:29). It is my aim in this essay to discuss some of the areas in which Abraham is especially relevant to the Jewish-Christian encounter.

In the shared Judeo-Christian tradition, Abraham is a major figure; references to him abound from antiquity to the present. One would expect therefore that Jews and Christians find considerable common ground and a convergence of their respective traditions in their discussion of Abraham. Looking at this issue historically, Jon Levenson has correctly observed that "the community of Torah (Judaism) and the community of Gospel (Christianity) would appeal to the same Scriptures and seek to practice virtues that overlap to a high degree. . . . This is as we should expect from traditions that each revere the memory of Father Abraham."[4] Certainly, Abraham is an inspiring figure around whom Jews and Christians find many areas of agreement. The biblical narratives about him contain many foundational theological themes and ethical teachings that have shaped the core of Judaism and Christianity.

On the other hand, Jews and Christians diverge in a number of ways in their understanding of Abraham. Just as the New Testament writers and the church fathers took the Jewish Scriptures and developed a Christian theology regarding Abraham, so the rabbis of the postbiblical era had their own distinct Jewish take on those same Scriptures. In terms of interpretation and emphasis, this has resulted in some significant areas of difference between the two faiths. In the end, Judaism and Christianity claim one father, Abraham. But as rival siblings, synagogue and church have understood and related to their father from different perspectives. Strong family resemblance and ties? Yes. Identical points of view? No.

This essay is arranged in three main sections. The first section establishes the importance of Abraham in Jewish tradition. The second section sets forth the importance of Abraham in Christian tradition. The third section concerns interpretation of Abraham. In this section, I have chosen five Abrahamic themes for comparison and contrast. Each of these themes illustrates theological convergence and divergence within Judaism and Christianity. It is my hope that this study of our father Abraham will

---

4. Jon D. Levenson, *The Death and Resurrection of the Beloved Son* (New Haven: Yale University Press, 1993), p. 219.

bring mutual enrichment and a deeper understanding and appreciation of Jews and Christians as people of God.

The Importance of Abraham in Jewish Tradition

Abraham is father of the Jewish people (Isa. 51:2). Hence he is often referred to as the first Jew, the "founder of the faith."[5] The annual Torah-reading cycle places particular focus on Abraham in the narrative of Genesis 11:26–25:11. In Ur of the Chaldees God reveals himself to Abraham and leads him out of an idolatrous way of life (cf. Josh. 24:2). Abraham keeps responding to God in faithful obedience. God promises Abraham numerous descendants, a land, and that the nations will be blessed through him. God sovereignly enters into a covenant relation with Abraham and establishes circumcision as a sign of that bond. Abraham faithfully walks with God, obeys him, and trusts him. God tests the depth of Abraham's commitment to him by telling him to bind his only son Isaac and prepare him for sacrifice. Abraham willingly obeys. At the last moment, however, God dramatically intervenes to save the life of Abraham's beloved son. Abraham passes this ultimate test. Consequently, the Jewish Scriptures sum up the life of Abraham by stating that God "found his heart faithful" (Neh. 9:8).

Abraham is the first person in the Bible to be called a Hebrew (Gen. 14:13) and the first to bear the title "prophet" (Gen. 20:7; cf. Ps. 105:15). In an address to all Israel, Joshua refers to the patriarch as "your father Abraham" (Josh. 24:3). In the prophets,[6] God calls Abraham "my friend" (Isa. 41:8). The Psalms speak of Abraham as God's "servant" (Ps. 105:42) and refer to the Israelites as "the offspring of Abraham" (Ps. 105:6) and "the people of the God of Abraham" (Ps. 47:9). Centuries later the Jewish sages succinctly summarized their great esteem of Abraham and his unique place in Jewish religion: "Five possessions has the Holy One, blessed be He, made especially his own. These are: the Torah, Heaven and earth, Abraham, Israel and the Holy Sanctuary" (Abot 6:10).

In the Talmud, God is referred to as *Rachmana,* "The Compassionate." Like father Abraham, children of Abraham are to show compassion,

---

5. Abba Hillel Silver, *Where Judaism Differed* (New York: Macmillan, 1956), p. 81.
6. Cf. Abraham J. Heschel, *The Prophets* (New York: Harper & Row, 1962), p. 311.

mercy, and kindness to others. "Whoever is merciful to his fellow-men is certainly of the children of our father Abraham, and whosoever is not merciful to his fellow-men is certainly not of the children of our father Abraham" (Babylonian Talmud, Bezah 32b; cf. Yeb. 79a). Humaneness, sensitivity to hurt, and hospitality to strangers are hallmarks of the Jewish tradition. In Genesis 18:1-15, Abraham, with the help of Sarah, warmly welcomes and entertains three visitors. It is therefore apropos that in the Psalms Abraham is twice characterized as God's servant (105:6, 42). Abraham's actions recounted in Genesis set a standard in Jewish tradition for the practice of hospitality. The rabbis, many centuries later, developed a teaching on hospitality built upon Abraham's example of servanthood to strangers. In Jewish tradition, hospitality, *hakhnasat orhim* (literally "bringing in of guests" or "gathering in of travelers"), became one of the most important functions of the home.[7]

Abraham also shows great concern for justice. In Genesis 18:16-33, Abraham, moved with justice and compassion over Sodom, engages God in dialogue. Appropriately, Martin Buber has characterized religious faith in terms of dialogue, an "I and Thou" relationship.[8] Abraham's passionate pleading with God to spare human life results in "one of the most famous and boldest intercessory prayers in all of Scripture."[9] What is all the more remarkable about Abraham's concern is the fact that he intercedes for an evil place inhabited by a people with whom he has no personal ties. Abraham is concerned that justice be tempered with mercy, hence he argues with God, pleading with him to agree that he will not bring destruction if ten righteous can be found. God repeatedly affirms his willingness to be merciful for the sake of the righteous. Abraham's nobility of character emerges with his anguished cry for justice. All human beings are his brothers, and he

---

7. For additional development of this theme see Marvin R. Wilson, *Our Father Abraham* (Grand Rapids: Eerdmans, 1989), pp. 219, 220. Also note the recently discovered synagogue mosaic (fifth to seventh century C.E.) at Sepphoris in Galilee, which may contain some of the earliest Jewish art known of the three angelic visitors to Abraham and Sarah (see Zeev Weiss, "The Sepphois Synagogue Mosaic," *Biblical Archaeology Review* 26, no. 5 [2000]: 48-61, 70).

8. See Martin Buber, *I and Thou*, trans. Ronald Gregor Smith (New York: Charles Scribner's Sons, 1937, 1958); trans. Walter Kaufman (New York: Charles Scribner's Sons, 1970).

9. Ronald Youngblood, *Faith of Our Fathers* (Glendale, CA: Regal Books, 1976), p. 43.

wants the Judge of all the earth to do right (Gen. 18:25). Abraham's dialogue with God sets a historic tone. As Abraham displayed God's attributes of justice and mercy, so the actions of Abraham's children must reflect the same.

Judaism also considers Abraham the "first great missionary in the world."[10] Abraham breaks with the deities of ancestral paganism and embraces the monotheistic ideal. The biblical record indicates that Abraham was a rich merchant-trader who roamed across the Fertile Crescent. Called to be a blessing to humankind, Abraham, through his journeying from place to place, bore the message of the one true God (cf. Gen. 12:2, 3). Commenting on a midrashic parable about Abraham, Chaim Pearl points out that because Abraham was a "'wandering Jew' Abraham could reach a wider population and so have greater influence."[11]

According to Samson Raphael Hirsch, the Israelites might have perished like their idolatrous neighbors had they not "received from Abraham the courage to be a minority."[12] Males who convert to Judaism recall Abraham through the covenant of circumcision that God instituted with the patriarch. The rabbis taught, "If a proselyte wants to become a Jew, he should not say: I am an old man. At this stage I am not becoming a Jew. Let him learn from Abraham, who performed circumcision when he was ninety-nine years old" (Tanhuma, Buber, Lekh-Lekha, on Genesis 3:24). Many converts choose for themselves the Hebrew name Avraham as part of their conversion.

In the liturgy of the synagogue, Abraham is remembered in the *Amidah* or *Shemoneh Esrai* prayer, recited in the three daily prayer services. The first paragraph of the prayer begins, "Blessed are you, Lord our God, and God of our fathers, God of Abraham, God of Isaac, and God of Jacob." The paragraph ends, "Blessed are you, God, shield of Abraham" *(magen avraham).* Why is Abraham singled out among the three forefathers? Abraham was the person responsible for creating an "indestructible spiritual inheritance of love of God for his descendants."[13] In addition, in

---

10. Cf. Solomon Schechter, *Some Aspects of Rabbinic Theology* (New York: Schocken Books, 1961), p. 84.

11. Chaim Pearl, *Theology in Rabbinic Stories* (Peabody, MA: Hendrickson Publishers, 1997), p. 70.

12. Quoted in Paul Carlson, *O Christian! O Jew!* (Elgin, IL: David C. Cook, 1974), p. 14.

13. Yitchok Kirzner, *The Art of Jewish Prayer* (Northvale, NJ: Jason Aronson, 1991), p. 62.

Jewish tradition the name of Abraham is connected with the concept of *zekhut avot* ("merit of the fathers"), the belief that mercy will be shown to the Jewish people for generations to come on account of the goodness of their ancestors.[14] *Zekhut* does not absolve individual Jews of moral responsibility based on the good deeds of the founding fathers. Rather, it is a reminder that patriarchs such as Abraham, and indeed the righteous few of any generation, can impact those who will follow them.[15] Prophetic literature may allude to the concept of *zekhut* in the phrase "turning the hearts of the fathers to their children" (Mal. 4:6; cf. Luke 1:17).

Like all human beings, Abraham had imperfections and weaknesses. Yet in assessing the measure of the man, most of the biblical and extra-canonical writings that reflect back on the Genesis narratives do not dwell on Abraham's failures. Rather, Abraham stands out as a man of virtue, devout in faith, a model of piety to be emulated.[16] In the Jewish wisdom literature of the early second century B.C.E., Ben Sira, in his "Praise of the Elders," sums up the significance of this great patriarch and righteous forebear of the Jewish people:

> Abraham was the great father of a multitude of nations,
>   and no one has been found like him in glory;
> he kept the law of the Most High,
>   and was taken into covenant with him;
> he established the covenant in his flesh,
>   and when he was tested he was found faithful.
>
>   (Sir. 44:19, 20)

God elected Abraham so that he might impact the world, an awesome task considering the grip that polytheism had upon his environment. Abraham was to bring the teaching of ethical monotheism to all his children after him. God says of the patriarch, "I have chosen him, so that he will direct his children and his household after him to keep the way of the LORD by doing what is right and just" (Gen. 18:19). Josephus sums up

14. See Shabbat 30a, where God instructs Israel to appeal to the merit of the patriarchs in the pleading of their cause to him.

15. Simon Gulstrom, *The Language of Judaism* (Northvale, NJ: Jason Aronson, 1988), pp. 203, 204.

16. In the mystical tradition of Judaism, the *gematria* of Abraham's name totals 248, equal to the number of positive commandments in the Torah. Thus father Abraham is viewed as one who perfectly fulfilled God's will.

the importance of Abraham as one who had a wise and righteous sense of calling: "Abraham, endowed with great sagacity, with a higher knowledge of God and greater virtues than all the rest, was determined to change the erroneous opinions of men."[17] Judaism and the Jewish people would not be as they are today without the revolutionary, ground-breaking influence of father Abraham.

The Importance of Abraham in Christian Tradition

The earliest Christian documents link the origin of the church to Abraham and his seed. The New Testament mentions Abraham by name seventy-two times. Only the name Moses, among Old Testament characters, appears more frequently. Thus for Christians, "he [Abraham], not Moses, is the real progenitor of the Hebrew people, the founder of the Church."[18] The opening words of the New Testament include the name of Abraham: "A record of the genealogy of Jesus Christ the son of David, the son of Abraham" (Matt. 1:1). In the verses that follow, Abraham is the starting point for Matthew's telescoped version of the ancestry of Jesus (Matt. 1:2-17). The descent of Jesus from Abraham was an important point in the church's teaching and preaching concerning Jesus as Messiah.[19] According to Paul, the blessing promised through Abraham to the people of Israel was particularly realized in Christ. In Paul's words, "the promises were spoken to Abraham and to his seed. The Scripture does not say 'and to seeds,' meaning many people, but 'and to your seed,' meaning one person, who is Christ" (Gal. 3:16; cf. Acts 3:25).

Paul writes to the church in Galatia, "If you belong to Christ, then you are Abraham's seed" (Gal. 3:29). In Paul's view, the church is made up of Jews and gentiles in one body, and Abraham is father of all (Rom. 4:11, 12, 16; Eph. 2:11-18). In Paul's letter to the Romans he uses the metaphor of an olive tree to symbolize Israel (Rom. 11:16-24). Gentiles are grafted into this tree and are nourished by its root (vv. 16-20). From the context of Romans 9–11, the root most likely represents the patriarchs, Abraham

17. Josephus, *Antiquities* 1.7.1.

18. Stuart Blanch, *For All Mankind: A New Approach to the Old Testament* (New York: Oxford, 1978), p. 82.

19. See H. Seebass, "Abraham," in *New International Dictionary of New Testament Theology*, vol. 1, ed. Colin Brown (Grand Rapids: Zondervan, 1975), p. 77.

being the deepest of those roots.[20] As stalwart founder of the original people of God, Abraham had an enduring faith. Through Abraham and his ancestors come a faith-filled, deep-rooted channel of blessing for gentiles, one that will not decay or become uprooted through the years.[21]

In Jesus' day, Jews considered it an expression of honor to be termed "children of Abraham" (Matt. 3:9; Luke 3:8). Abraham was "God's friend" (Jas. 2:23), a man whose "faith was made complete by what he did" (v. 22). Abraham's life of faithful obedience from the moment God called him serves as an inspiring witness to all believers (Heb. 11:8-12; 12:1). In addition, the book of Hebrews makes the point that the Levitical priesthood is descended from Abraham (Heb. 7:5).

In Luke's Gospel, Abraham has a prominent part to play in the story of the rich man and Lazarus (16:19-31). At the time of Jesus, Jewish tradition held that Abraham and other patriarchs remained alive with God and had the powers of intercession. In this Lukan story, however, Abraham refuses to intercede for the rich man. Rather, the account tells of judgment and torment for the rich man but the exaltation of Lazarus, a poor beggar, who is carried by angels to "Abraham's bosom" (Luke 16:22; NIV, "Abraham's side"). The expression "Abraham's bosom" apparently refers to a place of blessedness, honor, and repose for the righteous dead. Abraham refuses to hear the plea of the rich man, perhaps because the rich man did not apply the teachings of the Jewish Scriptures and hence live a life of faithful obedience as Abraham himself did (cf. Luke 16:29). Lazarus, in contrast, finds himself in a place of "tranquil intimacy with great father Abraham."[22]

The Gospels also portray Abraham as an eschatological figure. Abraham, Isaac, and Jacob appear together at a heavenly banquet, sitting at table with the righteous, feasting in the kingdom of God (Matt. 8:10-11; Luke 13:28-29). Jesus states, "People will come from east and west and north and south and will take their places at the feast" (Luke 13:29). This statement seems to allude to the "Apocalypse of Isaiah" where the Lord

20. See James D. G. Dunn, *Romans 9–16,* Word Biblical Commentary (Dallas: Word, 1988), p. 672; C. Maurer, in *Theological Dictionary of the New Testament,* vol. 6, ed. Gerhard Kittel and Gerhard Friedrich, trans. Geoffrey W. Bromiley (Grand Rapids: Eerdmans, 1968), p. 989.

21. See my discussion in *Our Father Abraham,* pp. 14-16.

22. John Nolland, *Luke 9:21–18:34,* Word Biblical Commentary (Dallas: Word, 1993), p. 829.

prepares a future banquet of rich food "for all peoples" (Isa. 25:6; cf. 2:2, 3). The Gospel writers thus emphasize the universality of the gospel message by opening the banquet door to include righteous gentiles, those who at one time had no table fellowship with Jews but now are allowed to share in the eschatological banquet with Abraham and the other patriarchs. In a profound sense, "Everything has been turned upside down."[23] To be sure, the promise to Abraham was that "all peoples on earth" will be blessed through him (Gen. 12:3).

The New Testament writers tend to take the high road in their theological and historical reflection upon the character of Abraham as set forth in the Genesis narratives. That is, in passages such as Acts 7:2-8 and Hebrews 11:8-19, the writers choose to emphasize Abraham's good qualities. They are not particularly interested in writing about the questionable or debatable aspects of Abraham's life."[24] In rather stark and provocative language, Philip Davies calls attention to this other side of Abraham: "For centuries Abraham has been regarded as a paradigm of how a good Jew or Christian should behave — although moving house all the time (Genesis 12:4, 10; 13:1, 18; 20:1; etc.), pimping off your wife (Genesis 12:10-16) and agreeing to slaughter your child (Genesis 22) are not usually highlighted as examples to be followed." Concludes Davies, "Alas, family values are not his [Abraham's] strong point."[25]

Certainly, every Bible character has flaws and failures, whether reported or unreported in the text. In my mind, the fact that the Bible records such incidents makes the message of the Bible more believable. These are the stories of real men and real women coming to know God. Revelation of God's will, however, is progressive. It is extraordinary how well characters like Abraham did, in view of how little light most of them had. True, the New Testament authors exercised selectivity in their use of Old Testament materials, and Abraham is a case in point. But the overall purpose of these authors is to give hope and build faith in the promises of God by showing how God has faithfully guided various individuals in the history of his people (Rom. 15:4; Heb. 11:39, 40).

One aspect of Abraham's character that is important to the New

23. Kuschel, *Abraham,* p. 75.

24. See Alden Thompson, *Who's Afraid of the Old Testament God?* (Grand Rapids: Zondervan, 1989), pp. 18-21.

25. Philip R. Davies, "Abraham and Yahweh: A Case of Male Bonding," *Bible Review,* August, 1995, pp. 24, 25.

Testament writers is his pilgrim life-style.[26] Even when Abraham dwelled in the promised land, "like a stranger in a foreign country, he lived in tents, as did Isaac and Jacob" (Heb. 11:9). Abraham said to the Hittites, "I am a stranger and sojourner among you" (Gen. 23:4). He accepted his status as a pilgrim. God gave him no inheritance in the promised land, "not even a foot of ground" (Acts 7:5). According to the writer of Hebrews, the true homeland of Abraham and the other patriarchs is a heavenly country, a new Jerusalem (see Heb. 11:10, 16; 12:22). "The earthly Canaan and the earthly Jerusalem were but temporary object lessons pointing to the saints' everlasting rest, the well-founded city of God."[27]

This theme of God's people viewing life as a pilgrimage and living it as Abraham and the patriarchs did is picked up in an early Christian document, the *Epistle to Diognetus:* "[Christians] dwell in their own countries, but only as sojourners; they bear their share of all responsibilities as citizens, and they endure all hardships as strangers. Every foreign country is a homeland to them, and every homeland is foreign. . . . Their existence is on earth, but their citizenship is in heaven."[28]

Many centuries later in England, the Pilgrims strongly identified with the memory of Abraham. The Pilgrims thought of themselves as "all the children of Abraham" and thus under the covenant of Abraham, fleeing "Egypt" (England), crossing "the Red Sea" (the Atlantic Ocean), and entering their own "promised land" (New England).[29]

In Catholic Christianity, Abraham is a key figure in the liturgy. In the offertory of every mass for the dead ("requiem mass") a prayer is included that the dead may come "into the holy light which Thou didst promise to Abraham and to his seed." At the end of the prayer are these words: "Grant them, O Lord, to pass from death unto life, which Thou didst promise to Abraham and to his seed." Furthermore, in the canon of every Catholic mass, the priest makes reference to "the sacrifice of our Pa-

26. Cf. D. J. Wiseman, "They Lived in Tents," in *Biblical and Near Eastern Studies,* ed. Gary A. Tuttle (Grand Rapids: Eerdmans, 1978), pp. 195-200.

27. F. F. Bruce, *The Epistle to the Hebrews,* rev. ed. (Grand Rapids: Eerdmans, 1990), p. 299.

28. *Epistle to Diognetus* 5:5-9.

29. Henry L. Feingold, "The Jewish Role in Shaping American Society," in *A Time to Speak: The Evangelical-Jewish Encounter,* ed. A. James Rudin and Marvin R. Wilson (Grand Rapids: Eerdmans, 1987), p. 46.

triarch Abraham."[30] In addition, the Vatican II document *Nostra Aetate* ("In Our Time"), which is a statement dealing with the relation of the church to the Jewish people, opens with a mention of Abraham: "As this Sacred Synod searches into the mystery of the Church, it remembers the bond that spiritually ties the people of the New Covenant to Abraham's stock." In the next paragraph it states, "She [the Church] professes that all who believe in Christ — Abraham's sons according to faith — are included in the same Patriarch's call."

In the early Christian controversy with Judaism, the church gradually distanced itself from appealing to Abraham as the father of Jew and gentile alike. Instead, Christian theology "moved increasingly toward the portrayal of a Christian Abraham who has abandoned and disinherited his children, the Jews."[31] Gradually, a largely de-judaized and gentile-dominated church claimed to be the true heir; it arrogantly began forcing Jewish people to the margin and thereby sought to remove them permanently from salvation history.

Tragically, this exclusion of the Jewish people, the proclamation that God has canceled his *berit olam* ("eternal covenant") with Abraham (cf. Gen. 17:7), has, over the centuries, contributed greatly to the church's general malaise and indifference concerning the Jewish people. Not only have Jews faced spiritual extinction through Christian insistence on their theological illegitimacy, but millions of Jews also faced physical extinction through Crusades, the Inquisition, and the church's deafening silence during the infamous Holocaust years.[32]

Interpreting Abraham: Selected Theological Themes

Election

Abraham marks a pivotal point in the history of biblical revelation. "A new start for humanity began with Abraham."[33] He lived in what the rab-

---

30. Cf. Walter M. Abbott et al., eds., *The Bible Reader* (New York: Bruce Publishing Co., 1969), p. 23.

31. Jeffrey S. Siker, *Disinheriting the Jews: Abraham in Early Christian Controversy* (Louisville: Westminster/John Knox, 1991), p. 27.

32. Kuschel, *Abraham*, pp. 128, 129.

33. Bernard J. Bamberger, *The Story of Judaism*, 3rd ed. (New York: Schocken, 1970), p. 292.

bis called an "age of chaos."[34] Yet God called Abraham to carry out his mission in the world. What appears at first sight to be particular (God chooses one man Abraham) is ultimately a call with the universal in view (all peoples on earth will be blessed through him; Gen. 12:3).

Scripture continually emphasizes that God is the source of Abraham's call. A. J. Heschel calls attention to the importance of divine election as a foundational pillar in Jewish theological thought: "We have not chosen God; He has chosen us. There is no concept of a chosen God but there is the idea of a chosen people."[35] In Genesis, God says to Abraham, "Leave your country . . . and go to the land I will show you" (12:1), and so he left (12:4). God confirms to Joshua and the people of Israel the fact of Abraham's call: "I took your father Abraham from the land beyond the River and led him throughout Canaan" (Josh. 24:3). Nehemiah states that God "chose Abram and brought him out of Ur of the Chaldeans" (Neh. 9:7). In the book of Acts, Stephen, a Hellenistic Jew, states, "The God of glory appeared to our father Abraham while he was still in Mesopotamia" (Acts 7:2). The writer of Hebrews says, when called to go he "obeyed and went, even though he did not know where he was going" (11:8). Thomas Cahill comments on the enormity of Abraham's act of obedience to God's call: *wayyelekh Avram*, "Avram went," are "two of the boldest words in all literature. They signal a complete departure from everything that has gone before in the long evolution of culture and sensibility. . . . [His was] a journey of no return."[36]

In sum, the emphasis in Genesis and the rest of Scripture is that God takes the initiative in reaching Abraham; the initial call comes from God.[37] In the poignant words of Stuart Blanch, "Abraham's life is a life impregnated throughout with an extraordinary sense of God's presence and God's will, for which there is no rational explanation nor ever can be; God speaks, and, listening, the dead receive new life."[38]

But it is important to ask, To what degree may human reason have come into play in the establishing of Abraham's relationship with God?

---

34. See Heschel, *God in Search of Man*, p. 303.

35. Heschel, *God in Search of Man*, p. 425.

36. Thomas Cahill, *The Gifts of the Jews* (New York: Doubleday, 1998), pp. 62, 63.

37. See Christoph Barth, *God with Us* (Grand Rapids: Eerdmans, 1991), pp. 38-55; also William LaSor, *Great Personalities of the Old Testament* (Westwood, NJ: Fleming H. Revell, 1959), pp. 13-21.

38. Blanch, *For All Mankind*, p. 81.

Does God find Abraham or does Abraham find God? Certainly the question can be argued from both perspectives. Throughout Scripture there is a tension between human reason and divine revelation, between free will and divine sovereignty. Post-biblical Jewish religious thought, however, emphasizes that Abraham came to know God by reason. The Talmud states that Abraham kept not only the 613 commandments of the written law (Kiddushin 82a) but also the oral law (Yoma 28b). This knowledge of revelation was not supernaturally given to Abraham but was deduced from his own reason. Accordingly, Samuel Sandmel bestows the epithet "philosopher-king" on Abraham.[39] He explains: "By means of introspection, Abraham discovered within himself a *logos,* and reasoning by analogy, concluded that there must be a Divine *Logos* in the universe."[40] Shlomo Riskin sums up the rabbinic discussion on Abraham's reasoning ability by concluding that "the Torah is eminently reasonable and logical, and that a profoundly intelligent and sensitive human being can arrive at an understanding of the Biblical theology and legal structure by means of his reason, and even without revelation. This is the axiom which lies behind the Mishnaic insistence that Abraham performed all of the commandments."[41]

Given this tension or paradox of Abraham either being sought by God or reasoning his way to him, I must side, in the end, with the former. While father Abraham is doubtless one of the most gifted people of Scripture, human reason, when all the theological dust settles, is not equal to God or capable of fully knowing him; neither can reason find him unless God by his grace assists him. In the overall scheme of Scripture, divine-human relationship (i.e., "walking with God," cf. Gen. 17:1) takes precedence over human reason (i.e., personal, intellectual quest to reach and understand God). This is an overarching perspective of Scripture in general and of the biblical Abrahamic materials in particular. Accordingly, Abraham Heschel has correctly summarized the issue: "Israel's religion originated in the initiative of God rather than in the efforts of man. It was not an invention of man but a creation of God; not a product of civilization, but a realm of its own. Man would not have known

39. Samuel Sandmel, *Judaism and Christian Beginnings* (New York: Oxford, 1978), pp. 291, 294.

40. Sandmel, *Judaism and Christian Beginnings,* p. 288.

41. Shlomo Riskin, "Keeping the Commandments," *The Jewish Advocate,* Oct. 14-20, 1994, p. 16.

Him if He had not approached man. God's relation to man precedes man's relation to him."[42]

Covenant

In the Old Testament, the most important metaphor to express God's relationship to his people is the covenant *(berit).*[43] In Genesis 15 and 17, God establishes a covenant with Abraham and his descendants. The New Testament writers, however, speak of a "new covenant" (Luke 22:20; 1 Cor. 11:25; Heb. 8:8). The theme of covenant thus becomes a significant issue of both convergence and divergence for Judaism and Christianity as Abrahamic religions.

In Genesis 15:9-21, through a mysterious covenantal ceremony, God establishes an enduring bond with Abraham and his descendants. God initiates this covenant and, by oath, confirms his promise to Abraham. The divine presence is symbolically manifested by a smoking firepot with a blazing torch passing between split animals (v. 17). The ceremony thus solemnizes the covenant; the parties, God and Abraham, are united by a bond of blood. Only God passes between the pieces of the animals. Abraham merely looks on, passive beneficiary of the covenant promise. "On that day the LORD made a covenant *(karat berit,* literally 'cut a covenant') with Abram" (v. 18). The unilateral, unconditional character of the covenantal agreement assures Abraham and his posterity that God's relationship with his people is permanent. The covenant with Abraham is sealed in blood. As Jeremiah 34:18-19 indicates, in a covenant ceremony the slaughtered animals dramatically serve as a type of self-maledictory oath for the parties involved. In essence, each partner in covenant is saying, "May I be cut off and as dead as these animals should I renege on the terms of this agreement."

In Genesis 17:1-27, circumcision is instituted as an external sign of the covenant. Circumcision is the oldest rite in Judaism. The commandment of circumcision is the first *mitzvah* in Torah specifically

---

42. Heschel, *God in Search of Man,* p. 198.

43. See Frederic W. Bush, "Images of Israel: The People of God in the Torah," in *Studies in Old Testament Theology,* ed. Robert Hubbard, Robert Johnston, and Robert Meye (Dallas: Word, 1992), p. 100.

given to Abraham and his offspring. Indeed, it is intended "for the generations to come" (v. 12). God said to Abraham, "My covenant in your flesh is to be an everlasting covenant" (v. 13). Thus, circumcision is referred to as "the covenant of Abraham."[44] God expects an active response from those binding themselves to the terms of the covenant. Anyone who is unwilling to have the foreskin cut off would be cut off from God's people; such refusal amounts to a breach of the covenant. Although from God's perspective his covenant is everlasting, never to be broken, from the human standpoint the covenant could be broken by disobedience, and its benefits could be lost (Gen. 17:7, 13, 19). As God establishes the covenant with the shed blood of animals (Gen. 15), so circumcision, a sign of that covenant, involves blood, a reminder of the seriousness of the obligation.

Circumcision binds one to the covenant and is a mark of Jewish identity.[45] Circumcision is far deeper, however, than merely a sign of religious, cultural, or national identity; its meaning is more profound than an outward mark on a physical body. Indeed, as Irving Greenberg has emphasized, "Because Abraham's covenant is built on values and concepts — transcendence, redemption, justice — Abraham's is more than a biological family."[46] In short, circumcision is a "symbol of the Jew's consecration and commitment to a life lived in the consciousness of that covenant."[47]

In the New Testament, Paul begins to tailor Judaism for gentiles in a number of ways. One of these ways is by turning circumcision into a metaphor, a spiritual concept. He speaks of a "circumcision of the heart," a term first employed by Moses (Deut. 10:16; 30:6) and the prophets (cf. Jer. 9:26). As a biblical figure of speech, "circumcision of the heart," as most Christians understand the expression, is an inward spiritual seal of righteousness through faith, accomplished through the indwelling work of the Holy Spirit (Rom. 2:29). It is a circumcision not "done by the hands of men" but "done by Christ" (Col. 2:11) and is based on faith in

---

44. See George Foot Moore, *Judaism*, vol. 2 (Cambridge: Harvard University Press, 1955), p. 18.

45. Robert L. Wilken, "The Christians as the Romans (and Greeks) Saw Them," in *Jewish and Christian Self-Definition*, vol. 1, ed. E. P. Sanders (Philadelphia: Fortress, 1980), p. 103.

46. Irving Greenberg, *The Jewish Way* (New York: Simon and Schuster, 1988), p. 72.

47. Nahum M. Sarna, *Genesis*, JPS Torah Commentary (Philadelphia: Jewish Publication Society, 1989), p. 125.

Christ (Gal. 5:6). In Paul's view, those spiritually "circumcised" are those who have put their faith in Christ; they have an inward "badge," but it is that of the Holy Spirit; they have confidence, but not by trusting in the flesh (sinful human nature) or in an outward physical identity which cannot save (Phil. 3:3-9).

The Council of Jerusalem convened about 49 C.E. (see Acts 15). The assembly met to decide the issue of whether gentiles should be required to be circumcised and to observe the entire law of Moses for salvation (v. 1). The council decided that circumcision should not be a requirement for gentiles (v. 10). In making its ruling, the council emphasized that salvation is a free gift of God; one cannot obtain it by mere conformity to any ceremonial ritual. This ruling sent a strong message to the Jewish community. By not requiring the ritual practice of circumcision, a basic teaching of the Torah, the church was understood by the Jewish community to be saying that it no longer considered itself part of traditional Judaism but rather apart from it. The old covenant, focused on Torah, had been modified; a new covenant, focused on faith in Christ, and interpreting the Hebrew Bible through Christian eyes, had now emerged.

For the first decade or two of the church's existence, gentiles who wished to belong to the church were required to convert to Judaism and uphold the law of Moses. For a gentile male, the thought of going through circumcision was not a particularly pleasant one; many adults did not want to undergo the physical pain involved.[48] Once the church removed the requirement of circumcision for gentile converts, however, Christianity began to grow rapidly; gentile response to the gospel message began to increase, though at the same time Jewish response to the gospel began to decrease. In light of Paul's special calling to reach gentiles, from the church's historic perspective the Jerusalem Council's decision was a critical move. That decision resulted in significantly advancing the Abrahamic promise that "all peoples on earth will be blessed through you" (Gen. 12:3; Gal. 3:8, 9).

48. Stephen Wylen, *The Jews in the Time of Jesus* (New York: Paulist Press, 1995), pp. 32, 33, 90, 91.

Faith

For Christians, Abraham is probably best known for his faith; many would call him a paradigm of faith.[49] Accordingly, those who believe God, as Abraham did, are "children of Abraham" (Gal. 3:7). The Abrahamic narratives in Genesis emphasize the patriarch's strong trust in God and his prompt obedience to every request God made of him (Gen. 12:4; 17:23; 21:14; 22:3). The New Testament epistles particularly characterize Abraham as a man of faith (see Rom. 4; Gal. 3; Heb. 11; Jas. 2). His commitment to and trust in the promises of God allowed him to venture into the unknown with the full expectation that God would meet him there. It is almost incomprehensible for us to grasp the extraordinary way Abraham's faith operated. He had "no tangible object in which to trust: he believed the bare word of God, and acted upon it."[50] In Thomas Cahill's words, "Out of an age of tall tales of warriors and kings, all so like one another that they are hard to tell apart, comes this story of a skeptical, worldly patriarch's trust in a disembodied voice. This is becoming, however incredibly, the story of an interpersonal relationship."[51]

In the story of this deepening relationship of trust, Genesis states, "Abram believed the LORD, and he credited it to him as righteousness" (15:6). That is, Abraham relies upon God and fully puts his confidence in him, and God is pleased and considers him righteous. Righteousness in the Bible centers on one being faithful to a relationship, acting the right way to please another. Thus, the meaning of the above text (cf. Rom. 1:16-17; 4; Gal. 3:6-9) seems to be that "a person's righteousness in relation to God is fulfilled when that relationship is characterized by faith."[52] In short, Abraham's behavior is consistent with the nature of the relationship established; his covenant fidelity renders him righteous before the Almighty.[53]

Jewish scholarship, while certainly not unanimous, tends to under-

---

49. Ronald Youngblood, *The Heart of the Old Testament*, 2nd ed. (Grand Rapids: Baker Book House, 1998), p. 92.

50. F. F. Bruce, *The Book of Acts*, rev. ed. (Grand Rapids: Eerdmans, 1988), p. 135.

51. Cahill, *The Gifts of the Jews*, p. 70.

52. William LaSor, David Hubbard, and Frederic Bush, *Old Testament Survey* (Grand Rapids: Eerdmans, 1982), p. 114.

53. William J. Dumbrell, *Covenant and Creation: A Theology of Old Testament Covenants* (Nashville: T. Nelson, 1984), p. 54.

stand Genesis 15:6 differently from the above. One such perspective is clarified by the rendering of this verse in the JPS translation of the *Tanakh:* "And because he [Abram] put his trust in the LORD, He reckoned it to his merit." Nahum Sarna comments on this translation: "Hebrew *tzedakah,* usually 'righteousness,' sometimes bears the sense of 'merit'. The idea is that Abram's act of faith made him worthy of God's reward, which is secured through a covenant."[54] In short, faith itself is seen by God as an act of merit. God credits or adds this meritorious act to the other good works of Abram's life.

In Pauline literature, Abraham becomes a prime illustration of one justified by faith. For Paul, faith is the means by which God declares all sinners righteous, and Abraham is Paul's example (Rom. 4:3; Gal. 3:6). In Paul's understanding, through faith God forgives Abraham (no human, including Abraham, is without sin) and Abraham thereby is enabled to stand in a new and right relationship before God. Abraham does not earn God's merit in the sense of works righteousness, but he trusts God who justifies him.[55] According to James Dunn, the key to understanding "credited to him as righteousness" (Rom. 4:3) lies in the Jewish theology of Paul's day, which links the covenant promise made to Abraham to Abraham's faithfulness under testing in regard to the binding of Isaac.[56] Such testing gave Abraham confidence before God. Paul is not attacking Judaism for belief in merit and reward for human effort to achieve salvation by good works. Rather, in quoting Genesis 15:6 in regard to Abraham's faith, Paul is arguing against the language of "payment due," for "the righteousness is surely reckoned in terms of grace, not of payment due."[57]

The epistle of James (2:23) also cites Genesis 15:6, removing it from the faith-works polarity that, unfortunately, certain Christian interpreters have mainly focused on in their particular reading of Paul. For James, the question is not "either/or" but "both/and." In short, "faith without deeds is dead" (Jas. 2:26). James refers to Abraham as one whom God considered righteous for what he did in offering Isaac on the altar (v. 21). Abra-

---

54. Sarna, *Genesis,* p. 113.

55. See Daniel Fuller, *The Unity of the Bible* (Grand Rapids: Zondervan, 1992), pp. 255, 256.

56. James D. G. Dunn, *Romans 1–8,* Word Biblical Commentary (Dallas: Word, 1988), p. 201.

57. Dunn, *Romans 1–8,* p. 204.

ham's "faith and his actions were working together" (v. 22). So, concludes James, "a person is justified by what he does and not by faith alone" (v. 24).

While certain Christian interpreters want to place faith and deeds worlds apart, some Jewish interpreters hold that faith and works "are one and the same."[58] In a Christian reading of the Scripture, James must not be hastily dismissed as if he is in conflict with Paul. A full reading of the New Testament reveals that faith involves both attitude (trust) and action (deeds). Faith is the basis of a relationship with God. Yet faith, if it is genuine, must produce good works to demonstrate that it is a living faith.

Abraham's faith and devotion to God are tested to the limit in the *Akedah,* the binding of Isaac. The climax of Abraham's story is "the Mountain Experience,"[59] that moment when God summons Abraham to "give up his entire future."[60] In James's reference to the *Akedah* (2:21), one is reminded that the Bible is not a work of reason but one of history and faith.[61] As for Abraham, "Whatever the cost, [he] is ready to carry it out because his faith is so strong and immovable."[62] *Akedah* remains an important word in Jewish life. It represents willingness to sacrifice that which is most cherished, dearest, or best in life, even life itself.[63] On occasion, during medieval times, Jewish parents willingly killed their own children as an act of martyrdom rather than submit them to baptism and forced conversion.[64] With utter abandonment to their faith, they saw themselves as repeating the test of Abraham, and being more faithful than he. The epistle of James is strong on the actions of Abraham. James emphasizes that Abraham is "considered righteous for what he *did*" (Jas. 2:21; italics mine), not for what he *thought.*

In the Abrahamic narratives, all too frequently the question of faith

58. See Burton L. Visotzky, *Reading the Book* (New York: Doubleday, 1991), p. 93.

59. Cahill, *The Gifts of the Jews,* p. 83.

60. John H. Marks, "The Book of Genesis," in *Interpreter's One-Volume Commentary,* ed. Charles M. Laymon (Nashville: Abingdon Press, 1971), p. 18.

61. See the discussion of this point in Paul Johnson, *History of the Jews* (New York: Harper & Row, 1987), p. 18.

62. Pearl, *Theology in Rabbinic Stories,* p. 58.

63. In parallel Christian tradition, in the Church of the Holy Sepulchre in Jerusalem, on a wall near the traditional location of Jesus' crucifixion, is a large Old Testament scene depicting Abraham's sacrifice of Isaac, a picture that in Christian theology illustrates the sacrifice of Jesus as God's beloved son.

64. Joseph Telushkin, *Jewish Literacy* (New York: Wm. Morrow & Co., 1991), p. 37.

becomes a matter of extreme divergence for Christianity and Judaism. Many are too easily prone to accept the oft-repeated stereotype that Christians are interested only in creeds (faith — what one believes and the one in whom they believe), while Jews are interested only in deeds (works — how one lives and how many *mitzvot* they perform). Some of this thinking about the other is understandable given the overall christocentricity of the New Testament narratives. Nonetheless, James is valuable for Christians and Jews in that with this epistle we come close to converging or "meeting in the middle." James is perhaps the least christocentric book in the New Testament. For James (*Ya'akov*, or Jacob, his Hebrew name), there is no great divide or major conflict between faith and deeds. If there are differences, they are more a matter of emphasis than of substance. Both faith and deeds are essential to the teachings of Judaism and Christianity. Both complement each other in the biblical narrative.

"Look to the Rock, . . . Abraham Your Father"

More than a millennium after Abraham and Sarah walked the Fertile Crescent, a cry comes from the prophets, a call to look back to father Abraham. The text reads,

> Listen to me, you who pursue righteousness,
>   you that seek the LORD.
> Look to the rock from which you were hewn,
>   and to the quarry from which you were dug.
> Look to Abraham your father.
>
> (Isa. 51:1-2)

The prophet begins his message with a sense of urgency. He employs three imperatives: first *shim'u*, "listen" or "hear," then the repeated verb *habbitu*, "look" or "focus intently upon." He calls for "maximum attention (v. 1), the concentration of both the literal ear and also the eye of the imagination."[65] His audience is those who "pursue righteousness" *(tzedek)* as the Torah commands (Deut. 16:20), those who seek to lead a righteous life through a right relationship with God and just actions to-

---

65. Geoffrey Grogan, "Isaiah," in *Expositor's Bible Commentary*, vol. 6 (Grand Rapids: Zondervan, 1986), p. 294.

ward others. In this passage, God's people are called to reflect on their origin, and Abraham is the name synonymous with origin. In this context it appears that the author may be intentional in linking Abraham both to his descendants and to righteousness (Isa. 51:1-2; Gen. 15:6). Accordingly, the calling of the children of Abraham, the covenant people founded on Abraham, is to reflect the way of the Lord, which is also the way of their father; it is *la'asot tzedakah*, "to do righteousness/justice" (see Gen. 18:19).

The prophet admonishes, "Look to the rock *(tzur)* from which you were hewn." Abraham represents the human platform upon which the covenant community is built. A midrash on this verse reads, "When God looked on Abraham who was to appear, he said, 'See, I have found a rock on which I can build and base the world,' therefore he called Abraham a rock *(tzur): Look to the rock from which you were hewn."*[66] Why is Abraham called a rock? The metaphor implies someone solid, steady, reliable, and enduring. The Lord himself is many times called a Rock (e.g., Deut. 32:4; 1 Sam. 2:2). So Abraham's descendents, quarried from Abraham the rock, are to reflect his faithfulness, his likeness.

Some intriguing similarities between Abraham and Peter raise the possibility of Peter being a "Second Abraham."[67] Let us look briefly at some of the imagery that may relate Peter to Abraham. On the occasion of Peter's confession at Caesarea Philippi, Jesus says to Peter, "You are Peter [Greek, *petros*] and on this rock [*petra*] I will build my church" (Matt. 16:18). Jesus may be pointing to himself as that rock on which he would establish his church, or the rock may be Peter's confession that Jesus was the Messiah, or the rock may be Peter himself. If it is the latter, then on Peter, like Abraham the rock, a new but enduring community of faith will be built (cf. Gal. 2:9). Paul states that the church is "built upon the foundation of the apostles and prophets, with Christ Jesus himself as the chief cornerstone" (Eph. 2:20). The word "foundation" *(themelios)* implies something solid or rock-like used to support a structure. In this interpretive scenario, the church is built upon the apostles (represented by Peter) and the prophets (represented by Abraham),[68] Christ being the cornerstone.

---

66. Hermann L. Strack and Paul Billerbeck, *Das Evangelium Nach Matthaus,* vol. 1 (Munich: C. H. Beck'sche, 1922), p. 733.

67. J. Massyngberde Ford, "Thou Art 'Abraham' and Upon This Rock . . . ," *The Heythrop Journal* 6 (1965): 289.

68. For the designation of Abraham as a prophet see Gen. 20:7; Ps. 105:15.

It is of further interest to note that both Abraham and Peter undergo changes of name[69] to indicate the coming into being of the people of God (Abraham; cf. Gen. 17:4-5) and the birth of the church (Peter; cf. Matt. 16:18; John 1:42). Further, both Abraham and Peter are associated with a new work of God promising to have worldwide influence: Abraham is to be "ancestor of a multitude of nations" (Gen. 17:4-5) and a blessing to all people on earth (12:3). On Pentecost, at the birthing of the church, Peter declares that God will pour out his Spirit "upon all people" (Acts 2:17). Further, Peter states, "in every nation anyone who fears [God] and does what is right is acceptable to him" (Acts 10:35). In addition, just as every member of Abraham's extended family in the flesh (Israel) are individuals cut from the rock (Abraham), so every member of the reconstituted and expanded Israel (the church) are individually likened to "living stones being built into a spiritual house" (Isa. 51:1-2; 1 Pet. 2:5).

The Gospels connect stones to Abraham. John the Baptist says, "Produce fruit in keeping with repentance. And do not begin to say to yourselves, 'We have Abraham as our father.' For I tell you that out of these stones God can raise up children for Abraham" (Luke 3:8; cf. Matt. 3:8-9). The Baptist's concern is that Jews not rely on their physical descent or ethnic privilege as protection from the wrath of God (Luke 3:7; Matt. 3:7).[70] The blessing of Abraham had become "Israel's pride and boast."[71] When the Baptist alludes to stones giving rise to "children of Abraham" (cf. Isa. 51:1-2), he is addressing his fellow Jews. The "children" the Baptist seems to have in mind, however, may not be Abraham's physical seed. Rather, he holds forth the possibility that God can reconstitute Israel of old and bring forth a new people of God, "hewed not from the rock Abraham but instead founded on the rock Peter."[72] The Baptist's emphasis, however, is on an inward change of heart, not an outward mission to the gentiles.

69. W. D. Davies and Dale C. Allison, *The Gospel According to Saint Matthew,* International Critical Commentary, vol. 2 (Edinburgh: T. & T. Clark, 1991), p. 624.

70. Nancy Calvert, "Abraham," in *Dictionary of Jesus and the Gospels* (Downers Grove, IL: InterVarsity Press, 1992), p. 4; also see Siker, *Disinheriting the Jews,* pp. 80, 84, 108-10.

71. Joseph A. Fitzmyer, *The Gospel According to Luke, I–IX,* The Anchor Bible (New York: Doubleday, 1981), p. 468.

72. Davies and Allison, *The Gospel According to Saint Matthew,* ICC, vol. 2, p. 624; Fitzmyer, *The Gospel According to Luke, I–IX,* p. 468.

Our Father Abraham

The expression "our father Abraham" increasingly becomes a theological hot potato as the church moves further from the confines of the Jewish womb that gave it birth. The right to claim Abraham as "father" becomes more and more defined by faith rather than descent. Whereas John the Baptist seems to hint at this (see Matt. 3:8-9; Luke 3:8), in the Fourth Gospel Jesus brings this controversy to the fore (see John 8:31-59). Abraham is mentioned ten times within this literary unit. In the debate between Jesus and his Jewish opponents, Jesus argues that the claim "Abraham is our father" is really a hollow presumption unless one performs deeds like Abraham did (v. 39). Not genetic descent but believing Jesus' word determines the true "children of Abraham." Jesus points out to his opponents that they are not like Abraham because they try to kill him (vv. 37-40). Jesus says they are children of the devil because they do not accept the truth he teaches (vv. 41-47). The debate is brought to a head over the question of his eternal existence (vv. 58-59). In sum, in the Johannine controversy with Judaism, the true "children of Abraham" are recognized by their "belief in and witness to Jesus as the Christ."[73]

In Paul's letters to the Romans and Galatians, a distinction is made between children after the flesh and children according to faith. There are children of Abraham by birth or natural descent and there are those who are spiritually his children through faith (see Rom. 4:1-24; 9:6-9; Gal. 3:6-29). In Romans 4, Paul focuses his attention on the inclusion of the gentiles in God's plan of salvation. Paul emphasizes the similarity of Christian faith to Abrahamic faith; "Paul did not assert that Abraham had faith in Christ, but Paul did assert that faith in Christ is like Abraham's faith on this side of the resurrection."[74] All who believe in Christ (Jew and gentile) are children of Abraham (Gal. 3:7, 29). "Through faith in Christ this divine blessing [of being children of Abraham] becomes really universal. It no longer remains limited to Israel but becomes truly comprehensive. God's promise of the blessing of the nations to Abraham has achieved a dimension which really spans the world."[75]

Does the above Christian vision of Abraham blessing the world di-

---

73. Siker, *Disinheriting the Jews,* p. 143.
74. Siker, *Disinheriting the Jews,* p. 196.
75. Kuschel, *Abraham,* p. 85.

verge from or converge with that of the Jewish vision? Isadore Twersky insightfully comments on the Jewish vision: "Messianism may be described as the ultimate triumph of Abraham, when true belief will be universally restored. The beginning and end of history are interwoven. The task of Abraham was to form a nation that knows God."[76] This, Twersky concludes, will mark "the end of history and the ultimate vindication and victory of Abraham's struggle."[77] Indeed, in the end there is a convergence of the Jewish and the Christian visions. To be sure, as this essay has sought to point out, there is a difference in the way Jews and Christians understand and relate to Abraham. But the "victory of Abraham's struggle" is a common vision shared by both.

Thus, "our father Abraham" expresses more than historic memories of a virtuous biblical character or present spiritual ties to a family of faith. The expression is ultimately an eschatological statement. Abraham is a symbol of hope; he binds Christians and Jews together with a common vision of the outworking of the kingdom of God: Abraham, "All peoples on earth will be blessed through you" (Gen. 12:3).

76. Isadore Twersky, *Introduction to the Code of Maimonides* (New Haven: Yale University Press, 1980), p. 451.

77. Twersky, *Introduction to the Code of Maimonides,* p. 451.

Salvation Is from the Jews

RICHARD JOHN NEUHAUS

The Samaritan woman said, "Sir, I perceive that you are a prophet. Our fathers worshipped on this mountain; and you say that in Jerusalem is the place where men ought to worship." Jesus responded, "Woman, believe me, the hour is coming when neither on this mountain nor in Jerusalem will you worship the Father. You worship what you do not know; we worship what we know, for salvation is from the Jews."

John 4:19-22

Despite its suggestive power, the striking statement of Jesus that salvation is from the Jews is seldom encountered in the now voluminous literature on the Jewish-Christian dialogue. The reason may be that the exchange is entangled in another dispute about supersessionism between religious communities, a dispute entirely apart from the Jewish-Christian relationship. It will be remembered that the Samaritans — the *shamerim,* which means "observant" — claimed to be the true Israel who remained loyal to YHWH when Eli allegedly seduced his brethren into constructing the apostate shrine at Shiloh instead of at God's chosen mountain, Gerizim, as recounted in 1 Samuel 1. After the fourth-century schism, Jews forbade Samaritans to make offerings in Jerusalem, to buy unmovable property, and to marry or circumcise a Jew. As John writes, "For Jews have no dealings with Samaritans" (4:9). In short, Jerusalem Judaism had definitively superseded the cult of Gerizim. Thus the exchange with the Samaritan woman at Jacob's well may be something of an embarrassment in a Jewish-Christian dialogue that is centrally concerned with the question of supersessionism.

Or it may be that in the Jewish-Christian dialogue there is little reference to the statement that salvation is from the Jews because the dialogue is not centrally concerned with the question of salvation. In any event, our passage has not been treated kindly by Christian commentators. A recent ecumenical Christian commentary on the passage says that Jesus is acknowledging that "God's salvation to humanity came historically through the Jews as a point of departure, not as origin or source. Salvation comes only from God."[1] "A point of departure" — it has a dismissive ring to it, almost as though Jews and Judaism are, for Christians, a dispensable accident of history.

Rudolf Bultmann, in a footnote in his commentary on John, gives our passage even shorter shrift. It is, he says, "completely or partially an editorial gloss," since the statement that salvation is from the Jews is "impossible in John [who] does not regard the Jews as God's chosen and saved people." "It is hard to see," he writes, "how the Johannine Jesus, who constantly disassociates himself from the Jews, could have made such a statement."[2] An interesting question that Bultmann does not address is why a later editor, presumably at a time when the lines between Jews and Christians had hardened, would have inserted such a statement. It seems improbable that an editor was trying to rectify what Bultmann views as the anti-Jewish bias of Jesus. It is more likely, I think, that Jesus said what he is said to have said, and that Bultmann's view reflects his difficulty, and the difficulty of too many other Christians, in coming to terms with the Jewishness of Jesus.

In his 1955 commentary on John, the estimable C. K. Barrett offers what may be taken as a more conventional supersessionist interpretation: "The saying does not mean that Jews as such are inevitably saved, but rather that the election of Israel to a true knowledge of God was in order that, at the time appointed by God, salvation might proceed from Israel to the world, and Israel's own unique privilege be thereby dissolved. . . .

1. *The International Bible Commentary,* ed. W. R. Farmer et al. (Collegeville, MN: Liturgical Press, 1998), p. 1468.

2. Rudolf Bultmann, *The Gospel of John: A Commentary,* trans. G. R. Beasley-Murray (Oxford: Basil Blackwell, 1971), pp. 189-90.

This eschatological salvation is in the person of Jesus in process of realization and the Jews are losing their position to the Church."[3]

St. Augustine, as we might expect, treats the passage more imaginatively. Samaritans were "aliens" to the Jews, he notes, and so it is that the woman at the well is a type of the church, which "was to come of the Gentiles, an alien from the race of the Jews." Thus the Jewish supersession of the Samaritans is reversed by the Samaritan identification with the church that supersedes the Jews. Of our passage Augustine says, "A great thing has he attributed to the Jews," but then he immediately adds, "but do not understand him to mean those spurious Jews [who rejected the Christ]." Citing Ephesians 2, he says that Samaritans and gentiles were strangers and foreigners to the covenants of God. When Jesus says, "We worship what we know," he is speaking "in the person of the Jews, but not of all Jews, not of reprobate Jews, but of such as were the apostles, as were the prophets." Citing Romans 11, he notes that "God has not rejected his people whom he foreknew," but by "his people" Augustine means only those Jews who are reconciled with the former aliens in Christ and his church.[4]

"Salvation is from the Jews." Few thinkers have pondered that idea, if not that specific passage, more deeply than Franz Rosenzweig (d. 1929), who was, as it were, reconverted to Judaism after a very close brush with becoming a Christian. Rosenzweig's view is frequently, if too simply, summarized in the proposition that Christianity is Judaism for the gentiles. Moreover, Rosenzweig was centrally concerned with salvation, as is evident in the title of his major work, *The Star of Redemption.* This touches on a perduring, and perhaps necessary, ambivalence in Jewish attitudes toward Christians and Christianity. In the historic statement of November 2000, *Dabru Emet* ("Speak the Truth"), signed by almost two hundred notable Jewish scholars, it is said that "through Christianity hundreds of millions of people have entered into relationship with the God of Israel." Then, toward the end of *Dabru Emet,* it is said: "We respect Christianity as a faith that originated within Judaism and that still has significant contacts with it. We do not see it as an extension of Judaism. Only if we cherish our own traditions can we pursue this relationship with integrity."

3. C. K. Barrett, *The Gospel According to John* (New York: Macmillan, 1955), p. 198.

4. Augustine, *On the Gospel of John,* Nicene and Post-Nicene Fathers, first series (Grand Rapids: Eerdmans, 1956), vol. 7, pp. 101, 106.

Yet it would seem that, if through Christianity hundreds of millions of people have entered into relationship with the God of Israel, Christianity must be, in some important sense, an extension of Judaism. Moreover, *Dabru Emet* makes clear that this relationship is one of worshiping "the God of Abraham, Isaac, and Jacob," underscoring that the God of Israel is not separable from the people of Israel. It follows that to be in relationship with the God of Israel is to be in relationship with the people of Israel. As is well known, in the documents of the Second Vatican Council, a favored phrase for the church is "the People of God." There is no plural for the people of God. Immediately following its denial of the view that Christianity is an extension of Judaism, *Dabru Emet* asserts, "Only if we cherish our own traditions can we pursue this relationship with integrity." Certainly there are distinct traditions that must be cherished and respected, but one may suggest that they are traditions within the one tradition, the one story, of salvation. That story is nothing less than, in Robert Jenson's happy phrase, "the story of the world."[5]

Our distinct traditions reflect differences within the one tradition of witness to the God of Israel and his one plan of salvation. It is misleading, I believe, to speak of two peoples of God, or of two covenants, never mind to speak of two religions. While it was not specifically addressed to Jewish-Christian relations, this was the truth underscored also by the statement in 2000 by the Congregation for the Doctrine of the Faith, *Dominus Iesus*. It is not Christian imperialism but fidelity to revealed truth that requires Christians to say that Christ is Lord of all or he is not Lord at all. From the Jewish side, when after the council the Catholic Church was formalizing its conversations with non-Christians, the Jewish interlocutors insisted that they not be grouped with the Vatican dycastery designed to deal with other religions but be included under the secretariat for promoting Christian unity. There were political reasons for that insistence, not least having to do with the politics of the Middle East, but that arrangement has, I believe, much more profound implications than were perhaps realized at the time.

The salvation that is from the Jews cannot be proclaimed or lived apart from the Jews. This is not to say that innumerable Christians, indeed the vast majority of Christians, have not and do not live their Chris-

5. Robert Jenson, "How the World Lost Its Story," *First Things* 36 (October 1993): 19-24.

tian faith without consciousness of or contact with Jews. Obviously, they have and they do. The percentage of Christians involved in any form of Jewish-Christian dialogue is minuscule. Not much larger, it may be noted, is the percentage of Jews involved. In addition, significant dialogue is, for the most part, a North American phenomenon. It is one of the many things to which the familiar phrase applies, "Only in America." In Europe, for tragically obvious reasons, there are not enough Jews; in Israel, for reasons of growing tragedy, there are not enough Christians. Only in America are there enough Jews and Christians in a relationship of mutual security to make possible a dialogue that is unprecedented in two thousand years of history. The significance of this dialogue is in no way limited to America. There is one people of Israel, as there is one church. Providential purpose in history is a troubled subject, and the idea of America's providential purpose is even more troubled, but I suggest that we would not be wrong to believe that this dialogue, so closely linked to the American experience, is an essential part of the unfolding of the story of the world.

> Remember not the former things,
>   nor consider the things of old.
> Behold, I am doing a new thing;
>   now it springs forth, do you not perceive it?
>
> (Isa. 43:18-19)

I think it is fair to say that neither Christians nor Jews would have seen this new thing or have acted upon it were it not for the unspeakable tragedy of the Holocaust. This is recognized in *Dabru Emet,* which says of the Christian understanding of Judaism, "In the decades since the Holocaust, Christianity has changed dramatically." It should be recognized that Judaism also has, at least in large part, changed dramatically, as is evident in, for example, a statement such as *Dabru Emet.* Following World War II and accelerated by strident attacks on Christianity, and on Catholicism in particular, by such as Rolf Hochhuth in his 1960s play *The Deputy,* Jewish-Christian "dialogue" was for some years conducted mainly in the accusative mode. In this mode, the chief duty of Christians was to engage in rites of self-denigration for wrongs committed against Jews and Judaism. Some Jewish organizations and a good many self-depreciating Christians are still trapped in that mode. And it cannot be denied that, without the Jewish prosecution and subsequent Christian defensiveness, the self-examination resulting in the changes alluded to by *Dabru Emet* may not have happened. It is true that God writes straight with crooked lines.

Those Jews for whom "Never again" means never enough of Christian self-denigration will continue to be with us, and we must try to contain our impatience, recognizing the burden of historical grievances and suspicions, and also the institutional interest of some organizations in exploiting such grievances and suspicions. But in recent years the dialogue is becoming more truly a dialogue, as both Christians and Jews are at last catching up with, for instance, the proposal of David Novak in his important 1989 book *Jewish-Christian Dialogue*. Indeed, it may be said that, through the convoluted ways of history, we are at last catching up with the 1920s dialogue between Rosenzweig and Eugen Rosenstock, which was emphatically a dialogue about salvation — the salvation that comes from the Jews.

Still today there are Jews who resist a dialogue about salvation because that is necessarily a theological dialogue, and they do not want Christians to make Judaism a part of the Christian story. Similarly, there may be Christians who resent efforts such as *Dabru Emet* that tend to make Christianity part of the Jewish story. Advancing the dialogue requires, I believe, our recognition that the Christian story and the Jewish story are of theological interest only as they participate in the story of the one God of Israel. Along the way there are many stories, but ultimately the story of salvation, like the phrase "the people of God," has no plural.

Today it is commonly said that Christianity needs to reappropriate its Jewish dimensions, including the Jewishness of Jesus, and that is undoubtedly part of the truth. But this should not be understood as a matter of taking some parts from the Jewish house next door in order to rehabilitate our Christian house. We live in the same house, of which Christians say with St. Paul that the Jewish Christ is the cornerstone (Eph. 2:20). To change the metaphor somewhat, we live in the house of the one people of God only as we live with the Jews of whom Jesus was — and eternally is — one. The second person of the Holy Trinity, true God and true man, is Jewish flesh, as is the eucharistic body we receive, as is the body of Christ into which we are incorporated by baptism. It is said that when John XXIII, then papal nuncio in Paris, first saw the pictures of the Jewish corpses at Auschwitz, he exclaimed, "There is the Body of Christ!"

All such insights are but variations on the words of Paul that must, for Christians, be ever at the center of our reflection on the mystery of living Judaism: "But if some of the branches were broken off and you, a wild olive shoot, were grafted in their place to share the richness of the olive tree, do not boast over the branches. If you do boast, remember it is not you that support the root, but the root that supports you. . . . So do not be proud, but stand in awe" (Rom. 12:17-18). "Salvation is from the Jews." This people is not, as the aforementioned Bible commentator suggests, a "point of departure" but remains until the end of time our point of arrival. By the appointment of the God whom we worship, we travel together, joined in awe of one another, sometimes in fear of one another, always in argument with one another, until that final point of arrival when we shall know even as we are known (1 Cor. 13:12).

When we Christians do not walk together with Jews, we are in danger of regressing to the paganism from which we emerged. Rosenzweig saw that gnosticism, pantheism, and the assimilation to the idolatry of culture and nation are constant temptations for Christians. In 1929 he was prescient in foreseeing what would happen in Germany:

> The nations have been in a state of inner conflict ever since Christianity with its supernational power came upon them. Ever since then, and everywhere, a Siegfried is at strife with that stranger, the man of the cross *(des gekreuzigten Mannes),* in his very appearance so suspect a character. . . . This stranger who resists the continued attempts to assimilate him to that nation's own self-idealization.[6]

Marcionism was not a one-time heresy. New Marcions are ever at hand to seduce Christianity into becoming a culture-religion, a practical morality, or but another spirituality of self-fulfillment. Christianity does indeed seek to engage culture, provide a guide for living, and propose the way to human flourishing, but, reduced to any of these undoubtedly good ends, it is not Christianity. Liberal Protestant theology beginning in the nineteenth century was much preoccupied with the question of "the essence of Christianity," and, not incidentally, was contemptuous of Jews and Judaism. Christianity is not defined by an essence but by the man of the cross, a permanently suspect character, forever a stranger of that

6. Quoted in David Novak, *Jewish-Christian Dialogue* (New York: Oxford University Press, 1989), p. 106.

strange people, the Jews. Through Jesus the Jew, we Christians are anchored in history, defined not by an abstract essence but by a most particular story.

With respect to Judaism, Christians today are exhorted to reject every form of supersessionism, and so we should. To supersede means to nullify, to void, to make obsolete, to displace. The end of supersessionism, however, cannot and must not mean the end of the argument between Christians and Jews. We cannot settle into the comfortable interreligious politesse of mutual respect for positions deemed to be equally true. Christ and his church do not supersede Judaism, but they do continue and fulfill the story of which we are both part — or so Christians must contend. It is the story that begins with Abraham, who in the eucharistic canon we call "our father in faith."

There is no avoiding the much vexed question of whether this means that Jews should enter into the further fulfillment of the salvation story by becoming Christians. Christians cannot, out of a desire to be polite, answer that question in the negative. We can and must say that the ultimate duty of each person is to form his conscience in truth and act upon that discernment; we can and must say that there are great goods to be sought in dialogue apart from conversion; we can and must say that we reject proselytizing, which is best defined as evangelizing in a way that demeans the other; we can and must say that friendship between Jew and Christian can be secured in shared love for the God of Israel; we can and must say that the historical forms we call Judaism and Christianity will be transcended, but not superseded, by the fulfillment of eschatological promise. But along the way to that final fulfillment we are locked in argument. It is an argument by which — for both Jew and Christian — conscience is formed, witness is honed, and friendship is deepened. This is our destiny, and this is our duty, as members of the one people of God — a people of God for which there is no plural.

We can do no better than Paul, who, at the end of his anguished ponderings in Romans 9–11, having arrived at the farthest reaches of analysis and explanation, dissolves into doxology:

O the depth of the riches and wisdom and knowledge of God! How unsearchable are his judgments and how inscrutable his ways! . . . For from him and through him and to him are all things. To him be glory forever. Amen. (11:33, 36)

Along the way to the eschatological resolution of our disagreements, Jews and Christians encourage one another to wait faithfully upon the Lord. Not all Jews and not all Christians agree with this way of understanding the matter. For instance, Christopher Leighton writes, "Plurality and difference are the inescapable realities of our existence, and any theological attempt to dissolve our diversity through appeals to a higher truth or a totalizing unity are suspect, even when projected against an eschatological horizon." He goes on to say that "The challenge for Christian theology is to accept, perhaps even celebrate, the gaps, the silences, the distances between us Christians and Jews." That is in some respects an attractive view and should not be dismissed as being no more than interreligious politesse. But it is, I believe, finally inadequate. "Totalizing" is, of course, a pejorative term, but it is precisely a definitive and comprehensive eschatological resolution that we await. Leighton is surely right to say, however, that along the way we should engage the Jewish people "as a mystery in whose company we may discover our own limits and in whose midst we may also discern new and unsuspected insights into ourselves, the world, and God."[7]

It is precisely that spirit of discovery and discernment that marks the Second Vatican Council's "Declaration on the Relationship of the Church to Non-Christian Religions" *(Nostra Aetate)*. Note that the declaration is about the church, not simply about individual or group relations. Here the mystery of the church encounters the mystery of the Jewish people. "As this sacred Synod searches into the mystery of the Church, it recalls the spiritual bond linking the people of the New Covenant with Abraham's stock" (no. 4). The church does not go outside herself but more deeply within herself to engage Jews and Judaism. This is consonant with Rosenzweig's observation that Christianity becomes something else when it is not centered in the Jewish "man of the cross." *Nostra Aetate* continues: "Nor can [the Church] forget that she draws sustenance from the root of that good olive tree onto which have been grafted the wild olive branches of the Gentiles. Indeed, the Church believes that by His cross Christ, our Peace, reconciled Jew and Gentile, making them both one in Himself (cf. Eph. 2:14-16)" (no. 4). Note that the statement that

7. Christopher Leighton, "Christian Theology after the Shoah," in *Christianity in Jewish Terms,* ed. Tikva Frymer-Kensky et al. (Boulder, CO: Westview Press, 2000), pp. 47-48.

the church draws sustenance from the Jewish people is in the present tense. It is not simply that she drew sustenance in her beginnings; she now, and perhaps until the end of time, draws sustenance. *Nostra Aetate* enjoins understanding, respect, study, and dialogue with Muslims and others as well as with Jews, but only with reference to the Jews does the declaration say that we are dealing with the very mystery of the church, and therefore the story of salvation.

At least for Catholics, *Nostra Aetate* marks the beginning of the present Jewish-Christian dialogue. That dialogue has produced many additional documents, official and unofficial, over the years. One may ask whether and, if so, how there have been advances over *Nostra Aetate* in Catholic understanding. That question necessarily engages the thought of John Paul II, who has, it is universally acknowledged, made unprecedented contributions to Catholic-Jewish relations. The extended reflection on Jews and Judaism in the pope's remarkable little book, *Crossing the Threshold of Hope,* observes that "The New Covenant has its roots in the Old. The time when the people of the Old Covenant will be able to see themselves as part of the New is, naturally, a question to be left to the Holy Spirit." A purpose of the dialogue, if not *the* purpose of the dialogue, he adds, is "not to put obstacles in the way" of Jews coming to that recognition.

Note that he speaks of when, not whether, this will happen. As though to leave no doubt on this point, he goes on to discuss "how the New Covenant serves to fulfill all that is rooted in the vocation of Abraham, in God's covenant with Israel at Sinai, and in the whole rich heritage of the inspired Prophets who, hundreds of years before that fulfillment, pointed in the Sacred Scriptures to the One whom God would send in the 'fullness of time' (cf. Gal 4:4)." Meanwhile, John Paul notes, the church is carrying out the mission of Israel to the nations. He quotes approvingly a Jewish leader who said at a meeting, "I want to thank the Pope for all that the Catholic Church has done over the last two thousand years to make the true God known."[8] We may recall in this connection that the Council's great Constitution on the Church, authoritatively setting forth her ecclesiological self-understanding, is titled *Lumen Gentium,* referring to the fulfillment of the vocation of Israel to be a light to the nations.

---

8. John Paul II, *Crossing the Threshold of Hope* (New York: Knopf, 1994), pp. 99-100.

A useful reference for understanding the state of authoritative Catholic teaching is, of course, the *Catechism of the Catholic Church.* The catechism has relatively little to say about Jews and Judaism in the post-biblical period, although, it must be admitted, the subject receives more attention than it probably does in the everyday piety, preaching, and catechesis of the church. We read that "The people descended from Abraham would be the trustees of the promise made to the patriarchs, the chosen people, called to prepare for that day when God would gather all his children into the unity of the Church" (no. 60). That hint of supersessionism is immediately tempered by reference to the branches being grafted onto the root of Israel. At another point the Jewish character of the early church is underscored, citing the statement of James in Acts, "How many thousands there are among the Jews of those who have believed; and they are all zealous for the Law" (no. 595). The discussion of the Second Coming refers to Romans 11 and "the 'full inclusion' of the Jews in the Messiah's salvation" (no. 674). The catechism's fullest statement is found under the title "The Church and non-Christians" and deserves quotation in full:

> And when one considers the future, God's People of the Old Covenant and the new People of God tend towards similar goals: expectation of the coming (or the return) of the Messiah who died and rose from the dead and is recognized as Lord and Son of God; the other awaits the coming of a Messiah, whose features remain hidden till the end of time; and the latter waiting is accompanied by the drama of not knowing or of misunderstanding Christ Jesus. (no. 840)

While the catechism is, of course, an authoritative presentation of magisterial teaching, one misses *Nostra Aetate*'s sense of the present tense relationship to the Jewish people from which the church learns and draws sustenance. Nor, in this connection, does the catechism's treatment of eschatological expectation suggest a promised understanding or resolution of differences beyond that which the church already knows and embodies.

One may usefully contrast David Novak's concluding thoughts on "the final redemption" in his book, *Jewish-Christian Dialogue:*

> Until that time, we are all travelers passing through a vale of tears until we appear before God in Zion. Jews and Christians begin at the same starting point, and both are convinced that we will meet at the all-

mysterious end. Yet we cannot deny that our appointed tasks in this world are very different and must remain so because the covenant is not the same for both of us. It is God alone who will bring us to our unknown destination in a time pleasing to him. . . . Our dialogue might be able to show the world that the hope it needs for its very survival can only be the hope for its final redemption. . . . From creation and revelation comes our faith that God has not and will not abandon us or the world, that the promised redemption is surely yet to come.[9]

Christians believe that the redemption that is surely yet to come has appeared in the Redeemer, Jesus the Christ. In the end time, the Messiah will not appear as a stranger. Along the way, we have known his name and named his name. Yet Novak's sense of heightened expectation of something new — as distinct from the confirmation of a completely foregone and foreknown conclusion — seems to me the appropriate mode of eschatological hope also for Christians. Aware that we do not yet know even as we are known, we realize that there is more to be known. Dialogue between Jews and Christians should be marked by an element of curiosity, by shared exploration of what we do not know, and perhaps cannot know until the end time.

For this reason, too, I believe our passage from John 4 — "Salvation is from the Jews" — should have a more prominent place in the dialogue than has been the case. The passage nicely combines the "now" and "not yet" of life lived eschatologically. The "now" is unequivocal. The woman said to him, "I know that Messiah is coming and when he comes he will show us all things." Jesus answers, "I who speak to you am he." The "now" and "not yet" are then exquisitely joined in the words of Jesus: "The hour is coming when neither on this mountain nor in Jerusalem will you worship the Father. . . . The hour is coming, and now is, when the true worshipers will worship the Father in spirit and truth, for such the Father seeks to worship him."

Here one can agree with Rudolf Bultmann in recognizing in these words an intimation of the vision of Revelation 21: "And I saw no temple in the city, for its temple is the Lord God the Almighty and the Lamb. And the city has no need of sun or moon to shine upon it, for the glory of God is its light, and its lamp is the Lamb. By its light shall the nations

9. Novak, *Jewish-Christian Dialogue*, pp. 155-56.

walk; and the kings of the earth shall bring their glory into it, and its gates shall never be shut by day — and there shall be no night; they shall bring into it the glory and the honor of the nations" (vv. 22-26). That is the mission of Israel fulfilled as *lumen gentium.*

Along the way to that fulfillment, Christians and Jews will disagree about whether we can name the name of the Lamb. And when it turns out that we Christians have rightly named the Lamb ahead of time, there will be, as St. Paul reminds us, no reason for boasting; for in the beginning, all along the way, and in the final consummation, it will be evident to all that the Lamb — which is to say salvation — is from the Jews. Salvation is from the Jews, then, not as a "point of departure" but as the continuing presence and promise of a point of arrival — a point of arrival that we, Christians and Jews, together pray that we will together reach.

The Church as Israel: Ecclesiology and Ecumenism

GEORGE LINDBECK

A Neglected Topic

Ecclesiology and ecumenism are inseparable, but their relationship has been little discussed. Much of the search for Christian unity in the twentieth century proceeded as if it were independent of the nature of the church. One reason for this is the decision of the central committee of the World Council of Churches in 1950 to focus on steps toward unity that seemed immediately possible and to postpone indefinitely the ultimately divisive issue of the relationship of individual churches to the "holy catholic church,"[1] as the Toronto statement put it. The present essay seeks to help remedy this omission by looking at the positive relation between the church as Israel and Christian unity.

That there is a positive relation is more surprising now than it would have been during most of Christian history. Since the Reformation, the idea of the church as Israel has been increasingly eclipsed by other ecclesiological perspectives (at least in the West; others more knowledgeable than I will have to speak of the East). Theologians long viewed the attribution of Israelhood to the church as merely figurative, but in the past half-century they have come to see it as much worse, as vicious, as a major contributor to the Shoah, the Holocaust. Supersessionist beliefs

---

1. See Morris West's article, "Toronto Statement," in *Dictionary of the Ecumenical Movement,* ed. Nicholas Lossky et al. (Grand Rapids: Eerdmans, 1991), pp. 1008-9.

that Christians alone are now the true Israel, the chosen people, because God has rejected the Jews, once pervaded Western culture and must be counted among the historical sources of the anti-Semitism that made Auschwitz and comparable crimes possible. If it had not been for conceiving the church as Israel, so the argument runs, Western societies and churches would have better resisted the Nazi efforts to exterminate all Jews everywhere. In view of these horrors, any suggestion that the concept has a positive aspect has become taboo.

And the taboo is rarely challenged. Even Christians who think Christianity has replaced Judaism as the religion God most favors do not generally make the supersessionist claim that the church is now Israel and the Jews are not. As already mentioned, thinking of the church as Israel has long been in decline. After the Reformation schisms, intra-Christian polemics dominated ecclesiology, and, as the disputants found the New Testament more useful than the Old for their partisan purposes, predicating Israelhood of the church quickly ceased to be traditional among both Roman Catholics and Protestants (except in some Calvinist enclaves where it took longer to disappear). That is one reason the recent taboo on this notion has not been challenged.

Another factor, going back more than two centuries, is also operative. Modern progressivism (represented most strongly by theological liberals on the Protestant side and, less strongly, by doctrinal developmentalists among Roman Catholics) deepened the aversion to seeing the church as Israel. According to Friedrich Schleiermacher, the most influential of liberals, "Christianity does indeed stand in a special historical connection with Judaism, but so far as concerns its historical existence and its aim, its relations to Judaism and Heathenism are the same."[2] The unlikeness of historic Christianity and historic Judaism, in other words, goes all the way down to their foundations, and from this it follows, as Schleiermacher elsewhere makes clear, that the unlikeness of Israel and the church must be complete. With the exception of the Nazi *deutsche Christen*, theological liberals have not been notable for anti-Semitism and have generally been more deeply committed than conservatives to full civil rights for Jews as individuals, but they are religiously farther removed from Judaism and more opposed to conceiving the church as Israel. They have not been

---

2. This sentence was quoted in the brochure announcing the theological conference from which this book of essays is derived.

in the least supersessionist in the sense of appropriating (or, more precisely, expropriating) Israelhood, for they have held it in contempt as, among its many faults, a form of primitive tribalism. There is as yet no evidence that the postmodern stress on diversity with its rehabilitation of "primal religions" is changing this liberal Christian distaste for the notion of chosen people.

This modern turn away from Israelhood by both traditionalists and liberals has been unfortunate for ecumenism and ecclesiology. Judging by the history that we shall review, the search for unity goes awry apart from a sense of the church as Israel, and the understanding of the church as Israel suffers in the absence of concern for visible unity. So it has been in the past, and there is no reason to suppose it will be different in the future unless the understanding of the church as Israel is somehow renewed.

One crucial condition for renewal is the severing of its connection with supersessionism (and, ultimately, the Shoah), and this separation gives hope for the future. As is repeatedly noted in the present collection of essays, more and more Christian communities, not least the Roman Catholic Church, have officially affirmed that God has not revoked his covenant with the Jews and have thereby rejected supersessionism (while continuing to insist in christologically orthodox fashion, at least in the Roman Catholic case,[3] that Jesus Christ fulfills, though he does not replace, the Torah as God's communally and universally normative self-revelation). To think of the church as Israel, therefore, need no longer be anti-Jewish; and, what is more, the churches desperately need this emphasis for their own intramural and ecumenical health. The historical evidence for this conclusion will be only sketchily narrated, but that is the burden of the tale as I shall tell it.

The Nature of the Church as Israel

The history we shall review is post-biblical, but it has New Testament starting points. The passage that for our purposes best illustrates the practice of treating the church as Israel is 1 Corinthians 10:1-11 (all biblical quo-

---

3. For the most recent reaffirmation of christological orthodoxy on these matters, see *Dominus Iesus,* a declaration published on September 5, 2000, by the Vatican Congregation for the Doctrine of the Faith.

tations are from the Revised Standard Version unless otherwise noted). Here Paul tells gentile Christians that "Our fathers" were in the wilderness with Moses (thus in effect including them in Israel). They were baptized "in the cloud and in the sea, and they all ate the same supernatural food and all drank . . . from the supernatural Rock which followed them, and the Rock was Christ." Yet, because of their disobedience, they suffered disasters as "warnings [literally, 'types'] for us." "Now," Paul concludes, "these things happened to them as *tupoi,* but they were written down for our instruction upon whom the end of the ages has come." The lesson to be drawn from these verses is that for Christians to practice being the church as Israel is for them to apply to their own community what they read about Israel in the *Tanakh,* the Old Testament. More pictorially expressed, it is a matter of seeing the church in the mirror of Old Testament Israel in the light of Jesus Christ. In this light, the light of the (at first unwritten) gospel, the Old Testament functioned as *the* ecclesiological textbook except where it was trumped by the New. This, in brief, is the practice of the church as Israel that came to prevail in the first centuries.

Examples of this practice may be helpful. In the twelfth chapter of Hebrews, for example, what happened to Israel long ago at Mount Sinai is happening now in a new and greater way and will happen over and over again until the Judgment Day when, according to verse 26, the heavens themselves (and not only the earth, as at Sinai) will tremble and shake. While awaiting this Last Assize, Christians are being liberated from Egyptian bondage, passing through the Dead Sea, wandering in the wilderness, crossing the Jordan, conquering Canaan, and living under judges, kings, priests, and prophets — some good and true, others false and evil — until the last trump sounds and the wheat and chaff are definitively separated.

Given such New Testament antecedents, it is not surprising that the songs and prayers of the later church are full of such imagery as in the ancient but still beloved Easter hymn of John of Damascus:

> Come ye faithful, raise the strain of triumphant gladness!
> God has brought his Israel into joy from sadness,
> Loosed from Pharaoh's bitter yoke Jacob's sons and daughters,
> Led them with unmoistened foot through the Red Sea waters.

The Old Testament types in this song were not mere metaphors to the eighth-century Christians for whom it was written. It would be strange if the Islamic rule under which they lived were not one of the referents of "Pharaoh's bitter yoke." More important, they had passed through the "Red Sea waters" in the baptismal font and thereby had become members of the community that is the body of Christ, partakers of the very flesh and blood of the one who was for them the summation of Israel. Not only spiritually but also in a sense physically they could experience themselves, through their participation in Jesus, as Israel, as "Jacob's sons and daughters."

Variety

A remarkable combination of ecclesiological diversity and ecumenical (i.e., catholic) unity characterized these Old Testament–oriented yet christocentric and incipiently trinitarian believers. When different groups of Christians in varied social, cultural, and historical settings saw themselves in the mirror of Israel, they inevitably projected their previously formed self-images and descriptive categories onto the sacred page. These varying preunderstandings, as Rudolf Bultmann called them, became interwoven with scriptural testimony into sometimes widely differing ecclesial outlooks. Christians in the Carthage of Tertullian and Cyprian and in the Alexandria of Clement and Origen, for example, may both have seen the church as Israel in the light of the New Testament's witness to Christ, but their visions were in part incompatible because of differences in the culturally conditioned lenses through which they looked. One cannot imagine Tertullian for a moment tolerating Origen's universalism, his belief in (or was it hope for?) the inclusion of all, even Satan himself, in the community of the saved; nor would Origen have had any sympathy for the exclusivist and rigorist enthusiasm of the Montanist schismatics whom Tertullian eventually joined. Yet both communities belonged to what we now anachronistically think of as the Christian mainstream. Despite diversity, the schisms in this mainstream were, with a single exception, minor or temporary in the first three centuries of Old Testament–oriented Christianity.

This exception, of course, was the sundering of gentile and Jewish Christianities after the destruction of the second temple in 70 C.E., but the rupture cannot be understood apart from the prior unity. The church had its geographical center in Jerusalem before the city's fall, and it was led by Torah-observant Jews who approved Paul's mission to the gentiles. It was natural for this mixed fellowship of Jews and gentiles to understand itself as the beginnings of that enlarged Israel foretold by Isaiah and other prophets when all nations will throng upward to worship on Mount Zion. If one were to diagram Israel and the gentiles as two Venn circles, then the church did not in the least resemble their intersection as if it were a hybrid, a new class or, most memorably, the "third race," as the later, second-century Epistle to Diognetus called the Christians. Rather, the non-Christian gentile circle, consisting of peoples that are no people (1 Pet. 2:10), was destined to disappear leaving only the Israelite one. The gentiles wane and Israel waxes as former gentiles are grafted, even though uncircumcised, into the olive tree (Rom. 11:17-24) and welcomed into citizenship in the commonwealth of Israel (Eph. 2:11-21). At the end of history, so this outlook suggests, church and Israel will coincide. Historic Israel, to whom the promises were first given, will not disappear but rather will fully respond to the call to be the gentile-welcoming assembly *(ekklesia)* of Israel in the new age.

If this is a plausible reconstruction of first-generation ecclesiology (and Israelology), then it was radically altered after Jerusalem's destruction by the distancing of gentile from Jewish Christians and the alienation of both from the synagogue. Hopes for the general conversion of the Jews and for gentile Christians entering into the fellowship of the visible commonwealth of Israel corresponded less and less with experience, with what was actually happening, and the remaining bonds of the shared scripture and belief in Christ, powerful though they were, did not suffice to keep Jewish and gentile Christians in communion. The preunderstandings of the two groups were too dissimilar. Even the shared word for "church," ecclesia, was understood differently. For the Jews, including those who knew no Hebrew, the Greek word could resonate with echoes of *qahal*, Israel assembled in the wilderness, for that is what it stands for in the Septuagint, while the connotations of the same word for the gentiles, unfamiliar with Septuagint usage, clustered around the assembly of the Greek *polis* in which Jacob's sons and daughters had no part. As they became the great majority, gentile Christians increasingly looked askance at the continued Torah observance of their Jewish fellow believers. Ultimately the few Jews within the church were canonically compelled to be non-practicing, that is, assimilated and in effect deprived of their Jewish identity. Completely forgotten was the need for Torah-observant Jewish participation in the church if it is to be truly Israel in the new age. Instead it was affirmed by universal practice, even if not always in theological theory, that the church can be Israel without Jews, and from there it is but a short step to the supersessionist absurdity of condemning Christian Jews for Torah-observance, that is, for worshiping God as did Jesus and the apostles.

When looked at in the context of Greco-Roman prejudices against Jews, however, Christian supersessionism seems almost philosemitic. There were multitudes of gentile Christians who rejected it, not because of its anti-Judaism, but because it was not anti-Jewish enough, and it is the reaction against this hyper anti-Judaism that shaped the later history of the church as Israel.

According to the rejectionists, there is nothing good enough in the Jews' ancestral religion to be worth keeping. For them, Israelhood is not a treasured identity that Christians eagerly appropriate (or, more commonly, expropriate); it is not attractive enough either to share or to steal. Christianity, on this view, does not replace Judaism by supersessionism but by a more extreme form of replacement theology. It does not acquire and putatively improve on the Old Testament heritage but repudiates it and is a fundamentally different religion.

The most familiar of the rejectionists in ancient times (there are, as we shall note, many modern ones) is Marcion, who flourished in the middle of the second century and is known only from his opponents. He was a literalist who, as deniers of multiple meanings usually are, was an uncharitable interpreter of the Jewish Bible (which, at the time he entered the scene, was still the only canonized scripture Christians had). That Bible, he argued, could not possibly be the word of the God known in Jesus Christ. It depicts a deity who bungled in creating the world and thereby filled it with misery and evil. Although concerned about justice, he was fierce, bellicose, and vindictive, utterly different from the infinitely peaceful, loving, and forgiving God revealed in Jesus Christ. Thus he must be a lower deity, and the Bible of the Jews must be false in treating him as supreme. Marcion's solution to the problems raised by his critique was to replace the Jewish Bible with a bowdlerized New Testament and to postulate, beyond the lower creator god worshiped by the Jews, a semi-gnostic highest god from whom Jesus came, and who is so far above the creaturely realm as to be blameless for its sorry state. Obviously the church could not be conceived as Israel in this dualistic cosmos. Israel's home is in the botched lower level besmirched with evils that the clumsy creator god of the Old Testament may not have intended but that he is unable to correct by his harshly legalistic rule, while the church, in contrast, dwells in the literally higher realm of the supreme god's unconditionally loving and forgiving grace. For the church to claim Israelhood is to crave descent into a lower level of being that it could not desire unless it first ceased to be the church. Contemporary progressivists who think of Israel and its religion as impossibly out-of-date or for some other reason objectionable are not dissimilar.

Multitudes found this anti-Jewish and anti-church-as-Israel version of the gospel appealing. According to some reports, there were sizable portions of the Empire and Rome itself in which Marcionites were for a time as numerous as "catholics" (in quotation marks because others, including Marcion and his followers, also claimed the title). If one adds to their number the gnostics and the early catholics who agreed with positions such as those of Barnabas (for whom "Israel" was totally metaphorical and applied only to Christians and never to Jews, not even in the Old Testament) and the Letter to Diognetus (in which the church is "the third race") it may well be that most gentile Christians in much of the second century did not think of the church as Israel. Much of the surviving literature in that period ranges from un-Israel-like to anti-Israel-like in its depictions of Christian community.

A change, gathering momentum from the middle years of the second century, is partly attributable to the reaction against Marcion. The communities oriented to the Old Testament were perhaps a minority among gentile Christians, but they led the way. It is to them that we owe the anti-Marcionite selection from older writings to form the New Testament. Moreover, they read the ancient scriptures through the lens of Jesus Christ as witnessed to by this new addition to the canon, and they came to view the church, Christ's body, in increasingly Israel-like terms. Adolf von Harnack says that the influence of the Old Testament in the third century brought Christianity "to the verge of becoming the religion of the book,"[4] and Jaroslav Pelikan reflects a historians' consensus when he speaks of "re-judaization."[5] Thus it was that the most Israel-like part of

---

4. Adolf von Harnack, *The Mission and Expansion of Christianity in the First Three Centuries* (New York, 1908), vol. 1, pp. 279ff.

5. Jaroslav Pelikan, *The Christian Tradition* (Chicago, 1971-89), vol. 1, pp. 25-26.

the Christian movement, the Great Church as it is commonly named, outdistanced rival forms of Christianity in the one hundred and fifty years after Marcion. By the time of Constantine, it had come to comprise the great majority of Christians. This raises the question of how the church's Israelization, as it is convenient to call it, helps account for this success.

Unifying Power

Adolf von Harnack stands virtually alone in addressing this question. He is still widely regarded as the greatest historian of the first Christian centuries, and yet the vivid passages he wrote a hundred years ago on the importance for the church's success of its self-understanding as Israel[6] have been neglected. Even he, however, writing in what for university scholars was a pre-ecumenical age, did not deal expressly with the crucial unifying power of the church as Israel. I shall therefore, using a data base somewhat larger than his, risk a hypothetical reconstruction of his answer to our question (an answer that, however historically plausible, would have regarded as theologically abhorrent, just as he did, patristic developments in general).

It was a specific text, the Jewish Bible typologically interpreted in Christian terms, that had the consensus, community, and institution-building power to make the Old Testament–oriented part of the Christian movement the overwhelmingly dominant and therefore catholic church. The gentiles who entered this biblical world developed in the course of time a Christian analogue to the Jewish sense of being a single people. They too claimed a cosmic destiny, and they also forged their identity and unity in circumstances as different as those of wandering in the desert, exercising kingly rule, living in exile, and returning from exile. What they lacked in ethnic cohesion was surpassed by, in their view, an even greater unity: Israel was for them the body of Christ. Those who belong to it are members one of another no less than of Jesus; and through Christ Jesus, they share in the most intense and intimate of all unities, that of the triune God. To desert this community is sadder than the betrayal of family, and Christians are called to follow the example of the

6. Pelikan, *The Christian Tradition*, passim, but esp. pp. 240-65.

prophets and of Jesus by surrendering life itself rather than separating themselves from God's elect and beloved people because of attacks from within or without. The enemy sows tares from within the field of the faithful according to the Lord's own parable (Matt. 13:25), and wolves and robbers assault the sheep from without (John 10:1-18); yet the Good Shepherd and his faithful ministers, beginning with the apostles, do not renege out of weariness nor desert out of fear. A stronger bond is hard to imagine, and it requires both the Israel-like external dimension and the christocentric internal one.

It is not surprising that gentiles who entered this biblical world developed a Christian analogue of the Jewish sense of being a single people. Their widely separated communities were bound together by ties of mutual helpfulness, responsibility, and openness to each other's correction. Because of this they were able to develop, not only congruent versions of a single rule of faith, but also unified (though not uniform) ministerial, liturgical, and disciplinary patterns and structures. If one remembers that it was a particular way of reading a particular text that made this unity possible, it does not seem farfetched to say, speaking nontheologically, that it was the Old Testament as much as the New that conquered the Empire in defiance of the normal laws of sociological gravity: nonviolently, despite persecution, and without special economic, social, cultural, or political advantages. Other texts in other contexts — the Qur'an and the Buddhist scriptures, for example — have also formed and sustained major transethnic communities, but never in comparable independence of external assistance. The people-and-unity-creating power of the Jewish scriptures as read by early Christians seems, with one exception, unparalleled.

The exception, not surprisingly, is rabbinic Judaism after the destruction of the second temple. What the rabbis did to make the Jews in diaspora an interconnected people, the catholics did for the gentile Christians. Both went far beyond their common scripture, and they did so in different directions, one by means of the oral Torah, and the other through the New Testament. Yet each group lived in the world of Israel's story and of Israel's God and claimed to be his chosen people. They thought their claims were mutually exclusive, but the Bible is a capacious instrument of God's Spirit: it bestowed its unity-and-community-building power on both.

Failure

Seeds of failure, however, were concealed in the harvest of success. The community-and-unity-building power of the church as Israel quickly changed its character after Constantine's triumph over Maxentius at the Milvian Bridge in 312 just outside of Rome. Much of the routed army perished in the river's flood, and Eusebius, writing shortly after the event, saw this event prefigured in the drowning of Pharaoh's hosts in the Red Sea. Constantine could even be compared to Moses, for he, too, gave all glory to God for the victory.

One can understand Eusebius's enthusiasm: the greatest persecution the church had ever suffered was a recent memory, and not four years had passed since the new Moses had led Christians out of hundreds of years of Egyptian bondage in which they had been suspect members of a *religio illicita,* a criminalized and illegal cult. Once Christianity became, not only licit, but imperially favored, Christians couldn't help but see a very different reflection of themselves in the mirror of Israel. The emperors who had once been Pharaohs now became Moses or, more frequently in later years, David, rulers of earthly anticipations of the heavenly kingdom. Christians had called themselves *peregrini,* pilgrims, but by the fifth century *romanii* was a favored self-designation. As a Jewish scholar puts it, "When the Romans became Christian, the Christians became Roman."[7]

More serious than change of reference, however, were unchanged descriptions of Jews and pagans. Even when these groups lost power, they were attacked with the same vehemently hostile biblical language, found in both Testaments, that Christians had previously employed against them when they were persecuting oppressors. Power relations had been reversed, and what had been cries of anguish in the mouths of the helpless became incitements to violence against the newly defenseless when repeated from positions of strength. It may well be, as has been recently and convincingly argued, that it was not theological impulses but political contingencies of a more imperial than ecclesiastical nature that caused this development,[8] but the fact remains that a religion that claimed toler-

---

7. G. Stroumsa, *Barbarian Philosophy: The Religious Revolution of Early Christianity* (Tubingen: Siebeck, 1999), p. 65.

8. H. A. Drake, *Constantine and the Bishops: The Politics of Intolerance* (Baltimore: Johns Hopkins University Press, 2000).

ance from heathen Caesars because it taught love of enemies became in less than a century far less accommodating to religious pluralism than the pagan empire had ever been.

The monarchic version of the Christian people as Israel reached its Western apogee in Charlemagne, who identified himself with tropological realism as a Christian King David set over church as well as state and divinely commissioned to rebuild the Christian kingdom, that is, the Roman empire. The Holy Roman Empire he founded was a sorry shadow of the original, but his other organizational accomplishments — the parish system, for example — laid the foundations for the civilizational unity of Western Europe. But the dangers in the lay — that is, princely — control of the church implied in Davidic (or in non-typological modern terminology, "Erastian") ecclesiology led to a reaction that tilted the Western church toward a papal model whose scriptural warrants, such as they were, were necessarily drawn from the New rather than the Old Testament (from, for example, Matt. 16:18). The practice of the church as Israel weakened, and sometimes the name was dropped entirely. As far as I have been able to discover, Thomas Aquinas, for example, never refers to the church as "new" or "true" Israel, much less as "Israel" *tout court* (although it is clear when he speaks of the church as the *populus dei,* the people of God, that Israel is the prototype).

In modern times, it was not only the name but the concept that disappeared from ecclesiology. One reason for this disappearance is the discrediting of Christian Israelhood by its polemical use among divided Christians. Conflicting parties within the mainstream laid exclusive claim to Christian peoplehood.[9] First, the Eastern and Western churches and then, much more extensively, Rome and the Reformation disputed with each other over which was the Northern and which was the Southern Kingdom. Both sides professed to be prefigured in Judah and Jerusalem and thus to represent, through Christ, the true New Israel, but this claim hardened their differences into irrevocability. Thus it was that conceiving the church as Israel intensified rather than moderated divisions. Perhaps the wars of religion would not have occurred without this hermeneutically intensified antagonism, and they certainly would not have been as

---

9. Earlier schisms within the catholic mainstream were over teaching (e.g., Athanasius vs. Arius) or leadership (Constantinople vs. Rome) within the one church, not over which of the contesting parties was the one and only *ecclesia.*

bloody. It was partly in reaction to these enormities that the church-as-Israel concept disappeared in all major traditions.

Under the influence of Enlightenment rationalism, itself a reaction against the wars of religion, everything within Christianity that was deemed to be specifically Jewish came increasingly under attack. Supersessionism in the classic sense of expropriating the *Israeliticam dignitatem*[10] was displaced by the repudiation of that dignity. Old Testament (i.e., Jewish) religion was rejected root and branch as primitive, legalistic, and intolerant. Whatever was good about it, such as the moral duties inculcated in the Ten Commandments, was simply part of the natural law or general revelation available to all human beings. There was nothing specific to Israelite religion that enlightened Christians wanted to appropriate or expropriate. In a move somewhat like Marcion's, they displaced a supersessionist by a rejectionist understanding of the relation of Christianity to Judaism. Christianity was no longer seen as a *people* that had replaced another people, the Jews, in God's plans for the world's salvation, but as a *religion* that had outgrown its anachronistic adherence to the Old Testament and is now becoming more and more an independent, tolerant, and thus superior faith. Thus anti-Judaism, in the sense of contempt for the religion of the Jews, became more virulent under Enlightenment influence even while Jews as individuals became more acceptable. Opposing this contempt by a non-supersessionist retrieval of Israelite dignity would be good for both Jews and Christians. The conditions under which such a retrieval might be possible are what we must now discuss in conclusion.

Retrieval

The most succinct scriptural warrant for the retrieval of the practice of viewing the church in the mirror of Israel is the text in 1 Corinthians that we have already looked at. Paul tells us that *all* the things that happened to "our fathers . . . were written down for our instruction, upon whom the

10. Henri de Lubac, *Catholicism* (New York: Sheed & Ward, 1950), chap. 2, n. 26, identifies this title as coming from the collect for Holy Saturday (after the fourth prophecy), which asks God "that the peoples of this world may become the children of Abraham and may be led in *Israeliticam dignitatem*." Needless to say, this collect can be prayed non-supersessionistically.

end of the ages has come" (10:1, 11). These instructions remain verbally the same as when first recorded, but they are multiple in meaning. God's scriptural word, so Paul believes, fits every conceivable context, and from this follows the possibility that seeing the church as Israel is a biblically mandated universal; it applies in the twenty-first century just as much as in the first. Yet this mandate has been forgotten.

What has gone wrong? The Pauline proof-text that commands believers to view the church in the mirror of Israel suggests an answer: Christian communities have regularly omitted the word "all" in their interpretations, as if not everything that scripture records about Israel is written for their instruction. They have focused selectively on the favorable prefigurations Paul mentions — on Christ the rock, on manna as type of the eucharist, on baptism under the cloud — and have neglected his more numerous warnings of the punishments for disobedience to which Christians are liable. This self-serving selectivity is not limited to the interpretations of this one passage: all the Old Testament denunciations of Israel's wickedness, prophetic threats of destruction and exile, and lamentations over Israel's God-forsakenness have only rarely been applied by Christians to themselves collectively (i.e., to the church) but frequently to the Jews. This procedure was expressed in medieval times as a hermeneutical rule: "all good elements in the texts (e.g., consolations, etc.) should be referred to Jesus Christ and his Church, while all bad elements (e.g., sufferings, punishments) should be referred to the Jews and to human sin in general."[11] The last clause provides a warrant for extending the rule to those who are not Jews, and thus Protestants and Catholics have abused each other's churches in the same language the Old Testament directs against unfaithful Israel, while reserving for their own communities the praises and the blessings.

Not everyone, to be sure, adhered to this self-serving rule, but most did. The practice gained ground and reached its climax in the Reformation controversies between Catholics and Protestants. Even after the abandonment, beginning in the seventeenth century, of this church-as-Israel exegetical triumphalism, the denominational divisiveness it spawned remains powerful. Each separated communion has too much invested in the

---

11. Rupert of Deutz (in *Patrologia Latina*, 167:1379) as paraphrased by Ephraim Radner, *The End of the Church: A Pneumatology of Christian Division in the West* (Grand Rapids: Eerdmans, 1998), p. 292, n. 30.

claim that it is fully even if not exclusively the church, to be able to admit that it could be in as sorry a state as God-forsaken Israel. The Christian reluctance to be as communally self-critical and penitent as Old Testament Israel (and much contemporary Judaism) remains alive and is a major barrier to non-supersessionist retrieval.

The difficulty of communal repentance was increased by the supersessionist conviction that the covenant with Israel has been revoked. This conviction presupposes that the election of the Jews as a people was conditional on their faithfulness: because they rejected the Messiah, God annulled his promises to them and transferred these to the church. When churches become equally unfaithful, so the logic of this reasoning implies, God will cast them out just as he has Israel. This makes their situation precarious. Individuals can throw themselves without reservations on God's mercy and be thereby freed to acknowledge the full extent of their misdeeds because of God's unconditional love and forgiveness, but communities cannot do this. They cannot admit that they ever flatly turn away from God, for then, like the Jews, they would no longer be God's elect people. It is not only communal impenitence that is strengthened by making election conditional, but also divisiveness. The difficulty of recognizing groups that are seen as deeply in error as parts of God's chosen people is greatly increased. Unless election is irrevocable for Israel, Christians cannot see their communities as the prophets saw Israel, as the adulterous spouse whom the Lord God may cast off for a time but has irreversibly promised never to cease loving, never to divorce.

When the church is identified by its faithfulness rather than by God's election, Christian communities look for some property within themselves that ensures that God will continue to acknowledge them as his own. In earlier times, the creedal attributes of unity, sanctity, catholicity, and apostolicity served as sufficient marks, but other signs were needed after the Constantinian establishment helped bring into being a church that was overwhelmingly composed of visible sinners rather than visible saints. This increased the pressure to support the church's high claims, by appeal not to the overall pattern of communal life, but to segregated aspects: to pure (ultimately infallible) doctrines, to uniquely (and in vulgar understanding, magically) efficacious sacraments, to divinely established institutions, to authentic gospel preaching and/or conversion experiences, to morality of either the individualistic or Social Gospel variety, and, most plausibly, to suffering, persecution, humility, and selfless service. The multiplication of these adversarially deployed marks of Christian authenticity escalated after the Reformation and further contributed to visible disunity.

If there is any merit in this analysis, the intra-Christian need for a non-supersessionist understanding of the church as Israel is undeniable. Supersessionism generated a communally impenitent triumphalism that has contributed not a little to reducing peoplehood to an individualism for which church membership is increasingly, even for Roman Catholics, a matter of changeable personal preference rather than of lifelong communal loyalty. In the absence of unity even of the external kind, there is little space for mutual love to flourish between churches. Separated denominations, confessions, or communions do not have the ability to consult and jointly decide regarding their common welfare. They no longer possess the means to correct and assist each other. Inter-communal responsibility becomes impossible, and competition unavoidable. To this day, jealously guarded denominational autonomy turns most ecumenical advances into a sham in spite of the intentions of their authors. It is no wonder that interest in unitive (as distinct from cooperative) ecumenism is disappearing. For those who think in these terms, the recovery of a non-supersessionist practice and understanding of the church as Israel is an indispensable though not sufficient condition for ecumenical advance.

I shall in conclusion simply list some of the ecumenically important consequences of this change in understanding that we have not yet noted.

First, as in Judaism, individuals are called to be part of the community, not primarily for their own personal salvation (though rejection of the call can be damning), but in order to contribute to the world's redemption by their membership in the body of Christ, the enlarged Israel, which God has unconditionally chosen to be his light to the nations for the redemption of the world.

Second, it follows from unconditional election and the world-historical mission the church shares with Israel that communal repentance for the disunity of Christians with each other and with the Jews is both possible and imperative. The need for penitence is ignored by the contemporary ecumenical strategy of arguing that separated denominations and confessions are equal (or at least adequate) expressions of the same basic faith and that they therefore have no excuse for remaining apart. That strategy is counterproductive. It functions to create contentment with division, for if each of the separated bodies is already adequately the church, why bother to unite? Worse than that, the strategy is triumphalistically false. No church in the present fissiparous situation is anything except dreadfully inadequate, and the pooling of failures can on occasion make things worse rather than better. Divided churches, as was previously noted, provide few occasions for mutual love to flourish. They do not have the institutional means to practice reciprocal aid, correction, and responsibility. Weeping and rejoicing together become impossible because each competing party takes satisfaction in the failures of the others to the degree these redound to its own advantage. Only by gazing at itself in the mirror of Israel can the church as a whole learn how to lament biblically for its intramural and extramural divisiveness and lovelessness.

Third, and finally, the biblically mandated role of individuals in helping the churches to become penitent is that of suffering and rejoicing on behalf of the church. "If one member suffers, all suffer together; if one member is honored, all rejoice together" (1 Cor. 12:26). Individuals are commissioned, as were the prophets of old, to warn God's people by their actions and by their words even when they are not listened to. Loyalty to God within disintegrating communities is the prophetic vocation in our day just as it was in ancient Israel. Prophets do not seek to find or establish new or purer churches, but rather to labor wherever they are on behalf of the masses who desert the shepherds or whose shepherds desert them. Whatever the cost, they do not leave the people among whom God has set them any more than did Elijah or Jesus. They complete in their flesh, as the author of Colossians puts it, "what is lacking in Christ's afflictions for the sake of his body" (1:24).

It is for Jews to discuss whether or not to welcome this nonsupersessionist understanding and practice of the church as Israel, but my guess, for what it is worth, is that many would agree with Jacob Neusner. He says that because "the Church long ago identified itself as Israel" there is hope that "in our day . . . it joins suffering Israel."[12] To this I would add only the obvious comment that the church can do this only by learning to see itself once again in the mirror of Israel while, in contrast to the past, fully acknowledging that the covenant with the Jews has not been revoked.

---

12. Jacob Neusner, *Christian Faith and the Bible of Judaism* (Grand Rapids: Eerdmans, 1987), p. xiv.

From Supersessionism to Parallelism in Jewish-Christian Dialogue

DAVID NOVAK

The Renunciation of Supersessionism

There is now a definite group of Christian and Jewish theologians who have been long engaged in a general theological enterprise, sometimes separately, sometimes together, where an important object of concern for the Christians has been Jews/Judaism and an important object of concern for the Jews has been Christians/Christianity. Some of us are still in the process of continuing our respective work in formulating Christian theologies of Judaism and Jewish theologies of Christianity. More specifically, a common conclusion that has already emerged from our long engagement is that we all, in a variety of ways, have renounced supersessionism.[1] I think all of us would agree that if one holds that God has exchanged the Jewish people for the church, thus canceling the election of Abraham and his progeny, there is no incentive whatsoever for Jews to formulate a positive theology of Christianity. Moreover, whatever Christian theology of Judaism there could be would have to be essentially negative, having eliminated Judaism from present engagement by seeing it as *already* superseded by the church once and for all.

Now it is obvious how Christians can be supersessionists and why

---

1. For the most thorough and theologically suggestive Christian treatment of this question, see R. Kendall Soulen, *The God of Israel and Christian Theology* (Minneapolis: Fortress Press, 1996).

the renunciation of supersessionism requires great theological skill. But how could Jews possibly be supersessionists — unless, of course, they are suicidal? No, we Jews cannot be Jewish supersessionists with any integrity, but many Jews can and certainly have been what I would call "counter-supersessionists." Jewish counter-supersessionists are those who listen to the argument of many Christians about the church having superseded the Jewish people as God's elect and then turn it on its head, thus seeing Judaism as the Christian antithesis. Indeed, on a more popular level, there are Jews who think that all they need to know and affirm of Judaism is that it is *not* Christian, which means they need know nothing of Judaism and next to nothing of Christianity. Moreover, the Christianity they set themselves against is usually bad Christian theology.

When practiced by learned Jews, however, Jewish counter-supersessionism can be as plausible as Christian supersessionism. Working out of a committed and knowledgeable background from within the Jewish tradition, these Jewish theologians do not constitute Judaism as the antithesis of Christianity. Rather, they constitute Christianity as the antithesis of Judaism. So, whereas Christian supersessionists assert that God has rejected the Jews and replaced them with the church, Jewish counter-supersessionists assert that Christians are a group of gentiles who erroneously — even arrogantly — think they are now God's people exclusively, having been first led to this position by a group of renegade Jews who removed themselves from Judaism. And the ultimate coup de grace of the Jewish counter-supersessionists is to assert that Christians do not worship the Lord God of Israel as do the Jews but, rather, another god altogether. Thus the longest and perhaps deepest Jewish debate over Christianity, one that began when the church became a decidedly non-Jewish community and that has by no means ended, has been the question of whether the Christians do or do not worship *our* God. If they do not, then they are idolaters ipso facto.[2]

The logic of this Jewish rejection of Christianity runs parallel to the logic of Christian supersessionism. Thus, when the trajectory of Christian supersessionism runs its full course, it usually results in the following conclusion: since Jews reject God as triune, and since God is essentially triune, therefore the Jews cannot be worshiping the same God as do the

2. See David Novak, *Jewish-Christian Dialogue* (New York: Oxford University Press, 1989), pp. 36-56.

Christians because of this rejection. Accordingly, Jews must be worshiping another god. That means Jews are no different than pagans — even worse since they cannot plead ignorance of the gospel. When the logic of the Jewish rejection of Christianity runs its full course, it usually results in the following conclusion: since Christians reject God as the One who elects — past, present, and future — the Jewish people forever, and since God cannot be conceived other than as the God of Abraham, Isaac, and Jacob, therefore Christians cannot be worshiping the same God as do the Jews because of this rejection. Accordingly, Christians must be worshiping another god. That means that Christians are no different than pagans — even worse since they began as renegade Jews.

That, then, is the logic of supersessionism, whether it be manifest in Christian rejections of Judaism or in Jewish rejections of Christianity. Clearly, the renunciation of supersessionism as either thesis or antithesis is the necessary precondition both for a more positive Christian theology of Judaism and a more positive Jewish theology of Christianity. Since Christianity began in the Jewish people, it would seem that the Christian reaction to Judaism precedes the Jewish reaction to Christianity. Christians, being the newer community, had to have made their assertions to the Jews before Jews could have responded thereto. But once Christians renounce supersessionist claims against the Jewish people — namely, when they acknowledge that *their* God's covenant with the Jewish people is perpetual — then Jews cannot very well say anymore that Christians have denied what cannot be denied of God, namely, that God elects Israel, who is, minimally for Christians, the Jewish people.

This does not mean, of course, that the rival assertions of Judaism and Christianity will be overcome by renouncing supersessionism and its Jewish counterpart; indeed, these rival assertions must remain with us until the end, when God will overcome all human rivalries. But it does mean that the Jewish-Christian relationship and its attendant discourse need no longer be primarily adversarial. For almost all Jews, the confrontation with non-supersessionist Christianity has required us to rethink the whole way we talk theology to Christians — that is, those of us who want to talk theology to Christians. Indeed, the fact that the renunciation of supersessionism has been carried on by Christian theologians committed to the truth of Christianity, over and above Christian diplomats interested in better political relations with Jews, means that our Jewish rethinking must be carried on with correlative theological *gravitas*. Since supersessionism has been a leitmotif of Christian theology from patristic times to this day, the renunciation of supersessionism by Christian theologians has required not only great theological ingenuity but moral courage as well. And this effort of mind and will has already brought forth fruit. The most important result heretofore of the renunciation of supersessionism, both as thesis and antithesis, is that some of us Jews can now talk theology not only *to* Christians — which has usually meant *against* Christians — but *with* Christians as well. And, I might add, we Jews who have also been involved in this post-supersessionist effort have had to argue against anti-Christian strains in Jewish theology and deal with the great suspicion of Christians and Christianity on the part of many of our fellow Jews.

The Mutual Theological Need

If the renunciation of supersessionism now enables Jews and Christians to talk theology with one another, then we should understand *why* we need to talk theology with one another.

For Christians, the answer, paraphrasing Karl Barth, goes something like this: The promises God made through Jesus presuppose that God has already been keeping his promises to Israel. Indeed, for Christians, Jesus was sent to fulfill God's ultimate promise to Israel of redemption and then to extend it to the world. Nevertheless, God's initial promise to Israel is that she will not die but live, and live with duration as a covenanted people. The promises made through Jesus, which the church accepts as normative, cannot be believed, therefore, if the Jewish people, who have a perpetual claim to be called *Israel,* are no longer present in the world.[3] The election of Israel as the Jewish people would only be terminable if one held with supersessionists as diverse as Baruch Spinoza and Friedrich Schleiermacher that the Jews elected God rather than that God elects the Jews.[4] Jewish election of God is contingent on the good behav-

---

3. For Barth's profoundly theological rejection of supersessionism, see Katherine Sonderegger, *That Jesus Christ Was Born a Jew: Karl Barth's "Doctrine of Israel"* (University Park, PA: Pennsylvania State University Press, 1992), pp. 131-33.

4. See David Novak, *The Election of Israel* (Cambridge: Cambridge University Press, 1995), pp. 22-49. For Schleiermacher's total dismissal of Judaism from Christian theological interest, see *On Religion,* trans. T. N. Tice (Richmond, VA: John Knox Press,

ior of the Jews; God's election of the Jews, however, means that the bad behavior of the Jews can only impede the covenant, not lose it. To paraphrase a striking passage in the Talmud: God and the Jews are stuck with one another. God is stuck with the Jews because he made an unconditional promise to them that cannot be annulled without God becoming incredible.[5] And the Jews are stuck with God because God is committed never to give up on them.[6] Whenever the Jews reject God's covenant with them, God keeps offering it to us again and again.

Were the Jews no longer present in the world as a covenanted people, then one would have to conclude that God broke his promise to them. But, if God broke his original promise to Israel, which is precisely the hidden premise of supersessionism, then how could the church — as the branch grafted onto the tree — possibly believe God's ultimate promise to her?[7] Only a Marcionite — who is the *reductio ad absurdum* of supersessionism — could posit that God's promise to the church comes *ex nihilo* and thus presupposes nothing before it. Only such a gnosticism could be so ahistorical, being a gnosticism that ignores *Heilsgeschichte,* the history of salvation. As the contemporary Protestant theologian Scott Bader-Saye astutely points out, "The problem with becoming a replacement people is that one has no assurance one will not meet the same fate as those who went before."[8] The Achilles' heel of the philosophy of religion of Hegel, who could be considered the greatest logician of supersessionism, is the historical presence and energy of Islam, let alone the refusal of Judaism to be deconstructed by Christianity or Islam.[9]

This recognition by Christians of their need for the Jews requires more than just pointing to the fact of Jewish national survival. It requires

---

1969), pp. 305-8. The essence of his extreme supersessionism is found in the following statement: "The truth rather is that the relations of Christianity to Judaism and Heathenism are the same, inasmuch as the transition from either of these to Christianity is a transition to another religion . . . we can no more recognize an identity between Christianity and Abrahamitic Judaism. . . . And neither can it be said that that purer original Judaism carried within itself the germ of Christianity" (*The Christian Faith,* trans. H. R. Mackintosh and J. S. Stewart [Edinburgh: T. & T. Clark, 1928], pp. 60-61).

5. *Babylonian Talmud* [hereafter "B."]: Berakhot 32a re Exod. 32:13.

6. B. Sanhedrin 44a re Josh. 7:11. See Novak, *The Election of Israel,* pp. 189-99.

7. See Rom. 11:17-21.

8. *Church and Israel After Christendom* (Boulder, CO: Westview Press, 1999), p. 96.

9. See *Lectures on the Philosophy of Religion,* trans. R. F. Brown, P. C. Hodgson, and J. M. Stewart (Berkeley: University of California Press, 1988), pp. 371-74.

that Christians who have renounced supersessionism actually talk with Jews in order to learn not only *that* the Jews have survived but also *how* the Jews have survived, indeed how we have thrived both physically and spiritually, which are two sides of the same coin. And at this point in history, it means learning how we have survived and thrived in spite of the Holocaust (and not because of it). In the present state of the world, especially, Christian spiritual survival in some societies, and even Christian physical survival in other societies, is just as precarious as Jewish survival has always been. Learning how God has not abandoned us to oblivion can greatly help you appreciate how God has not abandoned you to oblivion either. Learning what God has done for us in the past enables us to have faith in what God is yet to do for us in the future. By doing that for you, we Jews can fulfill God's assurance to Abraham that he and his progeny will "be a blessing" *(berakhah)* for the other peoples of the world (Gen. 12:3).[10] For Christians, to be able truly to learn from the Jews on this level surely requires that they formulate for themselves a Christian theology of Judaism. Having living Jews to talk with will prevent any such Christian theology of Judaism from becoming solipsistic, that is, a mere projection of what Christians would like Jews to be rather than what we truly are. As the contemporary Protestant theologian Clark Williamson puts it, "Jews, too, might serve the church critically by reminding it of what it is all too prone to forget, that it is called and claimed by the God of Israel."[11]

But why do we Jews need to talk theology with you Christians? Let us answer this question by inferring from the negative to the positive. Some Jews think that Jews do not need to talk theology with ourselves let alone with anyone else because Judaism has no theology. The most extreme advocates of this position are those Jewish secularists who think that Judaism has no *theo-logy*, no "God-talk," because Judaism has no God. I will leave it to these secularists to demonstrate how their position can be called "Judaism" with any true coherence. But there are religious Jews who think Judaism has no theology but only a law. Of course, once one asks them the source of this law's authority, and they answer "it is the law of God," their very justification of what they accept as normative can

---

10. See *Beresheet Rabbah* 39.2.

11. *A Guest in the House of Israel* (Louisville: Westminster/John Knox Press, 1993), p. 250.

be made only in theological terms.[12] Nevertheless, most of these religious Jews do not see any need at all to talk theology with non-Jews, especially Christians. What does a Jewish theologian like myself and a few others say to the people we worship with about our theological involvement with you Christians? What is our Jewish justification for the enterprise to which every speaker at this conference testifies by his life and work?

To eschew theological conversation with Christians, especially with those Christians who accept our most basic self-assertion of our chosenness, is to assume that we have nothing to say to the world outside ourselves. Many religious Jews have accepted the argument made by the late Rabbi Joseph B. Soloveitchik, who was a Jewish theologian par excellence, that theological discourse is totally self-referential, and that each religious tradition is like a Leibnizian monad, that is, each exists alongside the other, but there are no cognitive bridges between them.[13] In other words, when it comes to theological discourse, however defined, Jews can talk only to other Jews — and, it must be added, only to those other Jews who still believe that God elected Israel and revealed the Torah to her forever. But this assumes that Jews can make intelligible theological claims only on each other. The fact is, though, that even the most religious Jews make, indeed have to make, theological claims on the outside world. What are those theological claims? I would say that there are two such basic claims, one minimal and one maximal.

The minimal claim Jews have to make on the world is to allow us room to live our life as God's covenanted people. Now who in the world can understand this claim of ours, let alone justifiably respect it? And by "the world" I do not mean lone individuals in the world, which is surely an abstraction invented by modern liberalism, but rather communal persons, who we all are by nature. Therefore, the question is: Which members of which communities/traditions can understand, let alone respect, the minimal Jewish claim on the world for our communal survival, which is in essence a theological claim? Like Blanche Dubois in *Streetcar Named Desire,* none of us could survive without "always depend[ing] on the kindness of strangers."

---

12. My late revered teacher, Abraham Joshua Heschel (d. 1972), called such Jewish myopia "pan-halachism" or "religious behaviorism." See his *God in Search of Man* (New York: Farrar, Straus, and Cudahy, 1955), pp. 320-35.

13. See Novak, *Jewish-Christian Dialogue,* pp. 3-9.

The maximal claim Jews have to make on the world is to be "a light of the nations" (Isa. 42:6; 49:6), which means that the Jews are to be attractive to the gentiles because of our public teaching of the Torah and our observance of its commandments. And even though, for a variety of reasons, both political and moral, Jews have not engaged in active proselytizing for centuries, we have never ceased to accept converts from the gentiles.[14] In other words, we have cautiously welcomed those non-Jews who believe themselves elected as we have been elected by God. Indeed, one of the improvements of our living in liberal-democratic states, as opposed to either Christendom or Islam, is that we can now accept converts to Judaism without any political reprisals by the majority religions. However, it is the minimal claim rather than the maximal one that immediately figures in the current level of theological discourse between Jews and Christians in our society. Later, though, I shall briefly return to the question of Jewish proselytism.

Getting back to the minimal claim Jews make upon the outside world, it would seem that modern Jews have lived alongside those whose communal identity is either (1) fascist; or (2) communist; or (3) Islamic; or (4) liberal-democratic; or (5) Christian. Which community understands our claim for communal survival best, and which community can respect it most consistently?

We can certainly eliminate fascist communities from Jewish consideration since they have inevitably violated our basic human right to exist as persons, let alone to exist as a community. Communist societies have barely let us exist as persons, but certainly have done everything humanly possible to destroy our traditional/communal existence. As for Islamic communities, there was a time, not so long ago in fact, that Jewish communal claims were well understood by Muslims and fairly well respected by them. Because of that, there was a long history of successful Jewish communities in Islamic societies. Nevertheless, because of contemporary Jewish claims to national sovereignty in the land of Israel, which is seen as being within Islamic territory *(daar al-Islam),* almost all of contemporary Islamic territory is a place from which most Jews have chosen to flee. That is because of the inherently Islamic inability of most contemporary Muslims to understand, much less recognize, our claims to national sovereignty.

14. See Novak, *The Election of Israel,* pp. 177-88.

The vast majority of Jews today have seen our best chances for communal survival to be in liberal-democratic societies, in which our communal survival is tolerated as an essentially private matter. As for Christian societies, of which there are virtually no nation-states anymore, most Jews have bitter memories of our marginalization and vulnerability, both communal and individual, in the *ancien regime,* formerly known as "Christendom." Nevertheless, I would argue that Jewish communal existence, which is inherently and coherently covenantal, is also highly vulnerable in a liberal-democratic state that is not dependent on a larger religious culture. And in the West, that larger religious culture could only be predominantly Christian. In other words, Jewish communal existence functions best in a liberal-democratic state nurtured by a religious culture — and that is even true for Jewish communal existence in the State of Israel.

Moreover, since many Christians now recognize their inability to unilaterally constitute a culture that can nurture a liberal-democratic state without being subordinated to it, many Christians now realize that their cultural survival requires a new rapprochement with the Jews. Hence, the term "Judeo-Christian morality" — even "Judeo-Christian culture" — is not at all disingenuous. In political terms alone, this means that Jews, who are about 2 percent of the population of North America, now become 50 percent of the influence of the culture that surrounds the civil society and its states. But Jews cannot be an effective partner in that cultural enterprise unless we engage Christians theologically. That means we need a Jewish theology of Christianity, which is both true and politically beneficial, just as we need to encourage Christians themselves to develop a Christian theology of Judaism for the very same reasons. And that enterprise cannot be sustained, much less accomplished, unless we are in regular and deeply challenging theological conversation with one another.

Let me cite a concrete example of how Jews need to make a theological case to Christians for a matter of communal/covenantal survival in a liberal-democratic society, and why we need to do so before we can make an effective case in secular space. In Canada, where I now live, there is a public movement to outlaw the circumcision of infant boys. It is being promoted by some extreme civil libertarians and some gay men. I suspect some of the motivation for this novel prohibition is anti-Semitic since Jews would be its most conspicuous targets. Nevertheless, I can only guess at the anti-Semitism here and must, therefore, address myself to the public reasons given by the proponents of this radical legal innovation. They argue that circumcision is a form of mutilation, which can never be fully remedied. Even on medical grounds, they argue that the value of the procedure is too questionable to allow it to be performed on an unwilling infant. For this reason, it should be performed only on consenting adults. In fact, there are some men in Canada, who were circumcised as infants, who are already suing those who circumcised them for civil damages. Were the circumcision of infant boys to be proscribed by law, then those who circumcise or authorize others to circumcise their infant male children would be subject to criminal penalties as well. Of course, at present, this movement is little more than a journalistic curiosity. Nevertheless, considering the fact that numerous other religiously based social institutions — like marriage, for instance — are being radically redefined before our very eyes, today's journalistic curiosity becomes tomorrow's political and legal fact.

If this were to happen — God forbid — then no self-respecting Jew could remain in Canada with integrity, unless he or she wanted to have outlaw status. We Jews cannot survive as a covenanted community anywhere we are not allowed to circumcise our infant boys, in order "to bring them into the covenant of Abraham our father" *(le-hakhniso be-vrito shel Avraham avinu),* as the prayer recited by a Jewish father at the circumcision *(berit milah)* of his infant son states it.[15] It is an irrevocable commandment of the God who elected us and gave us the Torah forever. Since Canada is not the only place Jews can live today, leaving Canada to live somewhere else for this reason would be a real political option. It would seem morally preferable for a practicing Jew to opt for a society where he or she can be a law-abiding citizen over a society where his or her Judaism can be practiced only as a criminal act. Thus, when King Ferdinand and Queen Isabella outlawed the practice of Judaism in Spain in 1492, those Jews who quickly left Spain were far more morally admirable than those Jews *(Marranos)* who wanted it both ways by remaining in Spain and practicing Judaism in undetectable privacy.[16] Those who left as Jews survived as a Jewish community — former Spanish Jews became the *Sephardim* — but those who remained in Spain could not maintain the communal presence that individual Jews require for them and their children to survive as Jews.

15. B. Shabbat 137b.
16. See Cecil Roth, *A History of the Marranos* (Philadelphia: Jewish Publication Society of America, 1941).

For Jews to attempt to make our initial case to liberal-democrats (and by that I mean a much bigger group than the members of a particular American political party) for our communal right to circumcise our infant sons is a mistake. It is a mistake because the adherents of a liberal-democratic political ideology have no way of dealing with communal rights because they have no way of dealing with familial rights. A community, certainly for Jews, is the extension of a group of families into a clan. Every infant Jewish boy has the right to be circumcised on the eighth day of his life (barring medical complications), and therefore his father has the duty to circumcise him or authorize someone more skillful than himself to circumcise him. In the absence of a father to fulfill that duty, the community is obliged to do so *in loco parentis*.[17]

Since the Jewish communal/covenantal claim on the larger public for the exercise of the duty of circumcision is now being publicly challenged, to whom should the Jews first look for support? Muslims are an obvious choice since they too practice infant circumcision. Indeed, a Jewish-Muslim alliance on this issue might even contribute to a better atmosphere for lessening the political tensions between Jews and Muslims over the current situation in the land of Israel. Nevertheless, there are two problems with this suggestion. First, there is the political problem. As it stands now, there is such hostility between Jews and Muslims over the current situation in the land of Israel that any alliance seen to be of lesser political import is quite unlikely. Second, there is the theological problem. The problem is that Jews and Muslims circumcise infant boys for very different reasons. For Jews, circumcision is a direct command of God *(mitsvah d'oraita)*.[18] For Muslims, on the other hand, circumcision is only a matter of custom *(hadith)*.[19] Muslims can have a communal life even without circumcision. Thus in Indonesia, which has a very large Muslim population, the vast majority of Muslim men are uncircumcised, I am told. But such a situation would be unthinkable in Judaism. (Even the early Reform Jews in the middle of the nineteenth century, with their radical rejection of large parts of the Jewish religious tradition, quickly re-

17. B. Kiddushin 29a.

18. Lev. 12:3. Circumcision is even to be performed on the Sabbath if this is when the eighth day of the infant boy's life occurs (B. Shabbat 132a). See L. A. Hoffman, *Covenant of Blood* (Chicago and London: University of Chicago Press, 1996).

19. See J. Morgenstern, *Rites of Birth, Marriage, and Kindred Occasions Among the Semites* (New York: KTAV, 1973), pp. 48-66.

stored the obligation of circumcision after a very short period in which some of them criticized its necessity.)[20] Moreover, this has a lot to do with the fact that Judaism is a covenantal religion, whereas Islam is a voluntary religion. Islam has no theological notion of election. In Judaism, circumcision is "the sign of the covenant" *(ot ha-berit)*.[21]

Ironically, though, Christians, whose religion has consciously changed circumcision from a religiously mandated act to at best a medical option, can fully understand its covenantal significance for Jews. Indeed, Jesus himself had to have been circumcised on the eighth day of his life in order to be able to say that he "fulfilled" (Matt. 5:17) the Law.[22] Perhaps Christians who are supersessionists would be unlikely to support the right of Jews to circumcise their sons since Jews ought not to be keeping their eschatologically obsolete Torah and its tradition. If the covenant between God and the Jewish people is over, in the eyes of these Christians, then there can be little interest in, perhaps even hostility to, the circumcisional claim of the Jews. But those Christians who have truly overcome the errors of supersessionism, on the other hand, can certainly understand, respect, even actively support the right of the Jews to remain faithful to God's irrevocable covenant with us. That is the case because Christians have the only communal tradition in the world which, like that of the Jews, requires them to understand themselves covenantally.

But, in order for Jews to be able to make this argument to Christians in a cogently convincing way, there must be both a Christian theology of Judaism and a Jewish theology of Christianity in place. Jews need to recognize that a Christian theology of Judaism can cogently recognize the continuing validity of the Torah and its commandments for the Jews. And, if this Christian theology of Judaism is theologically foundational and not just an apologetics, then Jews need to know quite a lot about Christian theology to recognize such authentic Christian theology when we see it. Moreover, for the very same reason, if this Jewish theology of Christianity is theologically profound and not just good public relations, then Christians need to know quite a lot about Jewish theology. This need becomes especially acute when it is recognized from within that

20. See M. A. Meyer, "*Berit Mila* within the History of the Reform Movement," in *Berit Mila in the Reform Context*, ed. L. M. Barth (Cincinnati and New York: Berit Mila Board of Reform Judaism, 1990), pp. 141-51.

21. See B. Nedarim 31b-32a.

22. See Luke 2:21.

there is a need to call upon the other community, our nearest communal neighbor, for help during the precariousness of this yet-to-be-redeemed world. Members of the covenantal religions of Judaism and Christianity should be sensitive to the dialectic of theology and politics that constantly takes place within a covenant. That is, the transcendent thrust of politics — the way we order our human lives together — becomes most evident when we have to raise a theological issue in public. And the communal focus of theology becomes most evident when we have to raise a political issue for theology. One might well say: politics without theology is blind; theology without politics is dumb.

Thus, if there is to be a Christian theology of Judaism that learns of Judaism from Jews who are very much present and active, then it must be able to see why Jewish adherence to the commandments is not law in place of grace but, rather, a faithful Jewish response to God's most gracious commandments. As our teacher and colleague, George Lindbeck, writes,

> What is the nature and function of Torah? It is in the New Testament custodial in Israel and fulfilled in Christ, but what does this imply for later Christianity and its relations to Judaism? Is not Torah by analogical extension both custodial and fulfilled for Christian communities in this age before the end when fulfillment is not yet final; and does this not make Christians much closer to Jews than they have generally thought?[23]

Antecedents, Consequents, Parallels

So far we have seen how the consistent and persistent renunciation of supersessionism by Christians and counter-supersessionism by Jews enables both Christians and Jews to discover deeper truths of Christianity and Judaism respectively. And that effort could not have been possible, let alone effective, if Christians had been thinking only of Judaism without real Jews, and Jews had been thinking about Christianity without real Christians. We have also seen how this is good for the political survival of both Jews and Christians in the contemporary world, and that it is bene-

---

23. Lindbeck, *The Nature of Doctrine* (Philadelphia: Westminster, 1984), p. 123.

ficial because it is theologically truthful and not in spite of theologically accessible truth. Nevertheless, after all this is acknowledged and thought out, both Christians and Jews can fall into an easy error which, if left uncorrected, will lead both of us right back to the supersessionist dilemma. That error seems, at first, to be a new source of mutual respect, for it is found in the assertion of Christians to Jews: "we came out of Judaism," and the counter-assertion of Jews to Christians: "you came out of Judaism." These correlative assertions seem to be quite hopeful when first made; indeed, they seem to flatter both Jews and Christians. Yet they turn out to be erroneous on both historical and theological grounds.

Historically, these assertions are erroneous because the Judaism we know today, namely, Rabbinic Judaism — the Judaism of the Talmud and its ongoing tradition of interpretive application and expansion, is in many significant ways not identical with the Judaism out of which Christianity emerged. Instead, Christianity emerged out of the Old Testament as it was read in the last days of the second temple, especially by the Pharisees. This is the Judaism that later Rabbinic Judaism, the Judaism of the post-temple period, succeeded.[24] Thus it can be said, with a certain degree of historical confidence, that Christianity *and* Rabbinic Judaism are two different traditions that emerged at roughly the same time, and they were both responses to the imminently future or imminently past destruction of the temple as the center of the covenant between God and Israel. Historically, it is inaccurate to say that Christianity "came from Judaism," if one means the Judaism developed in the Talmud and related writings. Historically, our Judaism is no older than your Christianity; and your Christianity is no newer than our Judaism. Both Christianity and Judaism — and I mention Christianity before Judaism because the New Testament is an older text than either of the two Talmuds and the Midrashim — presented themselves as new revelations.

This point might become more clear if I explain my use as a Jew of the Christian term "Old Testament" when referring to what for me are *kitvei ha-qodesh*, "the Sacred Scriptures." Among ourselves, of course, we Jews would not use the term "Old Testament." And by now even Jewish

24. Thus the rabbinic teaching that the separate Oral Torah is normatively equal to, if not superior to, Scripture or "the Written Torah" (see, e.g., B. Gittin 60b re Exod. 34:27) is considered to be a doctrine fully formulated and emphasized after the rise of Christianity. Whether this was in reaction to Christianity or not, however, is debatable. See E. P. Sanders, *Jewish Law from Jesus to the Mishnah* (London: SCM, 1990), pp. 97-130.

scholars who interact with Christians do not have to say the "Old Testament" because these Christian scholars recognize it to be a problematic term for Jews. So, most of us use the neutral academic term "Hebrew Bible," which is a term that is neither Jewish nor Christian and therefore could be both. However, when Jews understand how Christian theology constitutes the relation of the New Testament and the Old Testament for Christians, we can see then how that relation is strikingly parallel to the relation, for us, of the Oral Torah (Talmud) and the Written Torah (Scripture). And when Christians understand how Jewish theology constitutes the relation of the Oral Torah and the Written Torah, they can then see how that relation is strikingly parallel to the relation of the New Testament and the Old Testament for them. In fact, what I want to suggest is that the Hebrew Bible functions very much like an "Old Testament" for the Jews too. Let me begin with the relation of the new and the old.

We usually assume that the new follows the old. If the new replaces the old, then the new has ontological priority over the old like the end has priority over the means.[25] If, on the other hand, the new simply emerges out of the old, then the old has priority over the new like the cause has priority over the effect.[26] This understanding of the relation of the new and the old is what lies at the heart of supersessionist and counter-supersessionist logic. That is, if the New Testament *replaces* the Old Testament and the church *replaces* the Jewish people as Israel, then the old has been overcome, that is *has been superseded,* by the new. Thus Christians saying "we came out of you Jews" cannot escape the strong practical conclusion: "So why have you Jews remained behind?" But if the New Testament only *emerges* out of the Old Testament and the church *emerges* out of the Jewish people as Israel, then the new has usurped the old. Thus Jews saying to Christians "you came out of us" cannot escape the strong practical conclusion: "So why have you Christians broken so far away?"

But for Christianity, at least as I have learned of it, the New Testament does not *follow* the Old Testament and the church does not *follow* the Jewish people in a necessary logical sequence, neither as a replacement nor as an emergence. Instead, the prime locus of authoritative revelation is in the New Testament. When that is fully established, Christians are

25. See Aristotle, *Posterior Analytics,* 85b29-35.
26. See Kant, *Critique of Pure Reason,* B124.

then to look back to the Old Testament, not as the source or ground of that christological revelation but rather as the set of conditions that made acceptance of the christological revelation possible. In other words, the "Old Testament" is "old" retrospectively, not as earlier "potential" or as a prior "cause." (Here is where philosophical terminology and conceptuality are important for theology, Christian or Jewish.) Here is where one can locate and intelligently refute the theological error of assuming the derivation of Christianity from Judaism. Thus both Judaism qua Oral Torah and Christianity qua New Covenant are *novi testamenti,* as it were.

This understanding of the old making the acceptance of the new *possible* enables Christians to see the New Testament as its original (as in the German *Ursprung*) revelation without a Marcionite rejection of history. The Old Testament "oldness" is not that of either potentiality or causality; rather, it is the "oldness" or historical priority (as in the German *Anfang*) of a necessary precondition, but one whose necessity is not known until after the fact of the truly original revelation.[27] Looking at the relation of Old and New Testaments in this way enables one to see "old" as meaning neither "passe" nor "sufficient." In talmudic logic this is called *bereirah,* that is, when the present defines the past in a way in which the past could never define the present.[28] Later talmudic logic called this process *ashmakhta,* namely, the "association" of norm and text, which is neither the derivation of the norm *from* the text nor the overcoming of the text *by* the norm.[29]

In this way, one can see how the New Testament is a *midrash* necessarily connected to the Old Testament. A *midrash* appears to be a rabbinic commentary on the text of the Bible. Nevertheless, very little *midrash* is what we would call "commentary" in the strict sense. (That had to wait for post-talmudic Jewish exegesis of the Bible, especially in the Middle Ages.)[30] Instead, most *midrash,* especially that which deals with immediately normative scriptural texts, is the attempt to *relate back* to scriptural foundations what had already been accepted in practice as the content of

27. This distinction is based on the ontological differentiation made by the Jewish philosopher Hermann Cohen (d. 1918). See his *Logik der reinen Erkenntnis,* 3rd ed. (Berlin: B. Cassirer, 1922), pp. 36, 79; also, *Religion of Reason Out of the Sources of Judaism,* trans. S. Kaplan (New York: Frederick Ungar, 1972), p. 69.

28. See, e.g., B. Eruvin 36b.

29. See, e.g., B. Hullin 17b.

30. See David Weiss Halivni, *Peshat and Derash* (New York: Oxford University Press, 1991), pp. 52-88.

the Oral Torah *(torah she-b'al peh)*.[31] Thus the later practices *(halakhot)*, which were very much considered to have been revealed as far back as the time of Moses, are the prime locus of the life of the covenanted community.[32] As the Jewish theologian Yeshayahu Leibowitz vividly put it, "the Oral Torah includes within itself the Written Torah."[33] That is why the very acceptance of one version of the biblical text as opposed to another is determined by the Oral Torah.[34] Indeed, the very sanctity of a written Torah scroll, whether it is fit to be read in the synagogue or not, is determined by the Oral Torah for the Written Torah, not by the Written Torah for itself.[35] And how intriguing it is to consider that Jesus of Nazareth, the word made flesh, and Rabbi Akibah, the greatest embodiment of the Torah, both died martyrs' deaths at the hand of the Romans.[36]

So, if Christians see Jesus to be the embodiment of the truly prior Oral Torah — "the word became flesh" (John 1:14) — then the Old Testament is what has made that possible for Christians to accept. And this is quite similar to the way the Written Torah is what has made the acceptance of the Oral Torah possible for Jews to accept. That is why both Christians in their way and Jews in theirs have been engaged in the midrashic process of relating the new to the old in our respective new revelations and traditions. In that way, then, the Hebrew Bible is very much your Written Torah as it is our Old Testament. But it is only in the thorough theological renunciation of supersessionism and counter-supersessionism that Jewish and Christian scholars can exchange this type of textual and historical information in a way that is neither adversarial nor capitulating. So, I would say: Christianity today need look to Judaism today as its source no more than Judaism today need look to Christianity today as its outcome. Both Jews and Christians today do, however, need to look to our common historical roots in the Old Testament and the Pharisaic Judaism of the late second temple period. And some of that theological research can be done mutually to the deep benefit of both communities in our perpetual search for the truth.

31. See, e.g., B. Kiddushin 41a re Deut. 24:1.

32. See B. Menahot 29b.

33. Leibowitz, *Judaism, the Jewish People, and the State of Israel* (Heb.) (Jerusalem and Tel Aviv: Schocken, 1976), p. 348.

34. See B. Sanhedrin 21b-22a.

35. See Maimonides, *Mishneh Torah:* Sefer Torah, 10.1.

36. See B. Berakhot 61b.

What we see from all of this is that it is best, both historically and theologically, to look upon ourselves as two traditions, related to the same sources, which have developed, often in the same worldly locations, with a striking parallelism. Being parallel to one another, our theological logic in talking with one another should be that of analogy rather than that of either causal inference or teleology. Analogy may not be as conclusive as deduction, and it may not be as comprehensive as teleology. Nevertheless, analogy has an openness and a range of possibilities that make it more attractive for truly personal discourse.

The Specter of Proselytism

Finally, let me make one last point about supersessionism, counter-supersessionism, and proselytism. Christian supersessionism lends itself to an easy way to proselytize Jews. It simply tells Jews that they are living in an irretrievable past. It thus tells Jews to become "full Jews," that is, to become Christians and leave Judaism behind. Even though Jewish proselytism is much more subtle and covert, it can use counter-supersessionism just as effectively. It can simply tell Christians to come home like prodigal sons. Thus, when a formerly Protestant friend of mine told me how by becoming a Catholic he felt as though he had come home, I had the temptation — and it was only a temptation — to tell him, "not quite." Now the renunciation of Christian supersessionism and its Jewish antithesis makes Christian or Jewish proselytizing of each other much harder. We cannot use either teleological or causal logic. That does not mean, of course, that either of us could abandon proselytism. Christians must hope that everyone will accept Christ. All Christians are to be seen as "born again" *(anagenesis)*. And Jews need proselytes to remind us that being chosen is best appreciated when our chosenness is what we would want for ourselves over and above the necessity of our birth to a Jewish mother. Indeed, Sarah, the first Jewish mother, is the archetypal convert: One "born again" *(ke-qatan she-nolad)*.[37]

There is always the chance that some Jews will finally accept the Christian revelation as original just as some Christians will finally accept the Jewish revelation as original. That is a chance we take in mutual theo-

---

37. B. Yevamot 22a and parallels.

logical discourse. It could even be a danger, and that is the reason why many traditional Jews want no part of our enterprise. Nevertheless, the renunciation of supersessionism by Christians suggests that Christians have no more arguments for our conversion than we have arguments for their conversion. That opens the ground for God to make the truly final demonstration of an end that will include us all, making our presently parallel lines converge in eternity.[38]

38. See Novak, *Jewish-Christian Dialogue*, pp. 155-56.

Recovering the God of History: Scriptural Life after Death in Judaism and Christianity

PETER OCHS

Where is God in our lives after the horrors of the Holocaust — or of what we prefer to call the Shoah (Hebrew for "total destruction")? Today, few Jewish thinkers seem prepared to talk again of our relation to a God of history. Of those who do speak of God, most refer only to a God of ethics or of creation: a God of principles, rather than one who is personally engaged in our social and political histories. For most who do speak of God, it seems too frightening to speak anymore of a God of history, the one whose covenant with Israel (our name for "the people Israel") renders God an inseparable partner to Israel's salvation history. It seems too frightening, because such a God would also have been God during the Shoah, and, in trying to comprehend that fact, we might have to undo the scriptural and rabbinic grounds of our faith.[1] Redescribing the God of

---

1. I will not take time in this essay to review the various theodicies composed by Jewish thinkers after the Shoah: including atheistic responses (such as Richard Rubenstein's),

My thanks to Robert Jenson and Carl Braaten for the opportunity to write this essay and to Robert Wilken for encouragement, advice, and comment. George Lindbeck and Kendall Soulen offered detailed comments on an earlier version of this essay and I made serious revisions at least in the direction of their comments. On the basis of suggestions from Prof. Lindbeck and other colleagues, I have also revised the clarifying glosses I offer for each of this essay's "lessons in scriptural reading." This assistance from my Christian colleagues reaffirms the closing theme of this essay: that the renewal of Jewish scriptural reading today is interrelated with the renewal of Christian scriptural reading.

Israel as a God outside of history is therefore a strategy for retaining faith when the alternatives seem too terrible to comprehend.

Only Job's sorry comforters would be unsympathetic to those who adopt this strategy. It honors the creature's own God-given instinct of self-preservation — preserving psychic health in the face of potentially traumatic reflections on what may appear to be divine violence or indifference, let alone divine emptiness. But our sympathy must have a time limit. In the long run, the strategy would prove to be as damaging to the Jewish people as a whole as it may, in the short run, have been protective of one generation's psychic health. In the long run, the strategy replaces biblically grounded theology with a form of instrumental reasoning that serves the needs of a particular time of mourning, but that cannot prepare the people Israel for renewed life after mourning, which is nothing less than a life after death.

Belief in resurrection is a central doctrine of the rabbinic Judaism that has guided Israel since the destruction of the second temple. This is a Judaism that renewed its life after the death of Israel's biblical institutions — temple, priesthood, and a national cult in the land of Israel — and that has the theological resources to renew itself after Israel's partial death in our own time. Removing God from history would, however, remove God from the economy of resurrection: condemning Jews to a life without rebirth, not only of the body, but also of the soul, and not only of individuals, but also of the people Israel as a whole. The soul of the people Israel is its faith. In a manner of speaking, this faith did die in the Shoah. Without a God of history, who is with us in our death, however horrible, as well as in our life, I fear there is no way for our

---

efforts to refer only to the consummate evil of Israel's enemies (such as Eliezer Berkovits's and Emil Fackenheim's), and efforts to bypass the question, to some degree, by speaking of God's absence from 1939-45 (such as Martin Buber's reference to *el mistater,* the God who, in Isaiah's words, "hid His face"). Buber's effort is perhaps the most noble of these, but David Halivni has recently composed the most telling response. He writes that *el mistater* remained a feature of the Deuteronomic theodicy of sin and punishment, since God hid his face in response to Israel's sin, and Buber certainly did not mean to blame the Shoah on the sins of Israel! For Halivni's entire theodicy, see David Halivni, "Prayer in the Shoah," trans. from the Hebrew by P. Ochs, *Judaism* 199, vol. 50, no. 3 (Summer, 2001): 268-91. Before Halivni's work, the most helpful theodicy was offered by Irving Greenberg, "Cloud of Smoke, Pillar of Fire: Judaism, Christianity and Modernity after the Holocaust," in *Auschwitz: Beginning of a New Era?* ed. Eva Fleischner (New York: KTAV, 1977), pp. 7-55, 441-46.

faith to be brought back to life. And, if it is not brought back to life, then I fear there is no new life for Israel, for I cannot identify the entity "Israel" without referring to the God in covenant with whom we *are* Israel.

If there were no renewal for Israel, I cannot imagine how there could be renewed life for the church. This is because I do not know what Christianity means without Israel, whose life demonstrates the faithfulness of the God of Israel and, thus, of the God whom the church knows in Jesus Christ. My fears on behalf of the Jewish people therefore lead me to have fears on behalf of Christianity as well. My Christian colleagues have already taught me about the centrality of Israel to the life of the church; I trust they will therefore share my concerns about Israel's health, for their sakes as well as mine. I do not yet know what they will say about what I am calling "the renewal of the church." If they teach that the church is not renewed periodically — even in times like these, after modernity and after the Shoah — then they may still affirm the arguments I offer in this essay about Israel in particular. If they do think of the church as experiencing periodic renewal, then they may also find analogues in Christian salvation history for at least some of my suggestions about the place of renewal and rebirth in Jewish salvation history.

Reading Scripture (Again) Is to Read Scripture in History

I have three relatively simple syllogisms to offer about why and how the Jewish people should rediscover the God of history. The first syllogism offers a general guideline:

(a) We Jews know the God of Israel only by way of our reading of Scripture (specifically, Tanakh, or the canonical book of Torah, Prophets [*nevi'im*], and Writings [*ketuvim*]).

(b) We read Scripture *as* Scripture only when we read it from out of our immediate communal and historical context, which means as the words of Torah whose meanings are guides to our immediate lives.

(c) We therefore know the God of Israel only as the God we know through our efforts to find in Torah a guide to living, today, in our immediate communal and historical context.

Combining this guideline (as major premise) with a certain observation about modern Judaism (as minor premise), the second syllogism offers a basis for understanding this generation's loss of the God of history:

(a) We Jews know the God of Israel as the God of history through the way we study Scripture from out of our immediate communal and historical context.

(b) However, long before the Shoah, modern Jews fell out of the habit of reading Scripture this way, *as* Scripture (or Torah), and read Scripture instead as a record of what they considered "past events" and "traditional beliefs." But neither past events nor traditional beliefs contained any precedents for knowing God from out of the context of Shoah, as total destruction.

(c) After the Shoah, the theologians of modern Judaism were therefore unprepared to consider the God of Israel the God of *this* history of Israel; they therefore tended either to speak of Israel independently of God, or to speak of God independently of Israel *in* history.

The third syllogism displays the lesson that follows from the first two, and by now this should be obvious:

(a) In fact, Jews do not yet know the identity of the God who was God during the Shoah, because they have not yet studied Scripture from out of the context of that terrible time. (On the whole, they have instead applied to that context their records of previous times of study.)

(b) In order to encounter the God of Israel once again after the Shoah, Jewish theologians must study Scripture anew, from out of the context of Shoah and of the life of Israel after Shoah. Most of us who write Jewish theology today did not live through the Shoah and cannot therefore rely on our own Torah study alone as the source of our acquaintance with the God who was the God of Israel during the Shoah and is our God today. Most scholars of Torah who did live through and survive the Shoah have not written theological works.

(c) In order to write Jewish theology today, those of us who did not live through the Shoah must therefore reexamine Scripture through the witness of Torah scholars who survived the Shoah, who studied Torah during and after the Shoah, and who have left us some evidence of their theological reflections. I believe we must regard this evidence as our evidence of the Torah's own witness to the Shoah and, thus, of the Torah's witness to the identity of God during the Shoah.

Thus, the formal argument that shapes this essay is that we know the God of Israel only by studying Scripture; that Scripture is studied *as* Scripture, or Torah, only when it is studied from out of the immediate historical context of the life (and death) of Israel; that the God we know in Scripture is therefore always the God of Israel's history; that, to renew Judaism today, we must renew the people Israel's relation to the God of history (which means its relation to the God who was God during as well as after the Shoah); that, to renew Judaism, Israel must therefore resume its rabbinic practice of studying Scripture as Torah *by* studying the witness of Torah itself to the Shoah; and that this witness is available to us only in the theological reflections of Torah scholars who studied Torah during and after the Shoah. Few of these scholars survived the Shoah, still fewer have written theological reflections, and even fewer are still with us today. I believe that our capacity to renew Judaism depends, in part, on our success in locating these scholars and examining their words as witnesses to the identity of our God.

This formal argument defines two tasks: recovering Judaism's practice of reading Scripture as Torah and re-encountering the God of Israel's history in that reading. This essay introduces the first task: how to read Scripture again. The second task remains the subject of a much longer project.[2]

Rereading Torah through the Witness of David Weiss Halivni

I could not offer more than the preceding, formal argument if I had not encountered the talmudist and Auschwitz survivor David Weiss Halivni and discovered, in his corpus of writings, an illustrative witness to the life

2. The "witness" for this more extensive project is presented in David Halivni, "Prayer in the Shoah." I am at work now on book-length commentary on Halivni's understanding of the identity of God after the Shoah (to be titled *Judaism after Shoah: Reflections on the Witness of David Weiss Halivni*).

of Torah during and after the Shoah and, thus, to the identity of Israel's God. Guided by that formal argument, I have concluded that, whatever else I think and believe, my studies of Jewish theological renewal must have their basis in a witness like his. But what if other witnesses differ from his? And what if other students of Halivni's read his witness differently than I do? I read his witness *as* a reading of Scripture, which means that I regard my own reading of Halivni as a commentary on a reading of Scripture. As I will suggest during this essay, to study Scripture *as* Torah is to study its words as possessing a depth that cannot be plumbed by any single reading.[3] I expect Halivni's witness to belong only to a particular context of reading; all the more so, I expect my commentary to reflect only one sub-reading. But, to the degree that these readings remain true to Torah, they should retain enough of the depth of Torah that their own words both clarify what they should clarify and also signal the depth that remains to be clarified by others in other settings. In the words of the rabbinic sages, "one word issues as many meanings,"[4] but also "deep speaks to deep,"[5] which suggests that the deep also speaks directly to a level of our comprehension that itself remains deep, or irreducible to clear and distinct propositions.

This essay's study of how to read Scripture again after Shoah begins with Halivni's reflections on what it meant to study Torah during and after the Shoah. The reflections are cited from his Holocaust memoir, *The Book and the Sword,* but my commentary draws on his broader corpus of writings, from his on-going magnum opus, *Mekorot u'Mesorot* ("Sources and Traditions," in Hebrew),[6] to his English-language theological and

3. For one thing, Torah speaks to each different historical context in ways that cannot be anticipated but make themselves known only *in* that context. For another, the word that Torah offers *to* each context is also refracted, again, to each particular community in that time, and that means to each collection of different individuals whose interrelations embody that community.

4. Babylonian Talmud *Sanhedrin* 34a: "Just as a hammer produces many sparks [when it strikes a rock,] so too a single word issues as many meanings."

5. "Where deep calls to deep" (Ps. 42:8), which the medieval commentator Rashi reads as "trouble calls to its fellow," which I read as a suggestion that, in the depth of the psalmist's troubled heart comes his capacity to hear the depth of meaning of a troubled word of Scripture, read in a troubled time, when "like a hind crying for water, my soul cries for You, O God" (Ps. 42:1).

6. Halivni, *Sources and Traditions: A Source Critical Commentary on the Talmud* (Hebrew) (Tel Aviv, 1968; Jerusalem, 1975, 1982, and continuing).

hermeneutical writings, most recently *Revelation Restored*.[7] My commentary addresses two questions: as exemplified in Halivni's work, how is it possible to study Torah in and after a time of death? And what patterns of Torah study may guide us in the renewal of Judaism after death? To explore the latter question, I adopt Halivni's way of reading Torah as a model for rereading a brief series of scriptural texts. My commentaries on these texts address two questions once again: how is it possible, in light of the Shoah, to study these texts as Torah? And what patterns of Torah study are recommended by these texts, as we reread them in this light? Our answers to these questions complete this brief study, suggesting how it is possible to renew the study of Scripture after Shoah, and therefore after a time of Israel's destruction and death. I then return to the question of Christianity, asking what Christian theologians would learn from the example of Israel's renewal through Torah study.

Rereading Scripture after Modernity

Before we begin, one more word is in order about why Israel needs to learn how to read Scripture once again. The Shoah did not itself break Israel's habit of reading Scripture as Torah. Instead, Israel appears to have lost its habit because most of those who may have known how to read perished in the Shoah, and most of those who remained had already learned from both modern and anti-modern Judaism how not to read.

The modern period of Jewish civilization has been marked by an increasing division between communal religious life, on the one hand, and academic study of Scripture, on the other. Gradually, the late medieval and the modern academy segregated what it considered the scientific study of Scripture from what we might today call the "performative" dimensions of Scripture, or the ways in which scriptural texts present themselves as commanding behavior. Academically trained theologians gradually followed suit, qualifying the performative dimensions of Scripture as strictly "confessional" or "subjective" and therefore outside the bounds of

7. Halivni, *Revelation Restored: Divine Writ and Critical Responses* (Boulder, CO: Westview Press, 1997). For a more scholarly version of the latter, see Halivni, "Reflections on Classical Jewish Hermeneutics," *Proceedings of the American Academy for Jewish Research* 62 (1995): 21-127. For a brief biographical sketch of David Weiss Halivni, see the appendix at the conclusion of this essay, pp. 146-47.

extra-denominational, formal study and criticism. At the same time, Jewish and Christian congregations not guided by such academics tended to pursue a contrary path: excluding academic, *or* academic-like, scholarship as vehicles of formational scriptural study. The result is a crisis in the modern study of Scripture: congregations tended increasingly to read Scripture naively, as a mirror of their own theological presuppositions; and academics tended increasingly to read Scripture without heart, which means independently of its consequences for congregational or communal life. Independent of such consequences, scriptural texts and commentaries appear only as records of past events and beliefs.

In these terms, modern Judaism — and I trust my colleagues would say the same of modern Christianity — tends to replace the drama, or happy tension, implicit in classical scriptural study with an unhappy dialectic, or battle, between what appear to be opposing forces of scientific criticism and uncritical communalism. The alternative to this dialectic is not some biblical monism but rather the drama of scriptural reading that is evident in the classical rabbinic literature (or, for Christians, early church and patristic literature) and that I trust we will see replayed in Halivni's work. This reading is both faithful and critical at once, addressing the historical realities of the day from out of a tradition of scriptural reading that will yield specific meanings and commands only as it meets the challenge of speaking directly to those realities.

How To Read Scripture Again in a Time after Destruction

Scriptural reading begins again, not with the text of Scripture itself, but with the context out of which it was written. To learn how to read Scripture again as Scripture, the first lesson is, ironically, that modern Jews must learn again how to read themselves. To redefine their lives through the text of Scripture, they need first to reread the concrete details of their own history as part of the story of Scripture. Our own reading of Scripture begins, therefore, with a reading of *The Book and the Sword,* Halivni's prototypical reflection on a Jewish "life of learning in the shadow of destruction."

The purpose of this memoir is to define myself spiritually in the light of the Holocaust. . . . My spiritual self is learning . . . as a highly stimulating pursuit permeated with divinity. Therefore I do not dwell too much on cruelties. I merely hint at them. The only cruelty that asserts itself again and again . . . is the gassing, . . . which still overwhelms my imagination.[8]

Halivni writes of his childhood, spent as a child prodigy in Talmud study in the Hungarian town of Sighet; of his teenage years, spent in slave labor camps, in Ebensee and Auschwitz; and of his adult years as a scholar of Talmud. His decision finally to write this book, so many years after the events, indicates his finally being prepared both to become a public witness to the events and, I believe, to ask, prayerfully, for the theological significance of the dreadful epoch in which he shared. The warrant and direction for my writing this essay come only from the existence of such a witness. In Halivni's study of Talmud during the years of Shoah — and in his oral teaching in the labor camps — I understand the Torah itself to have been present, literally, as a witness to the Shoah. In the way he studied Talmud after the Shoah, I understand the Torah to have displayed one illustration of its response to the Shoah. I say these things literally, because I am speaking of the historically situated reading of Scripture to *be* the presence of Scripture, as Torah, in the salvation history of Israel and, thus, to *be* the means through which God makes his presence known in this history.

For the overleaf of his memoir, Halivni composed a contemporary midrash that indicates, before any other words of recollection and reflection, how Scripture both continues and transforms itself through his witness.

The sword and the book came down from heaven tied to each other. Said the Almighty, "If you keep what is written in this book, you will be spared this sword; if not, you will be consumed by it" (*Midrash Rabbah Deuteronomy* 4:2). We clung to the book, yet were consumed by the sword.[9]

Halivni's text has many levels of significance. At the center of the text is a verse from the classical rabbinic midrash, or interpretation, that com-

8. David Weiss Halivni, *The Book and the Sword: A Life of Learning in the Shadow of Destruction* (New York: Farrar, Straus and Giroux, 1996), p. 166.
9. Halivni, *The Book and the Sword*, overleaf.

ments on the biblical book Deuteronomy, in this case commenting on a text from Isaiah that is read as commentary on Deuteronomy: "If you refuse and rebel, you will be devoured by the sword" (Isa. 1:20). But, before and after the rabbinic verse, Halivni has composed his own commentary: an ironic and tragic commentary on the rabbinic reading of Isaiah. "Follow this book," say the rabbis, "and you will live." "We did," says Halivni, "and we died." Halivni's textual performance is very brief in words, but profound in significance. The significance can only partly be located in the relationship between his own sentence and the plain sense of the rabbinic sentence. In its plain sense, Isaiah has offered a bit of Deuteronomic theodicy: you are rewarded for following God and punished for disobeying. The rabbinic midrash appears to raise the stakes of Isaiah's claim but without, in this instance, subverting the theodicy. The book will save you or it will condemn you. But Halivni's text subverts the plain sense of both the biblical and rabbinic texts in the same manner as most rabbinic midrash subverts the plain sense of the scriptural text it is commenting on.

A more typical example of this phenomenon is the rabbinic commentary that is often placed at the head of the texts from *Pirke Avot* ("Ethics of the Fathers") that appear in the daily prayer book, or *siddur:*

> All Israel have a portion in the world-to-come, as it is written, "your people shall all be righteous, they shall possess the land forever; they are a shoot of My planting, the work of My hands in whom I shall be glorified" (Isaiah 60:21). (*Mishnah Sanhedrin* 10:1)

One must imagine that the historical setting of this midrash from *Mishnah Sanhedrin* is a rabbinic reflection on the site of the destroyed temple in Jerusalem, sometime in the early second century. Imagine how a rabbinic sage would read the passage from Isaiah while gazing on the site of that ruin. He would have to read the plain sense of the scriptural text as counterfactual evidence either that the people Israel is no longer Isaiah's people Israel, or that God's promise is not fulfilled, or perhaps something even worse. The historical facts run counter to the plain sense. In one brief sentence, the rabbinic midrash restores a meaningful relationship between the word of God and the people of God in history by both subverting the plain sense and reaffirming a "deeper" sense of the Scripture: a discovery that the time of the promise is in "the world-to-come," not in this world of destruction. It is in the world-to-come that Israel will possess the land forever and will fulfill their portion as the shoot of God's planting. The "world-to-come" is not an explicit phrase in the Bible. By rereading various biblical tropes as types of the world-to-come, the rabbis uncover a dimension of the divine word that is addressed specifically to the historical context of Israel's life after destruction (in this case, the destruction of the temple). The disclosure of this dimension of Scripture heals what would otherwise be a rupture in Israel's relation to God. It heals by uncovering a word (the world-to-come) that coheres with the other words of Scripture but that appears at this time as the "new word" that both repairs apparent contradictions in the scriptural tradition and offers Israel a way to act meaningfully, once again, in a world that would otherwise have lost touch with the scriptural source of meaning.

We see, in this way, how the rabbis read Scripture as Torah. They read it, first, out of the anxiety of a moment in history that would seem to interrupt history as they know it. They turn to Scripture as a source of guidance in such moments but then discover in it words that seem, on one level, to undermine their faith in the very source of this guidance. But they read on because the plain sense is not all there is to Scripture; their traditional memory of what certain verses have meant in the past does not exhaust all there is to learn from those verses. This unhappy moment of encountering Scripture as counterfactual witness to the events of the day is therefore not extraneous to Scripture; it serves as the reader's entrée into Scripture's deeper dimensions. Moved, by suffering, to seek these dimensions, the reader becomes agent of the renewal of scriptural meaning *(chidush)* through which Scripture becomes the agent of God's renewing the community of Israel after moments of historical crisis and destruction. That Scripture is the word of God that renews Israel is therefore an axiom of the classical practice of reading Scripture, as is the understanding that this renewal does not mean "adding on to revelation" but only drawing out of the words of revelation meanings that were previously hidden but that have now found their time for disclosure. To read Scripture is therefore to renew Scripture as well as to renew the life of the community of readers.

Returning to Halivni's own practice of rabbinic midrash, readers may now see how Halivni's text reenacts the rabbis' innovative practice of reading, rather than simply citing it. As is evident in this case, to reenact the rabbis' practice of reading may mean to subvert the plain sense of previous instances of it: honoring one's ancient teachers, one might say, by appearing to disagree with them. In this case, the historical reality of the Shoah contradicts the plain sense of the rabbinic midrash in Sanhedrin. The Jews appear to have been punished rather than rewarded for their fidelity to the book. In a more recent publication, Halivni traces out the ultimate implication of his reading: the Deuteronomic theodicy can in no way apply to Israel's suffering in the Shoah, since Israel's death in the Shoah contradicts the terms of divine reward and punishment as set out in the biblical covenant.[10] I cannot take the time here to discuss the theodicy Halivni offers in its place, providing a new-old vision of the God of Israel's history without which I believe Israel cannot renew its history. But this vision of God is inseparable from the method of scriptural reading that engenders it, so that our study of Halivni's scriptural method should itself provide us with a sufficient glimpse of the force of his new vision.

This glimpse is best captured through Halivni's phrase "we clung to the book." For Halivni's reader, there is already more to say than that "we clung . . . yet were consumed," since the memoir is itself testimony to its *author's* still clinging to the word even after "we were consumed." The word is resurrected — and *his* word is alive — even though "we died." In classical rabbinic midrash, the biblical text stands, counterfactually, over against the present historical reality of destruction: the word promises, the reality condemns, and the midrash restores the promise by disclosing a word behind the word. In Halivni's midrash, the historical reality of destruction contradicts the rabbis' promise, and the promise is not restored. What is restored can be described only as a promise behind the promise, and this is the life of scriptural reading itself: the word spoken, the word contradicted, the word reread, the rereading contradicted, the rereading reread, and so on. Since it is Israel who rereads, this is also the life of Israel, who clings to the book, who dies, and who is resurrected clinging to the book.

Since the rabbinic model of Torah reading includes the subversion and recovery of the meaning of Torah, Halivni's clinging to the rabbinic practice engenders the possibility of his practicing a reading that subverts rabbinic Judaism itself — in *its* plain sense — while at the same time renewing it. If so, this briefest example of Halivni's reading would illustrate the following lessons of "reading Scripture again after destruction."

10. Halivni, "Prayer in the Shoah," pp. 268-91.

Lesson 1

Scripture is present to us only through the practice of reading Scripture as Scripture. In this sense, Scripture is itself the narrative of salvation history, because it is history that is disclosed through the heart, mind, and soul of a member of the people Israel who has suffered this history and has narrated it through his or her own reading of Scripture. In other words, Scripture becomes salvation history when we read Scripture as both a witness to the sufferings of our present-day community and an as yet undisclosed response to that suffering.

Lesson 2

Salvation history continues in post-biblical times, because the reading of Scripture as Scripture remains Israel's access to God throughout history and also because this reading always renews Scripture. To renew Scripture means both to restate the words of Scripture and to reenact the generative process of Scripture's disclosing the revealed word of God. In other words, post-biblical salvation history is history disclosed through the scriptural reading of a member of the people Israel who has suffered and has narrated it. There is, therefore, an analogy between Scripture and the writings of each witness to salvation history, writings that both imitate Scripture and renew or interpret it.

Lesson 3

To study Scripture as Torah is to engage in study as an activity of prayer — specifically, the kind of prayer that appeals to God in responding to an ultimate crisis of the day. In other words, to pray for help is to reread the plain sense of Scripture in the face of a historical reality that appears to contradict those words. To achieve an innovative, or midrashic, reading of Scripture as Torah is to have received an answer to one's prayers: to have received a transforming vision of the God who appears to condemn Israel in history and is now the God who may again redeem Israel in history (even if, as Halivni's words will suggest, Israel's work must itself contribute to this redemption). There is, therefore, no reading of Scripture as Scripture without suffering, nor without the expectation that there is One who will redeem us from this suffering.

There are several corollaries of Lesson 3:

Lesson 3a

The Redeemer to whom we pray must also be the One who created this world in which we suffer and the One whose revealed word is disclosed through our reading of Scripture. (For only a God who created our world could also redeem the suffering we experience in it.)

Lesson 3b

There must be some relationship that binds the Creator-Revealer-Redeemer to those who read Scripture in this prayerful way, otherwise there would be no warrant for this prayerful study. In the language of rabbinic Judaism, this relationship bears several names: creation (which binds creature to Creator), Torah (which binds Israel to the Revealer), and covenant (which binds Israel to the Redeemer God of history), among others.

Lesson 4

Yet the Shoah exceeds the conditions of suffering that prompt prayerful study in the tradition of rabbinic Judaism.

I cannot derive this last lesson as an inference from any text or experience or principle but must derive it only from what I learn from Halivni's witness and other witnesses like him. "We clung to the book, yet died by the sword." What the Torah promised is contradicted by experience, and what the rabbis learned from this contradiction is now contradicted by Halivni's experience. The implication must be that his experience confounds the logic of prayerfully studying Torah, for he has experienced the absence of God's redeeming presence and has no clear reason to anticipate God's redemption in the future. Perhaps this is why he wrote his memoir so many years later. But he did write it and wrote it prayerfully. That is his contradiction, but his writing may wrest a new form of prayerful study from this contradiction. He named his memoir *The Book and the Sword* after an image of his own making, composed in the manner of rabbinic commentary on Scripture, but through an inversion of the rabbis' own reading of Scripture. As reader of his composition, I am led to suspect that contradiction is inherent in his exegetical and theological method. And I take the time to derive lessons from his method, because, once having perceived these lessons in his salvation history, I find reason to read them into analogous histories that bear witness to each of the horrible destructions in Israel's history. These extend from his witness back through the history of Israel's sufferings in Europe, through the prototypical rabbinic witness to the destruction of the second temple, to the prototypical biblical witness to the destruction of the first temple. And, in each case, I can, in light of his work, now reread the Jewish literatures that follow each of these disasters as comparably contradictory: ironically prayerful monuments to God's absence as Redeemer. These contradictions seem somehow to mark the path of Jewish salvation history; and, while I can in no way *understand* this path, I (also ironically) cannot imagine our recovering Jewish religious life after the Shoah through any other path.

Not insightfully, therefore, but with anguish, learning only from what I have been shown, I turn to derive a few more lessons from Halivni's witness.

Lesson 5

To study Torah prayerfully, but after a major destruction of the people Israel, is to anticipate redemption but in a way that contradicts what explicit Jewish tradition would lead one to expect.

Recognizing this contradiction entails two corollaries:

Lesson 5a

Study after destruction requires drawing a distinction between the plain sense of Torah *(peshat)* and the interpreted sense *(derash)* that is disclosed through the present study itself. The *peshat* may stand counterfactually over against the reality of our historical condition; the *derash* redeems (affirming that, despite what appears to be the case, God nevertheless redeems and that witnesses like Halivni are therefore not wrong).

The plain sense, you see, appears to be contradicted by present-day experience. Therefore, classical rabbinic study distinguished between the plain sense of Torah as Scripture — with its contradictions — and the rabbinic *derash* that offers a means of resolving the contradictions in *its* time of witness. Subsequent study, at least study after the Shoah, may also draw a distinction between the plain sense of rabbinic *derash* and the study that now reinterprets *derash* as well.

Lesson 5b
One must account for the role of the interpreter and the interpreter's community in rereading the plain sense brought forward by the tradition. Redemption despite destruction is not achieved through additional revelations to individuals, nor by simply returning to previous readings, nor by jettisoning the past.

There is no doubt that both the classical rabbinic sages and Halivni's community of interpretation brought something to the study of Torah that contributed to the new sense of Torah that emerged through their interpretations. But it is as yet not at all clear what they brought and how it relates to the process of prayerful study. We will see later that modern scholarship and the anti-modern reactions against it both founder in their efforts to follow this corollary. Some interpreters founder by imagining that, in such times of great change, their individual, new readings are authorized by some direct revelation from God. In imagining this, they ignore the uncertain presence of God's redeeming hand in times of terrible destruction and overlook the significance of what they themselves bring to their studies after destruction. Other interpreters founder by imagining that their study requires no innovation but is fully guided and warranted by the plain sense of previous traditions of study. These interpreters ignore the aporias and uncertainties that belong to the conditions of prayerful study after destruction. A third and final group of interpreters founder by imagining that their new readings are determined solely by autonomous reasoning, fully independent of prior traditions or of divine presence. These, I am afraid, ignore most of what we have already said about the prayerful character of this study and of its place in the traditions of scriptural study.

Let us turn, then, to three prototypical sets of texts in the Jewish tradition of prayerful study to see what we have so far only intimated: that, both despite and in light of its innovations, Halivni's witness both imitates and reinterprets prior Jewish witnesses to salvation history.

Texts of Distress

At a quicker pace, I would like first to overview all of the distressful aspects of these histories of destruction.

Mitzrayim: Bondage in Egypt

> The Israelites groaned in their bondage and cried out and their cry for
> help because of their bondage went up to God. (Exod. 2:23)

We may say that this is Israel's witness to its primordial event of loss,
marked by exile, enslavement, and the dissolution of the patriarchal/ma-
triarchal, Abrahamite religion.

Chorban: First Destruction

> I reared up children and brought them up,
>   but they have rebelled against me. . . .
> The Lord's anger burns against his people.
>
> (Isa. 1:2; 4:25)

> How solitary sits the city,
>   once so full of people. . . .
> Bitterly she weeps at night,
>   tears are upon her cheeks. . . .
> Jerusalem has become unclean.
>
> (Lam. 1:1-2, 17)

Here is witness to Israel's paradigmatic destruction: the burning of Israel's
temple, the end of its monarchical theo-polity and political independence, the exile of its priests and intellectuals to Babylonian captivity.

Chorban: Second Destruction

An image dominates even more than a text: the burnt temple (70-71 C.E.);
Jerusalem razed and salted (135 C.E.). But texts abound:

> When Rabbi Joshua looked at the Temple in ruins one day, he burst
> into tears. "Alas for us! The place which atoned for the sins of all the
> people Israel lies in ruins!" (from Avot de Rabbi Natan 11a, in *Machzor
> for Rosh Hashanah and Yom Kippur*, ed. J. Harlow)

It was decreed for Israel that they study words of Torah in distress, in enslavement, in wandering and in uncertainty, suffering for lack of food. (Midrash Eliayahu Rabbah)

These late midrashim present themselves as witnesses to the destruction that marks the emergence of our Judaism, which is rabbinic Judaism. The biblical promises are broken, so it seems. "Because of our sins, we are exiled from the land." *Galut.* The end of direct biblical jurisdiction over Israel's life.[11]

Scriptural Reading as a Witness to Destruction

The plain sense meanings of this first set of scriptural texts offer textual evidence for our first five lessons about scriptural reading. Each scriptural text gives witness to a period of Israel's terrible suffering, disclosed by way of Israel's heart, mind, and soul rather than only its physical — or journalistic — eyes. Each witness is therefore also a form of prayer, since it refers the suffering to Israel's relation with God and elicits the reader's concern about the past and future character of this relation. The overall sequence of these texts both within and beyond the corpus of the Tanakh suggests several new lessons.

Lesson 6
Israel's salvation history — including its scriptural record — narrates destructions of its entire theo-political order and not merely of its population.

Placed in a sequence, we read narratives of the end of Israel's patriarchal/matriarchal order, of its monarchical order, and of its priestly order.

---

11. If we were to add the next stage of the salvation history, it could be given the heading "*Galut* in Muslim Afro-Asia and Christian Europe, with Its Refrain of Pogrom, Forced Conversions, and Displacements." Sorest in memory are sufferings in Christian Europe: the massacres of the crusades, the expulsion from Spain, the Chmielnicki pogroms of eighteenth-century Poland, the pogroms of nineteenth- to early twentieth-century Russia and the Soviet Union.

Lesson 7

Israel's salvation history narrates a spiral of destructions — that is, both a cycle of destruction and some progressive change in the character of these destructions as Israel witnesses them. They are characterized by progressive changes of explanation, moving from the amoral (Egypt), through the moral (first Chorban), to an account of both "sin" and mere "fate" (second Chorban).

In the Exodus account, Israel suffered without apparent sin. It prays (cries) for help, and God hears and sends a redeemer. In prophetic accounts of the first Chorban, Israel suffers for its sins, but also suffers beyond measure. As very briefly sampled here, late rabbinic accounts of the second Chorban both imitate features of the prophetic accounts of Israel's sins and add a new voice: Israel seems fated to its suffering as if there were no apparent reason for it. The second Chorban appears to challenge Israel's relation with God in unforeseen ways.

Lesson 8

As witness to its terrible destructions, Israel's scriptural readings therefore appear to mark the termini of identifiable epochs in Israel's relation with God as that relation is embodied in all of its theo-political, theo-societal, and theological institutions.

We thereby arrive at what might appear to us as an awe-ful response to our prayerful inquiry into the meaning of this past century of destruction. While this is apparently our worst experience of suffering, periods of destruction like this are not unprecedented in Israel's salvation history, and there is — God help us! — no scriptural warrant for our assuming this sad cycle of history has ended. There is scriptural warrant, however, for our reading the epoch of Shoah as the terminus of a particular epoch of Judaism: what we might call the epoch of modern Judaism. Let us consider the implications of this possibility.

The End of Jewish Modernity

If the bodies of the people Israel were destroyed in the Shoah, Israel's religion had already been sent into spiritual exile two hundred years earlier

— not destroyed, but separated into the dialectical poles of Jewish modernism and ultra-Orthodox anti-modernism. These poles define present-day Judaism as well. This is why, if we remain within the dialectic of modern Judaism, there is no hope for rebirth and thus no means of ending our traumatic period of mourning for the Shoah.

The non-orthodox Jewish theologian Eugene Borowitz narrates such a history of Judaism as it goes into and out of modernity:

> After more than a millennium of ostracism and persecution, European Jews were astounded when the French Revolution signaled a turn to political equality in Europe, including even Jews. . . . Emancipation revolutionized Jewish spirituality, for whenever Jews were permitted to modernize, they did so avidly, and uncomplainingly accepted its accompanying secularization.
>
> The startling effects of this fundamental shift of cultural context cannot be overemphasized. Freedom from segregated existence brought on a transition from a life oriented by revelation, tradition, and a sense of the holy to one in which religion became privatized if not irrelevant or obsolete. This . . . meant that, as the realm of religiously neutral activity expanded, the twin questions of Jewish identity and continuity became increasingly troublesome. Jews began to ask, "What does it mean to be a Jew today? Why should one undertake its special responsibilities?"[12]

By what criteria would modern Jews now choose which aspects of their Jewishness to retain and which to discard? According to Borowitz, modern Jews chose criteria offered by Western Enlightenment sources rather than traditional, rabbinic sources: sharply separating private and public spheres; relegating religion to the private sphere; and adopting, for the public sphere, the rules of scientific reason, modern statehood, individual rights, and universal ethics.[13] For Borowitz, however, this "Jewish modernism" also contained the seeds of its own self-negation, since it represented a particular form of social assimilation that could not over time adequately serve the people Israel's covenantal norms of community and traditional religious law:

---

12. Eugene Borowitz, *Renewing the Covenant: A Theology for the Postmodern Jew* (Philadelphia: Jewish Publication Society, 1991), pp. 3-4.

13. Eugene Borowitz, *Exploring Jewish Ethics* (Detroit: Wayne State University Press, 1990), pp. 26ff.

As the twentieth century waned, doubts about modernity's beneficence arose throughout Western civilization. People were profoundly disturbed by the deterioration of the quality of life. . . . The Enlightenment, the intellectual credo of modernity, had promised that replacing tradition with rational skepticism, hierarchy with democracy, and custom with freedom would bring messianic benefit — and certainly it hasn't.

On a much deeper level, this loss of confidence in Enlightenment values has come from the collapse of its philosophical foundations. All the certainties about mind and self and human nature that once powered the bold move into greater freedom now seem dubious.[14]

There is no simple alternative, however, since the dominant theologies that supported pious practice in the modern era emerged as reactions against Jewish rationalism rather than as transformatory responses to it. I do not mean that *pious practices* are reactionary — they share, rather, in the timeless dimensions of Torah as a way of life; I am referring, instead, to the reactionary forms of orthodox argumentation that were developed to defend such practices against secular critics. Examples include popular Hasidism, as well as the varieties of esoteric kabbalism that lie behind it; neo-Orthodoxy, when it appears only as a means for traditionally religious Jews to make use of the socioeconomic vehicles of life inside of modern civilization; and the expanding varieties of contemporary ultra-Orthodoxy, combined in Israel with political or ethnic nationalism. These orthodoxies tended to replace Jewish religious tradition with the idea of it — that is, they tended to replace the humanly unpredictable evolution of traditional Jewish life and law with artificially constructed systems of communal and hermeneutical order.

There is therefore reason for us to conclude, sadly, that there is no way for Jews to move beyond the dialectic of modernity without allowing its inner logic to die. From this perspective, a salvation history of Israel's death in the Shoah may indeed mark the terminus of the epoch of modern Judaism. To acknowledge the fact of Israel's physical death in the Shoah is to acknowledge the incapacity of modern Western civilization to prevent this death. If so, this is to recognize that, unredeemed, the modern West — which includes modern Western Judaism and Christianity — offers no home for us; it is a place of death.

14. Borowitz, *Exploring Jewish Ethics,* pp. 26ff.

The salvation history of our day therefore reiterates the narratives of Israel's previous destructions, marking the end of a moment in our collective life. There is also a significantly new feature in our history, however, which you may have sensed already. In all of Israel's previous narratives of destruction, Israel suffered alone, facing by itself the end of one epoch of its civilization. This time, however, the end of modern Judaism may very well parallel the end of modern Christianity as well. This is, at least, the lesson I learn from an expanding circle of powerful Christian theologians who work at the centers of their respective church communities, but who are also at the center of a potentially transformative movement of postliberal theology. Let us turn next to consider the significance of their work for our studies of both scriptural reasoning and religious renewal today.

The End of Modern Judaism Is Also the End of Modern Christianity

The dominant voices in the circle of postliberal Christian theologians are in fact included in the symposium that gave rise to this book. George Lindbeck and Robert Jenson are two of its most established and influential voices in theology, Kendall Soulen one of the strong new voices in scriptural theology — and I trust Richard Neuhaus, Carl Braaten, Robert Wilken, and David Burrell would not mind being included in the circle as well. (And it may be noteworthy that this movement is led by Lutherans, in the United States and Germany. Most of the other strong contributors are Catholics [with Lutheran ties], Anglicans [in the United Kingdom], and Methodists. And Karl Barth is the theologian cited most often by all of them.) Together, along with a supporting cast of students and colleagues throughout the United States and Europe, these theologians have shown the people Israel that it is not alone, neither in facing an end to one of its epochs nor in drawing on its scriptural sources as resources for possible religious renewal.

I am not suggesting that Judaism and Christianity are united or unified in this transformative moment in Israel's salvation history. But I am appealing now to the beliefs that drew both David Novak and me to the projects of *Dabru Emet* and *Christianity in Jewish Terms*:[15] that, in a

---

15. *Dabru Emet* ("Speak the Truth," from Zechariah) is the name of a "Jewish State-

historically unprecedented way, this circle of Christian theologians has helped lead the church to a qualitatively new epoch in its relations with the people Israel; that this movement renews in radical ways Christianity's commitment to its sources in Israel's covenant, history, and Scripture; that this Christian renewal signals the potential terminus of the modern epoch of Christianity, including both its liberal and its reactionary, anti-liberal aspects; and that a postliberal Christianity is partner to the Judaism that is emerging now after destruction. This means partner in renouncing and seeking to repair and redeem the moribund civilization of the secular, modern West and, therefore, partner in the scriptural reasoning that may serve as an instrument of this redemptive work.

From the perspective of my reading of Judaism after Shoah, I read the works of my Christian colleagues in this symposium as witnesses to the renewal of Christianity after Shoah and after modernity. This leads me to derive from their writings a series of six lessons in "Christian scriptural reading" that parallel the eight lessons I have offered about Jewish scriptural reading. I do not, in fact, presume that my Christian colleagues would assent to my drawing these lessons from their work. I frame these lessons only as my way of sharing an appreciative Jewish reading of their Christian teachings and inviting their responses to these questions: Would they find it meaningful to speak of their work, as I have, as contributing to a "renewal of Christianity"? It is controversial enough to read Jewish salvation history, as I have done, as a story of the cycles of Judaism's death and resurrection; would it be more — or less — controversial to speak analogously of the cycles of Christianity's renewal?

---

ment on Christians and Christianity" that four of us printed in September 2000 as a *New York Times* full page ad, signed by one hundred Jewish religious leaders. This statement is included on pp. 179-82 of this volume. The statement said that it was time for Jews to take Christianity seriously as a theological dialogue partner. We also published a scholarly book, with thirty Jewish and Christian contributors, that explored the theological background to our statement in greater depth: *Christianity in Jewish Terms,* ed. T. Frymer-Kensky, D. Novak, P. Ochs, D. Sandmel, M. Signer (Boulder, CO: Westview Press/Perseus for the Institute for Christian and Jewish Studies, 2000).

Some Jewish Lessons about Christian
Scriptural Reading after Modernity

Lesson C-1

Christian scriptural reading after modernity is, in part, a critique of the dualistic and dichotomous character of modern Christianity. Modern Christianity fails in its efforts to correct and redeem the imperfections of premodern Christianity, because its efforts perpetually divide into mutually exclusive alternatives. One locates the sources of correction in received traditions (unchallenged by critical inquiry); the other locates them in the self-validating claims of certain individual critics. The latter alternative is subdivided again, between the self-validating claims of biblical literalists and those of autonomous reasoners (or conceptualists).[16]

In his book *The Eclipse of Biblical Narrative,* Hans Frei, of blessed memory, introduced a highly influential genealogy that traced this particular dualism to the work of eighteenth-century Lockians and neologians.[17] Following their lead, most modern Christian thinkers became what Frei called "mediating theologians," who sought to mediate the two poles of received and revealed knowledge, but always in favor of the revealed. Advocates of revealed (or what some call foundational) knowledge divided, in turn, into advocates of the literal sense of Scripture and of autonomous reason. Lindbeck contributed to and extended this genealogy, and his book *The Nature of Doctrine* is perhaps the best known manifesto of scriptural reading as a form of Christian theology.[18] Jenson's more recent two-volume *Systematic Theology* also joins in this genealogical critique and extends it into a project of what we might call trinitarian scriptural reading.[19]

16. As I read them, each of the latter two would subdivide again, in Lindbeck's terms, into "propositionalist and expressivist" varieties of literalists and of conceptualists.

17. Hans Frei, *The Eclipse of Biblical Narrative: A Study in Eighteenth and Nineteenth Century Hermeneutics* (New Haven and London: Yale University Press, 1974).

18. Among many other sources, see also George Lindbeck, "The Story-Shaped Church: Critical Exegesis and Theological Interpretation," in *Scriptural Authority and Narrative Interpretation,* ed. Garrett Green (Philadelphia: Fortress Press, 1987), pp. 161-78, esp. p. 161; and Lindbeck, *The Nature of Doctrine: Religion and Theology in a Postliberal Age* (Philadelphia: Westminster Press, 1984).

19. Robert W. Jenson, *Systematic Theology,* vol. 1: *The Triune God,* and vol. 2: *The Works of God* (New York and Oxford: Oxford University Press, 1997, 1999).

According to both Lindbeck and Jenson, the mediating theologians' inner divisions generated modern Christianity's sterile and destructive battles between the religion of liberal academia and fundamentalist or literalist orthodoxies. Jenson argues, in volume 1 of the *Systematic Theology,* that modern theologians have failed in their efforts to unify a divided church and that this division threatens the life of the church itself. Divided among themselves, furthermore, the modern theologians tend to be dominated by advocates of autonomous reason over scriptural tradition, grace over law, and, ultimately, the epistemologies of the academy over those of the church denominations. In *The Nature of Doctrine,* Lindbeck argues that academic Christian theologians are themselves divided between "propositionalist" and "experiential-expressivist" tendencies. One group argues that the doctrines that govern Christian lives can be disclosed in clear and distinct statements that are either true or false. The other group argues that what God wants of us is disclosed, ultimately, to the individual heart, and enters into public discourse only probatively, hypothetically, and relative to the contexts of interpretation. Modern Christianity has failed to locate any successful method for mediating between these two models or, all the more so, for repairing the divisions of Christian church and Christian academy.

Lesson C-2
Christian scriptural reading does not simply reject the various poles of modern theology but redeems them by drawing them back into relation by way of the divine word that alone is their mediating ground. This is the word of Scripture — of the Old Testament, of the Gospel narratives that interpret its meaning for the church, and of the chain of subsequent literatures that interpret this meaning specifically for subsequent communities of the church, from the Pauline letters to the patristic commentaries and on to the contemporary commentaries and theologies that regenerate Christian scriptural reading. Academic scholarship, including historical-critical studies, has a proper — and necessary — place among this chain of interpretive literatures; it is simply not privileged over other modes of scholarship.

In Jenson's words, the error of the mediating theologians was to think that their own reasonings could unify the divisions of the church. For Jenson and Lindbeck and all other postliberal Christian scholars, God alone is mediator, in the presence of Jesus Christ as disclosed through the texts and interpretations of the Gospel narratives.[20]

Lesson C-3

Christian scriptural reading therefore renews/resurrects the premodern tradition of Christian scriptural theology, but in a way that both encompasses and transforms the practices of the modern Christian academy and modern Christian congregational life.

As resources for their theological work, these Christian scriptural readers draw, at the same time, on historical-critical studies of the Bible and of Christian salvation history; on their participation in community-specific practices of Christian life; and on tradition-specific and academic disciplines of reasoning. No one of these resources dominates the other, because the Word that guides this reading belongs irreducibly to the triune life of God. Trusting in this Word, Lindbeck can therefore say that historical-critical scholarship protects the church against denominational misreadings of the gospel, without betraying what he considers his own Christian orthodoxy. And Soulen — as well as Jenson and Lindbeck — can, with comparable assurance, offer far-reaching ethical, hermeneutical, and source-critical arguments against supersessionist exegeses.

Lesson C-4

As both a means and a consequence of renewing/resurrecting Christianity's primordial traditions of scriptural theology, Christian scriptural reading renews/resurrects Christianity's identity with the people Israel and fosters a new relationship of the church to contemporary Judaism.

As evidence, here are some sample citations from Lindbeck:

> One need not be a theologian or even a Christian believer to suspect that the Christian communities that have the greatest chance of survival and success will in the long run be those that understand themselves as Israel in continuity with the catholic tradition and in commitment to ecumenical unity.[21]

20. Jenson, *Systematic Theology,* vol. 1, p. viii.
21. Lindbeck, "The Church as Israel: An Experiment in Ecumenical Ecclesiology," unpublished manuscript, p. 9.

The roles of the two Torahs and of rabbinic commentaries in Judaism[22] are not without value for resolving church-dividing Christian differences over the interrelationships of the two Testaments and of church tradition.[23]

Lesson C-5 (which is also Lesson 9 for Judaism)
Thus, finally, Christian scriptural reading suggests that, like Jewish salvation history, Christian salvation history can also include cycles of renewal. Since these mark certain ends of history, but not final ends, we might label them "meantime end-times," that is, times that qualitatively end one epoch of Christian salvation history and initiate a subsequent epoch. Like Judaism, Christianity might experience this time after modernity and after Shoah as a time of renewal, change, and revival. This lesson about Christian scriptural reading may therefore contribute a new lesson to Jewish scriptural reading: that Judaism as well as Christianity experiences meantime end-times in its salvation history. In the present day, moreover, we may say that both Jews and Christians are entering one of these meantime end-times, characterized in this case by parallel and interrelated forms of scriptural reading, which redeem the failings of their modern epochs by re-engaging modern scriptural reading with its premodern sources.

This may be the most challenging claim of this essay. It suggests that popular distinctions between Jewish and Christian eschatologies should be modified. In popular Jewish understanding, Christianity looks to the resurrection of Jesus Christ as fulfilling Jewish eschatology: that is, that we are now in the end-time for which Jews prayed, but that this end-time is temporally thick, extending from the time of Christ's resurrection to the time of a second and final coming. This meantime, the time of the church, would be an eschatologically homogeneous time, a time of bringing the world to realize what the apostles have already beheld. In popular Christian understanding, Judaism looks to the long run of future history as the time of bringing humanity from this world of sin and suffering to the time of messianic fulfillment. This time, the time of Israel's history,

22. In a note, Lindbeck cites the example of David Halivni's reading of rabbinic Judaism in *Revelation Restored.*
23. George Lindbeck, "What of the Future? A Christian Response," in *Christianity in Jewish Terms*, p. 365.

would also be eschatologically homogeneous, a time during which the world comes to know the God who created the world and spoke the Torah. The typical conclusion is that Christianity believes it lives in the end-time; Judaism does not.

Lesson C-5, which would apply to Jewish as well as Christian scriptural reading, revises these popular beliefs without necessarily contradicting them. According to this lesson, both Judaism and Christianity participate in temporally extended meantimes that are not eschatologically homogeneous. These meantimes are, instead, marked by meantime end-times, or disruptive moments when the people Israel, within its salvation history, and the church, within its, may suffer the end of a given epoch of history and also the beginning of another epoch. As noted in Lesson 2, such disruptions are marked by and recorded in the writings of witnesses to salvation history. These writings imitate Scripture itself as the narrative of salvation history, and, according to patterns disclosed within the texts of Scripture, they interpret Scripture within the contexts of their own histories. Thus, both scriptural documents and the written witnesses that interpret them mark what Arthur Cohen called the "caesurae of history," the meantime end-times of salvation history.

For both Jews and Christians, the present day may therefore mark a moment of transition, from a time of death to a time that revives each religion into an unexpected and new epoch of religious life. Unique, perhaps, in the salvation histories of Judaism and Christianity, these revivals may be taking place together, which means at least in parallel ways and possibly in interrelated ways. Each religion's revival may display parallel and possibly interrelated forms of scriptural reading, while applied to different scriptural traditions and with differences of detail and theme. From this perspective, the previous or modern epoch seems to be characterized, in particular, by the disruption of premodern patterns of scriptural reading. If so, then the revival of scriptural reading might itself be one significant feature of the epoch to follow modernity.

Will Christian theologians accept these claims? Jenson's essay "Toward a Christian Theology of Judaism"[24] may provide a Christian proof-text of at least one aspect of Lesson C-5: that Christians and Jews may live in parallel meantimes. Jenson writes,

24. Jenson, "Toward a Christian Theology of Israel," *Pro Ecclesia* 9, no. 1 (Winter 2000): 43-59.

In general, the two [Judaisms], the one the Judaism of the rabbis, and the other the church, were born and made their way through history in a kind of lock-step and in theological and structural mutual mirroring.[25]

This means, he says, that the time of the church is neither the final end-time nor independent of the end-time:

The time of the church is after all not a piece of the kingdom; we do not now enjoy the final vision of God. Yet neither is the time of the church simply a continuation of this world's history. The time of the church is a time within the advent of the Christ to fulfill Israel's history. . . . Until the last judgment and our own resurrection, the Christ has not yet come in the way that consummates Israel's mission. . . . God institutes the church by not letting Jesus' resurrection be itself the end, by appointing the famous "delay of the parousia."[26]

The church is, in this view, a detour that mirrors the detour that is rabbinic Judaism; in Jenson's words, "Christianity should interpret continuing Judaism as another such detour occupying the same time as the church, paired with the one that is the church for reasons that may even be in some part knowable."[27] I believe this leaves out only one feature of Lesson C-5. Jenson does not say explicitly that, during this meantime, both Christianity and Judaism may enter non-final end-times. I infer, however, that the practices of all the postliberal Christian scriptural readers warrant such a claim, at least for the present day. Lindbeck, Jenson, Soulen, and also Wilken, and I believe Braaten and Neuhaus — and I could add Stanley Hauerwas and Bruce Marshall, and Daniel Hardy and David Ford over in the UK — all promote a Christianity that is freed from the dualisms and divisions of modern Christianity as well as from modern and premodern anti-Judaism and supersessionism. Is this not to acknowledge epochs within Christian salvation and meantime ends and meantime beginnings?

If the God of history is to reenter Jewish theology and renew Jewish life after Shoah, then, I believe, Jews need first to understand this time af-

---

25. Jenson, "Toward a Christian Theology of Israel," p. 50.
26. Jenson, "Toward a Christian Theology of Israel," pp. 48-49.
27. Jenson, "Toward a Christian Theology of Israel," p. 50.

ter Shoah and after modernity as a non-final end-time, through which one cycle of Judaism has died and another must be born. I say "must be born," because Jews cannot be passive vessels of any rebirth but only active participants. A rebirth of Judaism is found only in the renewal of Jewish scriptural reading. Effort, will, and works are not sufficient for this renewal, but they are necessary elements of it: we must engage in the work of reading and study, of contributing to the communal practice that makes such study possible, of attending prayerfully to our historical condition, and of awaiting the word through which this condition may be redeemed. A symposium like this makes us sense that, this time, the Jews may not be alone in their waiting.

Epilogue: Texts of Resurrection and Revival

The scriptural texts that initiated our study of scriptural reading were texts of distress that served as prototypes for the people Israel's latest and most horrifying encounter with destruction. By now, however, our study has led to the expectation that such an encounter could also be followed by an epoch of religious revival. Are there scriptural prototypes for such a revival, as well? Let us conclude this study by revisiting the same three sets of texts and observing how, within them, distress and death are replaced by revival and resurrection.

Mitzrayim

> The Lord continued, "I have marked well the plight of My people in Egypt and have heeded their outcry because of their taskmasters." . . . "I have come down to rescue them. . . . I will send you." Moses said, "Who am I that I should go?" . . . He said, ehyeh imach, "I will be with you." . . . "Thus shall you say to the Israelites, 'ehyeh sent me to you.'" (Exod. 3)

The patriarchal/matriarchal religion of Abraham died in Egypt, but it was reborn as the Mosaic religion of the God whose name is with Israel in its suffering, and whose word unites the people of Israel under the legislative force of Torah.

143

Chorban: First Destruction

> But you, Israel, My servant, Jacob, whom I have chosen, Seed of Abraham my friend — You whom I drew from the ends of the earth. . . . To whom I said: You are My servant. . . . Fear not, for I am with you. . . .
>
> This is My servant, whom I uphold, My chosen one, in whom I delight. I have put My spirit in him, He shall teach the true way to the nations. . . .
>
> Who formed you, O Israel: Fear not, for I will redeem you. . . . You are Mine. (Isa. 41–43)

> Ezra opened the scroll in the sight of all the people, for he was above the people; as he opened it, the people stood up. Ezra blessed the Lord, the great God, and all the people answered, Amen, Amen, with hands upraised. Then they bowed their heads. . . . Jeshua, Bani . . . and the Levites explained the Teaching to the people, while the people stood in their places. They read from the scroll of the Teaching of God, translating it and giving the sense; so they understood the reading. (Neh. 8:4-8)

The religion of monarchy and prophet died in the first destruction. In the very place of exile, however, in Babylon, the religion of Israel was reborn as the religion of second Isaiah, Ezekiel, and Ezra: a religion of scribal priests who would redact and reteach the Torah as well as maintain it, and whose reteaching would gradually become the legislative voice of Torah within the second commonwealth.

Chorban: Second Destruction

> All Israel have a place in the world to come, as it is written, "Your people shall all be righteous, they shall possess the land forever; they are a shoot of My planting, the work of My hands in whom I shall be glorified" (Isa. 60)

> Moses received Torah from Sinai and transmitted it to Joshua, and Joshua to the elders, the elders to the prophets, the prophets to the members of the Great Assembly. . . .
>
> Simeon the Just was one of the last members of the Great Assembly.

He used to teach: The world rests on three things: on Torah, on service to God, and on acts of lovingkindness. (Pirke Avot 1)

Hillel taught: Do not separate yourself from the community. . . .
  Rabbi Tarfon used to teach: You are not obligated to finish the task, neither are you free to neglect it. (Pirke Avot 2)

The religion of biblical Israel — the religion of temple service, defined by the literal word of the written Torah and lived by Israel only on its holy soil — died in the second destruction. The religion of rabbinic Judaism — a religion that inherited the Torah teachings of the scribal priests and the central beliefs of their Pharisaic defenders — was born in its place. These central teachings are belief in the resurrection of the dead, belief in life in the world to come *(olam haba)* as well as in this world, and belief that the Torah that God gave Moses on Sinai displays two and not only one dimension of meaning: the *peshat* or plain sense meaning of the Written Torah *(torah she b'chtav)* and its interpreted and performative meaning, or *derash,* collected in the Oral Torah *(torah she b'al peh).*[28]

---

28. If, once again, we were to add the next stage of salvation history, it could be illustrated by the following redemptive texts:

Galut in Muslim Afro-Asia and Christian Europe, with Its Refrain of Pogrom, Forced Conversions, and Displacements

God both creates and destroys; indeed, he destroys by creating and he creates by destroying. . . . Consider the comment attributed to R. Abbahu on the verse, "There was evening and there was morning, the first day" (Gen 1) "From here [we learn that] the Holy One, blessed be He, created worlds and destroyed them, until He created these. He said: These give me pleasure, but those did not give me pleasure." (Genesis Rabbah 3)

According to a bold idea expressed in the Zohar and further developed in the Lurianic material of the sixteenth century, the first act of divine creativity involves the elimination of the forces of impurity from the Godhead. This act of catharsis of evil is related to the attribute of judgment or divine limitation, which is referred to in the Lurianic kabbalah by the technical term *tsimtsum* (withdrawal). . . . From this perspective, we can speak of divine suffering at the very core of existence. If God did not suffer his own death as the infinite, there would be no existence outside of the infinite God. (Elliot Wolfson, "Listening to Speak," in *Reasoning after Revelation,* ed. S. Kepnes et al. [Westview, 1998])

Appendix

For those who may not know his work, let me introduce Halivni in some more detail. (The information presented here is drawn from my "Preface to David Halivni's Prayer in the Shoah," *Judaism* 199, vol. 50, no. 3 [Summer, 2001]: 259-67.)

David Weiss Halivni, Lucius Littauer Professor of Classical Jewish Civilization at Columbia University and former head of the Talmud Department of the Jewish Theological Seminary, is recognized as one of the post-war generation's greatest Talmudic scholars. Until the past decade, when he began to write his theological and methodological studies in English, he was widely known only among Hebrew readers of *Mekorot u'Mesorot* — a technical, wondrous play of hypothetical reconstructions of the Talmud text's history of redaction. His recent writings in English have explained how it is possible for one to apply the scientific tools of textual and historical analysis to the Talmudic literature while at the same time respecting the sanctity of that literature as the source of traditional religious practice.

The center of Halivni's overall work concerns the bond between academic rabbinic scholarship and rabbinic practice: a link that he fears is often missing today in both the academy (lest "religious interests" lead scholars to lose "scientific or critical objectivity") and the traditional or *yeshivah* worlds (lest "scientific interests" lead pious Jews to lose the "purity of Torah"). He observes that academic scholarship that is not connected to rabbinic practice tends to lose contact with the overall purposes of Jewish textual study, as well as with the guidelines for responding to textual questions for which there are no clear-cut, "scientific" answers. He adds, on the other hand, that when *yeshivah* learning avoids using the tools of critical scholarship, it fails to imitate the *talmud torah* of the Mishnaic and Talmudic sages, who made use of the powerful interpretive tools of their age to help them discern the subtler meanings of the Torah texts. In this context, one could say that the overall goal of Halivni's work has been *tikkun torah* as his way of "mending the broken bond" that links Torah study and Torah life.

Consistent with this goal, he has devoted his energies to practical, communal work as well as to scholarship. He is cofounder and rector of a rabbinical seminary — the Institute of Traditional Judaism in Teaneck, New Jersey — and he has become Rav of a Shabbat minyan in the Upper

Westside of Manhattan (with a growing congregation of observant Jews, many of them students and young professionals). This practical side of Halivni's work is worth noting, because his study of Torah reflects theological judgments that cannot simply be deduced through some formal method of inquiry. His judgments are made by a whole person — grounded, to be sure, in a life of text study, but offered just as intently for the sake of upholding living communities of Jews. To form such judgments, moreover, he has had to reflect on a lifetime of experiences, including those that bring memories of unimaginable suffering.

Halivni spent his childhood in the Jewish community of Sighet, in the Carpathian Mountains. He was famous for his Talmudic erudition even as a child, and even before his rabbinic ordination at the age of fifteen. But Hungarian Jewry had already begun to suffer the effects of Nazism several years before this, and in 1944 he was deported, first to a ghetto, then to Auschwitz, later to the forced labor camp of Wolfsberg in Gross-Rosen, then to the death camp of Ebensee. Most of his family perished in Auschwitz, and he writes that, of his grandfather's sixty-five children and grandchildren, only five survived the camps. Inside the camps, he continued to teach Mishnah from memory, but, as he recounts in his memoirs, the environment was hardly one in which he could open his mind to new levels of learning Torah.

Did God Forgive Adam?
An Exercise in Comparative Midrash

JON D. LEVENSON

I

Among the hoary stereotypes about Judaism that are still alive and well today in Christian or post-Christian lands, the notion that its God is a God of wrath and judgment, rather than love and forgiveness, is surely one of the most widespread. It is closely connected to the image of Judaism as a religion of law as that term is generally understood in the modern West — a religion, that is, of rules and procedures that may or may not serve a larger moral purpose but, in and of themselves, are cold, mechanistic, and unfeeling: like God, like religion. Theoretically, I suppose, there could exist a community of warm, generous, forgiving people devoted to this angry, merciless God and to the fulfillment of the rigid legalistic norms that they believe he has revealed. The historical record exhibits, however, a remarkable correspondence between the stereotype of Judaism to which multitudes of Christians have subscribed and the stereotype of the Jews that those Christians hold. The demand of the most memorable Jew in Western literature, Shakespeare's Shylock, for his "pound of flesh," for example, is hardly unrelated to the Jewish God's equally unforgiving, equally legalistic character. "I stand for judgment," Shylock tells the Venetian duke, "Answer; shall I have it?" Some verses later in the same scene, we encounter a highly revealing *double entendre,* one that encapsulates the connection of Judaism to the Jews in a mere five words. "I stand here for law,"

Shylock announces.[1] Whatever Shakespeare may have meant by that last sentence, in the light of the history of the Christian view of Judaism, Shylock does indeed stand for law, for the Jewish Torah as perceived by its Christian enemies, with all its odious and repugnant features. There is, to be sure, something to the distinction between anti-Judaism and anti-Semitism, but the historical record argues that the distinction is rarely observed: like God, like worshipers; like Judaism, like Jews.

To a small degree before the Holocaust and increasingly afterwards, some Christians have striven mightily and honorably to correct these stereotypes. I am thinking, to give but one example among many that might be cited, of the "Guidelines for Lutheran-Jewish Relations" promulgated by the Evangelical Lutheran Church in America. "Blame for the death of Jesus should not be attributed to Judaism or the Jewish people," it advises, "and stereotypes of Judaism as a legalistic religion should be avoided."[2] It is not difficult to find the source of the first misconception. The notion that the Jews are to blame for Jesus' execution is found in the New Testament itself. "And the whole people said in reply," reports the Gospel according to Matthew, "His blood be upon us and our children" (Matt. 27:25).[3] A wide range of historians, including some devout Christians, have argued compellingly that the report is highly unlikely, its main purpose being to shift the blame for Jesus' death from the Romans, who had political power, to the Jews, who lost what little they had with their defeat in the war of 66-73 C.E.[4] In short, what the Gospels, in their own diverse ways, depict as the Jewish scapegoating of Jesus actually involved no small measure of Christian scapegoating of the Jews. Nonetheless, for millennia Christians not only credited this charge but also interpreted it maximally. They thought it referred not just to the Jews who supposedly demanded Jesus' death, and not just to their Jewish contemporaries who were far from the scene at the time, but even to the descendants of the

1. *The Merchant of Venice,* Act IV, scene i.

2. Evangelical Lutheran Church in America, "Guidelines for Lutheran-Jewish Relations," n.p. (cited 20 December 2001). Online: http://www.elca.org/ea/interfaith/jewish/guidelines.html

3. Unless otherwise noted, all scriptural quotations are taken from the New American Bible. The edition I have used is *The Catholic Study Bible* (New York: Oxford University Press, 1990).

4. See E. P. Sanders, *Jesus and Judaism* (Philadelphia: Fortress Press, 1985), pp. 294-318.

malefactors, presumably throughout all their generations.[5] Some Christians so interpret it to this day.

The second stereotype of which the Lutheran statement warns, "Judaism as a legalistic religion," also has roots in the New Testament, as in the following example:

> Woe to you, scribes and Pharisees, you hypocrites. You pay tithes of mint and dill and cummin, and have neglected the weightier things of the law: judgment and mercy and fidelity. [But] these you should have done, without neglecting the others. Blind guides, who strain out the gnat and swallow the camel! (Matt. 23:23-24; cf. Luke 11:42-44)

Here again, the actual historical record is more complex; indeed, the difficulty of determining just what "Pharisees" meant in the time of the evangelists makes this one of the most obscure and controverted points in New Testament studies. Jesus' actual historical relationship to the Pharisees (a somewhat different question) is not much clearer.[6] Whatever be the resolution of this longstanding conundrum, it is crucial to recognize that it is irresponsible in the extreme to identify Judaism in its broad sweep with the mindless observance of legal minutiae, to the exclusion of larger issues of justice, compassion, and faithfulness. That some Jews succumbed to the universal temptation of mindless observance of ritual is, of course, likely. That whole parties of Jews did so strains credulity. But even if this be the case, a generalization of this sort about Judaism, even about Judaism in late antiquity, is dangerously irresponsible. Note, for example, that both the Babylonian and the Jerusalem Talmuds include passages that speak ill of that subgroup of the Pharisees whose observance of Torah is exaggerated for effect or motivated by a desire for reward.[7] The proper motive for Torah observance, rather, is love, the love of God who gave the Torah to Israel and, not incidentally, commanded Jews to love their neighbors as themselves (Lev. 19:18). According to a passage in the Jerusalem Talmud (also known as the Palestinian Talmud, or the Talmud of the Land of Israel), the model for emulation is not Job, who acted from fear

---

5. One classical discussion is Jules Isaac, *The Teaching of Contempt: Christian Roots of Anti-Semitism* (New York: Holt, Rinehart, and Winston, 1964); see especially pp. 109-47.

6. See, e.g., Sanders, *Jesus and Judaism,* pp. 270-93.

7. *b. Sota* 22b; *y. Ber.* 9:5.

of punishment, but Abraham, who acted from love, not fear, and transformed his baser instinct into a positive one.[8]

Though the two stereotypes are related (as we have seen), the image of Judaism as a legalistic religion must, nonetheless, be carefully distinguished from the equally widespread notion that the God of the Jews is a God of wrath and judgment, rather than forgiveness and mercy. One difference is that whereas the former stereotype has some rooting in the New Testament, that anthology does not speak of two Gods, in the manner, let us say, of the opposition in Israelite prophetic literature between the God of Israel and the Canaanite Baal.[9] The claim of the early Christians was not that a new God had revealed himself to them, but rather that the God of Israel — the God of the Jews — had revealed himself more fully, indeed definitively, in the one that the Christians called "Jesus Christ." This claim of a fuller revelation is the foundation of what has come to be known as Christian "supersessionism," the theology that sees the putative new revelation as transcending and surpassing the old, rendering it obsolete. This does not imply that the old revelation was not "holy and righteous and good," to use Paul's words about the Law (Rom. 7:12), in its allotted time. Nor does it deny that the new revelation depends in some important sense upon the old. It is to imply, however, that the status of the old has changed dramatically in light of the new and fuller disclosure.

Although supersessionism is often presented as a uniquely Christian phenomenon, the question it answers is universal: If the preceding order was altogether adequate, why should a new one have come into existence and why should anyone adhere to it? Indeed, the religion of the Hebrew Bible itself displays elements of supersession.[10] I am thinking, for example, of the report that God first disclosed his proper name only to Moses, and not to Abraham, Isaac, and Jacob before him (Exod. 6:2-3), or of Moses' injunction to Israel to institute a new altar law once they have crossed into the promised land after his death and to follow it forever (Deut. 12:8-14). The difference is that, whereas the Hebrew Bible offers, in general, a high estimation of Isaac, Jacob, and Moses[11] (though none of them is

8. *y. Ber.* 9:5.

9. E.g., 1 Kings 18:1-40.

10. See Jon D. Levenson, "Is There a Counterpart in the Hebrew Bible to New Testament Anti-Semitism?" *Journal of Ecumenical Studies* 22 (1984): 242-60.

11. See R. W. L. Moberly, *The Old Testament of the Old Testament* (Minneapolis: Fortress Press, 1992), pp. 79-146.

portrayed as flawless or God-like), the New Testament and (even more) subsequent Christian tradition deliver fierce attacks on the Jews and their religion. This is the unhappy legacy that many faithful Christian groups are struggling to overcome.

Such Christians instinctively turn to the anathematization of Marcion for support. Marcion, a formidable Christian writer of the early second century C.E., saw a radical discontinuity between Judaism and Christianity, based on the notion that the God of the Hebrew Bible and the God of Jesus were not identical. It was, of course, the God of Jesus whom Marcion believed to be the higher and truer deity, the God of the Gospel rather than of the Law, the God of love rather than mere justice, of the spiritual world and not the carnal. Thus, when the church branded Marcion and his teachings (which long survived him) heretical, so the reasoning goes, it reaffirmed its connection to Judaism and its God and distanced itself from supersessionism.

This appeal to the anathema on Marcionism has a point, but logically, it need not undermine Christian supersessionism in the least. There is no reason that an affirmation that the same God spoke and acted in the Old as in the New Testament must undermine the orthodox Christian belief that Christianity represents a higher and fuller revelation of God than Judaism, even the Judaism of the Old Testament. And, indeed, that conviction was dominant in the church that anathematized Marcion's teachings, a church in which supersessionism was every bit as *un*problematic as it is problematic among sensitive Christians today.

Marcion has often been seen as a radical Paulinist, one who made Paul's antithesis of faith in Jesus Christ versus the works of the Law the keynote of his whole theology, refusing to allow the other notes and different perspectives that existed in the early church to compromise the pristine gospel of the apostle to the gentiles. Whether Paul, had he lived to hear Marcion, would have regarded the new theology as a logical extension of his own is open to considerable doubt. What cannot be doubted, however, is that Paul at times also sees a sharp opposition between the old order and the new, with the old representing the negative pole and the new representing the positive. Paul's interpretation of human history from its beginning to its end is probably his most pointed example of this chronological dualism, the dualism of the ages:

Therefore, just as through one person sin entered the world, and through sin, death, and thus death came to all, inasmuch as all sinned — for up to the time of the law, sin was in the world, though sin is not accounted when there is no law. But death reigned from Adam to Moses, even over those who did not sin after the pattern of the trespass of Adam, who is the type of the one who was to come. But the gift is not like the transgression. For if by that one person's transgression the many died, how much more did the grace of God and the gracious gift of the one person Jesus Christ overflow for the many. And the gift is not like the result of the one person's sinning. For after one sin there was the judgment that brought condemnation; but the gift, after many transgressions, brought acquittal. For if, by the transgression of one person, death came to reign through that one, how much more will those who receive the abundance of grace and the gift of justification come to reign in life through the one person Jesus Christ. In conclusion, just as through one transgression condemnation came upon all, so through one righteous act acquittal and life came to all. For just as through the disobedience of one person the many were made sinners, so through the obedience of one the many will be made righteous. The law entered in so that transgression might increase but, where sin increased, grace overflowed all the more, so that, as sin reigned in death, grace also might reign through justification for eternal life through Jesus Christ our Lord. (Rom. 5:12-21)

What is most striking for our purposes is the unrelieved grimness of the old order, the order that "reigned" from Adam to Jesus, in Paul's theology of history. On the basis of the other passages in Paul's letters (including the previous chapter) in which it is faith that conveys righteousness, one would have expected an exception to be made for Abraham and the mode of spirituality of which he had become emblematic.[12] In that case, Paul would have seen sin as reigning over all from the time Adam first opened the door to it — except, that is, for those who, like Abraham, had faith and were thus reckoned as righteous. But such is not the case in our passage, in which Abraham is conspicuous for his absence. Romans 5:12-21 is thus a major obstacle in the way of the Lutheran reading of Paul, the reading that sees justification by faith as the heart and soul of the apostle's theology. When Paul concentrates on Abraham and faith, it is for another

12. See also Galatians 3.

situation, when he must counter the argument that the Torah ("the Law") and its commandments must be observed — the heart and soul of Judaism, if you will. But that claim is not at issue in his review of human history here in Romans 5.

Not that the inadequacy of the Torah is absent from his mind here. "Death reigned from Adam to Moses" (v. 14), but Moses did nothing — here the contrast with rabbinic tradition is diametric and striking — to reverse the process. Indeed, it is striking that Paul moves from this verse directly to his introduction of his antidote to those dire things that he associates with Adam — sin, disobedience, condemnation, and death. The antidote is "the gracious gift of the one person Jesus Christ" (v. 15), the new Adam through whom the effects of the old Adam are, by some unspecified process, more than reversed. In other words, where we expect to find a reflection on Moses, we find instead an extended reflection on Jesus. To be sure, the Torah does make a cameo appearance in v. 20 ("the law entered in so that transgression might increase"), but this negates rather than affirms any notion that the Torah might serve as an antidote to the negatives associated with Adam. Paul's point is that the Torah functions as a kind of bill of indictment, itemizing and tabulating sin in the form of individual violations of its hundreds of commandments. This is, in a way, a positive role, I suppose, since persons of conscience want to know exactly what they have done wrong. But in Paul's theology, the Torah — whatever its original or even currently positive role — in no way contributes to healing the catastrophic rupture in the divine-human relationship that the story of Adam reports. For Paul, the Torah is part of the problem; it is not part of the solution.[13] Here, as we have remarked and will see again, the contrast with rabbinic Judaism could not be sharper. For the rabbis, the Torah is a sign and even an agent of healing in the relationship between humankind and God.

The grim view of life between Adam and Jesus that Paul propounds in Romans 5:12-21 (and subsequent Christian theology forcefully develops) has given many the impression that Paul is deeply pessimistic. The impression has been especially strong among Jews, who often contrast

13. In the post-Holocaust world, the idea has grown that Paul's negative view of the Torah applies to gentiles but not to Jews. The severe weakness in this well-intentioned but inattentive reading of Paul is succinctly summarized in Brendan Byrne, "Interpreting Romans Theologically in a Post-'New Perspective' Perspective," *Harvard Theological Review* 94, no. 3 (2001): 227-41, esp. p. 228, n. 10.

Paul's supposed pessimism with the optimism about human potential supposedly characteristic of Judaism.[14] Judaism, we are told, has no doctrine of original sin; people are as good or as bad as they choose to be, and God is not so much a judge exercising mercy upon sinners as he is humankind's partner in the upbuilding and perfecting of the world.

Later, we shall have occasion to challenge this cheery view of Judaism. Our point at present is that the popular contrast also misconceives Christianity. In the text under discussion, for example, Paul is emphatic that the power of sin has been broken. Obedience has replaced disobedience, justification has replaced condemnation, and eternal life has replaced death, the inevitable consequence of sin in Paul's theology. The pessimism accurately describes the old order. The new order, the order that "Jesus Christ our Lord" has brought about in Paul's own lifetime, is a bright and happy one indeed. Or, rather, it is for those who move from the old to the new, from the Adamic mode of being to the Christic.

But what precisely is it about the new Adam, "Jesus Christ our Lord," that has worked this dynamic reversal, transforming universal punishment into (possible) universal acquittal, judgment into mercy? Many Christians will have an immediate answer, based on other New Testament authors or other Pauline texts. Some will point to faith, citing Paul's assertion in the preceding chapter that the story of Abraham demonstrates that "faith is credited as righteousness" (Rom. 4:5). On this reading, Jesus' faith — "the faith of Christ" in the sense of the faith Christ himself has, a faith foreshadowed in Abraham's — makes sinners righteous and thus defeats death and awards the palm to eternal life. The problem, however, is one on which we have already remarked: in Romans 5:12-21, "death reigned from Adam to Moses, even over those who did not sin after the pattern of the trespass of Adam" (v. 14), and that includes Abraham. Faith, in fact, is nowhere mentioned in this passage; Paul here provides no exemption for those who rely on faith rather than the works of the Law. Until Jesus' time — which is Paul's own time — death reigned

---

14. See, e.g., Abba Hillel Silver, *Where Judaism Differed: An Inquiry into the Distinctiveness of Judaism* (Philadelphia: Jewish Publication Society, 1957), pp. 165-66; Trude Weiss-Rosmarin, *Judaism and Christianity: The Differences* (1943; rpt. New York: Jonathan David, 1972), pp. 48, 39; and Joel S. Kaminsky, "Paradise Regained: Reflections on Israel at Sinai," in *Jews, Christians and the Theology of the Hebrew Scriptures,* ed. Alice Ogden Bellis and Joel S. Kaminsky (Atlanta: Society of Biblical Literature, 2000), pp. 15-43, esp. pp. 15-18, 39-43.

over *all,* the faithful Abraham included. The Torah, as we have seen, itemizes for Paul the sin of which death is the just wage. But replacing Torah with faith does not, in this passage, constitute an effective strategy for attaining righteousness.

In order to account for the sudden reversal that, according to the passage, has taken place, other Christians, persuaded that the classical Augustinian-Lutheran emphasis on faith fails to explain our text, will point to the theology of Jesus' death as sacrificial. According to this familiar line of thinking, Jesus' death served as an expiation for sin and thus converted the moral debits of those who believe in him into the equivalent of moral credits. This idea is so well known in the history of Christianity, from the Gospels on, that it hardly needs documentation. And, indeed, a variety of it is prominent in Paul too, appearing, for example, in Romans itself:

> But now the righteousness of God has been manifested apart from the law, though testified to by the law and the prophets, the righteousness of God through faith in Jesus Christ for all who believe. For there is no distinction; all have sinned and are deprived of the glory of God. They are justified freely by his grace through the redemption in Christ Jesus, whom God set forth as an expiation, through faith, by his blood, to prove his righteousness because of the forgiveness of sins previously committed, through the forbearance of God — to prove his righteousness in the present time, that he might be righteous and justify the one who has faith in Jesus. (Rom. 3:21-26)

The problem, however, is that Romans 5:12-21 displays none of the characteristic language of sacrificial redemption — no "expiation" *(hilasterion)* there, no redemption "by blood," indeed, no "forgiveness of sins," either. This is not, of course, to deny that Paul believed in the expiatory power of Jesus' life-blood or in the efficacy of faith to effect righteousness, for that matter. It is, rather, to say that importing those notions into the midrash of the two Adams in Romans 5:12-21 is an unjustified act of harmonization that silences the powerful theology that Paul therein articulates.

The answer to the question of what effects the momentous reversals of Romans 5:12-21 lies in the structure and language of the text itself. The generative contrast in this passage is, I submit, that between "the disobedience *(parakoē)* of one person," namely, Adam, and "the obedience *(hypakoē)* of one," namely, Jesus (v. 19). If so, then those who stress faith against works have radically misunderstood Paul here (and doubtless elsewhere as well). For the factor that moves God from condemnation to exoneration, and humankind from sin to righteousness and from death to life eternal, truly is a deed, a "work," if you will — the work of Jesus' eschatological obedience undoing the fruits of Adam's protological sin.[15] This is not to deny that the grace of God is essential to Paul's vision in Romans 5:12-21, just as it is elsewhere. Here, however, grace takes the form of God's imputing the righteousness of Jesus to the credit of those whose own behavior resembles not his, but Adam's (vv. 15-19). From their perspective, from the perspective of the exonerated sinners, this is indeed an altogether free gift: they have done nothing to deserve it and everything to merit the dire fate of Adam instead. But from God's perspective, the gift is not at all unmotivated. What motivates it is "the obedience of one," the act, the deed, the "work" of Jesus that undoes the calamitous act of Adam. The exoneration is thus earned, but not by those who profit from it. It is simultaneously God's just response and a gracious gift — and as such, by the way, it has striking parallels in Judaism.[16]

Given the symmetry of this tale of two Adams, one should expect the deed that turns the tide at the end to be the opposite of the deed that put humankind on their lethal course in the beginning. Now, Adam's catastrophic offense derived from a desire (certainly his wife's and probably his own as well) to be "like gods [or, God] knowing good and evil" (Gen. 3:5).[17] It was, in other words, born of a Promethean refusal to accept the subordinate status of creaturehood. Adam sought the divine knowledge of his creator and got, of course, more than he had bargained for (cf. Ezek. 28:1-19). It has often been noted that the Pauline (or, more likely, pre-Pauline)[18] hymn in Philippians 2:6-11 portrays Jesus in quite the opposite way:

15. However unfamiliar or objectionable this may sound to Lutherans or those who have absorbed a Lutheran understanding of Paul, it will not be so to all readers. My student and research assistant, J. Randall Short, who has expertly reviewed the manuscript of this essay, tells me that "this is basically what I am accustomed to hearing in Calvinistic contexts."

16. See Solomon Schechter, *Aspects of Rabbinic Theology: Major Concepts of the Talmud* (New York: Schocken, 1961), pp. 170-98.

17. I depart from the New American Bible to facilitate the point I am making.

18. See Dieter Georgi, "Der vorpaulinische Hymnus Phil 2,6-11," in *Zeit und Geschichte,* ed. Erich Dinkler (Tübingen: J. C. B. Mohr/Paul Siebeck, 1964), pp. 263-93.

Who, though he was in the form of God,
did not regard equality with God something
to be grasped.
Rather, he emptied himself,
taking the form of a slave,
coming in human likeness;
and found human in appearance,
he humbled himself,
becoming obedient to death,
even death on a cross.
Because of this, God greatly exalted him
and bestowed on him the name
that is above every name,
that at the name of Jesus
every knee should bend,
of those in heaven and on earth and under
the earth,
and every tongue confess that
Jesus Christ is Lord,
to the glory of God the Father.

If the contrast holds, then whereas Adam sought to make himself the equal of God, casting off servitude and the fear of death (death being the punishment specified for disobedience to this command in Gen. 2:16-17), Jesus divested himself of his divine nature and accepted servitude and death as well, a gory one at that. The great paradox is that, in Paul's thinking, this resulted in Jesus' revivification, exaltation, and lordship — the very things he, unlike Adam, had not sought (cf. 1 Kings 3:10-14).

In Romans 5:12-21, the two figures on which all history turns, Adam and Jesus, are more than historical. Each is the first of many others who will partake of his nature and whose nature is also somehow determined, or at least influenced, by the archetypal figure. Paul, in short, here sets out two modes of human existence, the Adamic and the Christic, hoping, as befits an apostle, that his readers and hearers will choose to move from the former to the latter — from the condition of natural humanity, defined by disobedience, sin, condemnation, and death, to that of eschatological humanity, defined by obedience, righteousness, acquittal, and eternal life. As Karl Barth puts it in his commentary to our passage, "If a man be *in Adam,* he is an old, fallen, imprisoned creature: if he be *in*

Christ, he is a creature, new, reconciled and redeemed."[19] The homiletical power of this schema cannot be gainsaid; Christian preachers have benefited from it for nearly two millennia.

The assumption that the two existential modes, the Adamic and the Christic, are contemporaneous is one that Paul shares. What he does *not* share is the assumption that they have always been so.[20] For were the Christic mode available before Jesus' pivotal act of self-emptying — were human beings able, that is, to pass from condemnation to acquittal without his intervention — then Jesus accomplished nothing original, and the good news that Paul proclaims, though good, is hardly new. To the extent that Jesus becomes a metaphor for certain eternally available modes of being (as many liberal Christians make him),[21] the wind goes out of the sails of Paul's evangelism. For in Paul's thinking, the Christic option is very new indeed, and in dramatic opposition to what preceded it in the period from Adam to Jesus. The very contemporaneity of the two modes of being, the sinful and lethal Adamic and the righteous and life-conferring Christic, is a new situation brought about by Jesus' recent challenge to Adam's fateful disobedience.

Within this christocentric understanding, one can indeed speak, as Christians do, of the good news that God's "forgiveness" (though Paul does not use that term) has triumphed. The other side of the coin, however, is the bad news that sin had reigned unchallenged from Adam to Jesus, Abraham's faith and Moses' Torah notwithstanding. The good news, to put it directly, is that Jesus saves. The bad news is that everything else damns, since there was no forgiveness before his great reversal of universal sin. To any reader of the Scriptures (as Paul would call the book that Christians would later term the "Old Testament"), this is, to be sure, a puzzling claim. For Paul's Scriptures offer abundant evidence that their God is, in the words of Exodus 34:6-7, "a merciful and gracious God, slow

---

19. Karl Barth, *Epistle to the Romans,* 6th ed. (London: Oxford University Press, 1933), p. 165.

20. Contrast Barth (*Epistle to the Romans,* p. 171): "Adam has no existence on the plane of history and of psychological analysis. He exists as the first Adam, as the type of the second Adam who is to come, as the shadow cast by His light."

21. See, e.g., John Hick, *Disputed Questions in Theology and the Philosophy of Religion* (London: Macmillan, 1993), pp. 35-57, for an attempt to found a Christology on the mode of religiousness of the historical Jesus rather than on the putatively objective effects of his life and death.

to anger and rich in kindness and fidelity, continuing his kindness for a thousand generations, and forgiving wickedness and crime and sin." What would Paul say, for example, about Cain, who, despite having committed cold-blooded murder, escapes the death penalty and lives by the protection of the selfsame God to whom his slain brother's blood called out (Gen. 4:8-16)? Or of David, whose life is similarly spared, though he is guilty of adultery and murder (both capital offenses in biblical law), and who is allowed to keep the woman with whom he has sinned and even to beget his heir through her (2 Sam. 12:7-25)? Or of Abraham, whom, as we have seen, Paul describes elsewhere as declared innocent by virtue of his faith (Gal. 3:1-22; Rom. 4:1-25)? It might be countered that in the cases of Cain and David, the Scriptures speak only of a gracious reduction of the penalty, and not of forgiveness. But even if this be so, what are we to make of the case of Abraham, in which they speak (at least in Paul's reading) of full-fledged justification?

The answer lies in Paul's famous affirmation that "the wages of sin is death" (Rom. 6:23). Whatever boons God may have conferred on Cain, David, and Abraham, all three of these scriptural figures are dead. None has been resurrected, as Paul believes Jesus has, and therefore the wages for their sin are still being paid. Only with Jesus' resurrection is death, "the last enemy," vanquished (1 Cor. 15:20-28). Only then is sin, which Paul associates inextricably with death, truly reversed.

Now the origins of the Christian anti-Jewish stereotype with which we began our investigation should be clear. All one has to do to produce the stereotype is to name the old order, the order from Adam to Jesus, "Judaism," and the new order, the one inaugurated by the risen Christ, "Christianity." So doing, one finds that the God of the Jews is a God of judgment and wrath, forgiving no one, whereas the God of the Christians is a God of mercy and reconciliation, offering forgiveness to all who move from the old mode of being to the new. The good news of Paul's gospel is the bad news that Judaism offers no hope of salvation. This entails another piece of bad news — that those Christians who can conceive of Judaism only through the schema of Christian salvation history will (even if their intentions are the best and the kindest) inevitably subscribe to a grossly distorted and pernicious image of Judaism.

II

In Judaism, the issues of sin and forgiveness, death and life, though they pervade the liturgical year, lie at the very center of the dynamics of Rosh Ha-Shanah, the autumnal New Year's festival. Rosh Ha-Shanah (which in Jewish law is a two-day festival, even in the land of Israel) begins the ten days of repentance, which conclude with Yom Kippur, the day of atonement. The governing notion is that God judges the world on Rosh Ha-Shanah, deciding its fate, "who shall live and who shall die," in the words of one of the most gripping and haunting texts in its liturgy. If the verdict is negative, repentance, prayer, and charity can still set it aside. On Yom Kippur, the fate inscribed on Rosh Ha-Shanah is sealed.

Two themes dominate Rosh Ha-Shanah, a cosmogonic and a forensic. The cosmogonic theme hails the New Year's Day as the anniversary of creation, or, as the liturgy puts it, as "the birthday of the world." The forensic theme speaks of it as the day of judgment, a kind of dress rehearsal for the cosmic Last Judgment and for the day when each of us will at last have to give an accounting of his or her life before the court of our all-seeing and inerrant Maker.

The two themes come together in striking fashion in a rabbinic passage that, like Romans 5:12-21, centers on the sin of Adam and the manner by which it can be reversed:

> "On the first day of the seventh month you shall keep a Sabbath rest" (Lev 23:24). This bears on what is written in Scripture: "Your word, O LORD, endures forever; it is firm as the heavens" (Psalm 119:89). It was taught in the name of R. Eliezer: The world was created on the twenty-fifth of Elul. [The view of Rab agrees with the teaching of R. Eliezer. For we have learned in the Shofar Benediction composed by Rab: "This day, on which was the beginning of work, is a memorial of the first day, 'for it is a statute for Israel, a decree of the God of Jacob' (Psalm 81:5). Thereon also sentence is pronounced upon countries, which of them is destined to the sword and which to peace, which to famine and which to plenty; and each separate creature is visited thereon, and recorded for life or death."] Thus you are left to conclude that on New Year's Day, in the first hour the idea of creating man entered His mind, in the second He took counsel with the Ministering Angels, in the third He assembled Adam's dust, in the fourth He

kneaded it, in the fifth He shaped him, in the sixth He made him into a lifeless body, in the seventh He breathed a soul into him, in the eighth He brought him into the Garden of Eden, in the ninth he was commanded [against eating of the fruit of the tree of knowledge], in the tenth he transgressed, in the eleventh he was judged, in the twelfth he was pardoned. "This," said the Holy One, blessed be He, to Adam, "will be a sign to your children. As you stood in judgment before Me this day and came out with a free pardon, so will your children in the future stand in judgment before Me on this day and will come out from My presence with a free pardon." When will that be? "On the first day of the seventh month" (Lev 23:23.)

(*Leviticus Rabbah* 29:1)[22]

The passage is a *petichta'* (literally, "opening," often rendered into English as "proem"), that is, a brief discourse apparently intended to open the public Torah reading. In this case, the reading begins at Leviticus 23:23, which speaks of the sanctity of the first day of the seventh month, a day that rabbinic tradition will come to call Rosh Ha-Shanah.[23] The convention of the *petichta'*, however, requires the rabbinic preacher to end with the first verse of the lection that he is introducing and to begin his own introductory discourse with a verse far afield from it — or at least ostensibly so. For a major part of his challenge is to work from the introductory to the concluding verse by a chain of midrashic logic that is compelling and, ideally, fresh and unexpected. And this is exactly what our *dashan* (rabbinic preacher) does in the passage under consideration.

He begins with Psalm 119:89, but certainly assumed that his congregation knew the ensuing verses:

Your word, O LORD, endures forever;
   it is firm as the heavens.
Through all generations your truth endures;
   you have established the earth, and it stands firm:

22. The translation is taken from *The Midrash Rabbah,* ed. H. Freedman and Maurice Simon (London: Soncino Press, 1977), *Leviticus Rabbah,* pp. 369-70. I have adjusted the biblical citations to the New American Bible. The same midrash, with only very minor differences in wording, can be found in the *Pesikta de-Rab Kahana* 23:1.

23. In rabbinic Judaism, the autumnal Rosh Ha-Shanah is one of four New Year's Days. The counting of months begins on a less well known vernal New Year's Day six months earlier — hence the anomaly of a Rosh Ha-Shanah, or New Year's Day, on 7/1.

According to your ordinances *(mishpateyka)*
    they still *(hayyom)* stand firm;
    all things serve you.

(Ps. 119:89-91)

In these verses, the ancient Jewish community listening to this *petichta'* for Rosh Ha-Shanah could not but have heard allusions to both the cosmogonic and the forensic themes that jointly dominate the theology of the occasion. In verse 89, they could hear of God's creating the heavens through his word, a word that their tradition at times regarded as preexistent and identified with the Torah.[24] Similarly, in verse 90, they hear of God's creating the earth. So much for the cosmogonic theme. With some slightly creative philology, verse 91 can be read — and almost certainly was so read by the rabbinic author — as an allusion to Rosh Ha-Shanah as a day of judgment:

For judgment *(mishpateyka)*, they stand
this very day *(hayyom)*;
everyone is your servant.

I hasten to note that this is not the plain sense interpretation of the verses, which make no reference at all to Rosh Ha-Shanah. In fact, in the Hebrew Bible, the first day of the seventh month is never identified as a New Year's Day or in any way associated with either the cosmogonic or the forensic themes of the rabbinic autumnal New Year. To say this, however, is not to say that the interpretation fails, but rather to say that if it succeeds, it succeeds as *midrash,* not as a plain sense exegesis *(peshat).*

Immediately after the citation of Psalm 119:89, we hear a teaching of Rabbi Eliezer, probably Rabbi Eliezer ben Hyrkanus, a major figure in Palestinian Jewry a generation or two after the destruction of the temple (he died about 120 C.E.). Rabbi Eliezer held that the world was not created on Rosh Ha-Shanah, as one might have thought, but six days earlier, on the twenty-fifth of the twenty-nine-day month of Elul.[25] The material

---

24. E.g., *Ber. Rab.* 1:1.

25. Elsewhere (e.g., *b. Rosh Hash.* 11a), he is said to have defended an autumnal date for creation against Rabbi Joshua's advocacy of a vernal date. See Jon D. Levenson, *Creation and the Persistence of Evil: The Jewish Drama of Divine Omnipotence,* rev. ed. (Princeton: Princeton University Press, 1994), pp. 66-77.

163

I have placed in brackets, probably an interpolation,[26] goes on to connect with certain key aspects of the Rosh Ha-Shanah liturgy. When the interpolation is finished, we read an hour by hour account of the creation and sin of Adam on the sixth day of creation. The midrash, in other words, telescopes the events of Genesis 2:4–3:24, the creation of Adam (and Eve),[27] into 1:26-28. It is not, that is, that groups of men and women were created simultaneously on the sixth day of creation, as Genesis 1 would have it, nor that Adam was created according to a time schema independent of the six days of Genesis 1, as in Genesis 2. Rather, the creation of man in 1:26-28 is interpreted to incorporate the events narrated in 2:4–3:24, even the eating of the fruit of the forbidden tree.

As we have had occasion to note, it has often been observed, mostly by liberal apologists for Judaism, that the Christian doctrine of original sin finds scant resonance in Jewish tradition.[28] If the point is that Judaism is optimistic about human nature, regarding the impulse to sin as unrooted in our innate constitution, then the observation is altogether in error and fails to reckon not only with the theological anthropology of the Hebrew Bible but also with the pervasive rabbinic idea of the *yetzer ha-ra'*, or "evil inclination." This is the inborn force within all of us that requires us to engage in a lifelong struggle if we are to do the right thing.[29] In the text at hand, the chronology of Adam's first twelve hours of life profoundly underscores the falseness of the optimistic view. Given his one and only command in the ninth hour, Adam violates it in the tenth! So much for humankind's innate goodness and the alleged optimism of Judaism about human nature.

The creation of Adam over the course of the twelve hours that constitute the day appears in about a dozen passages in rabbinic literature. In almost all of them, after the trial in the eleventh hour (rabbinical courts did not meet at night), he is "driven into exile" when sentence is pronounced in the twelfth, just as one would expect from the conclusion to

---

26. My student David Lambert points out that the citation contradicts Rabbi Eliezer's case, since it appears to assume that creation began on Rosh Ha-Shanah.

27. Note that Eve is blamed for the sin in the Garden of Eden neither here nor in Rom. 5:12-21. Rather, in both texts she is simply unmentioned. Whether this is a comfort or an irritation to the feminist critics of the rabbinic and the early Christian traditions I will leave to them to decide.

28. See n. 14.

29. See Schechter, *Aspects of Rabbinic Theology,* pp. 242-63.

the Garden of Eden story in Genesis 3:22-24. For therein Adam (presumably along with Eve, who is unmentioned) is banished from the Garden of Eden and denied access to the Tree of Life and thus to immortality. What is extraordinary in our passage is that in the twelfth hour — at the last minute, as it were — he goes out from God's presence not condemned, but exonerated, "with a free pardon."[30]

As with Paul's similar midrash in Romans 5:12-21, we must ask what brought about the change. To judge only from the text before us, God's forgiveness would appear to be a free act of grace. Adam, undeniably guilty, goes out a free man. A closer look, however, suggests that his pardon is not quite so arbitrary after all, for it is intended as a "sign" of what is possible on Rosh Ha-Shanah — the exoneration of the guilty, or, in Paul's terminology, "justification." And in rabbinic theology what brings that about is something that is not peculiar to Rosh Ha-Shanah, but available perpetually — *teshuvah,* that immensely difficult psychosocial process designated in English (for lack of a better term) as "repentance." "Returning" or "turning around" might be more accurate.[31] Repentance is not simply a human "work," though it requires enormous effort on the part of sinners. It is, rather, the product conjointly of human effort and the grace of God. This is nicely shown in a midrash on Song of Songs 5:2 ("Open to me, my sister, my beloved, my dove, my perfect one!"):

> Said the Holy One (blessed be He) to Israel: Open to me one opening of repentance, [as narrow] as the point of a needle, and I will open to you openings that wagons and chariots can come through.
>
> (*Song of Songs Rabbah* 5:2)

---

30. For a list and synoptic analysis of passages that deal with the creation, sin, and trial of Adam over the twelve daylight hours of the sixth day, see Anthony J. Saldarini, *The Fathers According to Rabbi Nathan* (Leiden: Brill, 1975), pp. 303-5. Only in our passage (and its variant in *Pes. Rab. Kah.* 23:1) and in *Pesikta Rabbati* 46:1 and *Midrash. Psalms* 92:3 is the outcome other than expulsion from Eden. In the latter two texts, Rosh Ha-Shanah or the Sabbath intercedes to the benefit of Adam condemned. Only in *Lev. Rab.* 29:1 (= *Pes. Rab. Kah.* 23:1) does he emerge a free man, however. On the Second Temple background of the rabbinic and the Pauline views of Adam alike, see John R. Levison, *Portraits of Adam in Early Judaism: From Sirach to 2 Baruch,* Journal for the Study of the Pseudepigrapha Supplement Series 1 (Sheffield, UK: Sheffield Academic Press, 1988).

31. See Schechter, *Aspects of Rabbinic Theology,* pp. 313-43.

Similarly, another midrash notes the opposition between Jeremiah 3:14 ("Return, rebellious children, says the LORD") and Psalm 90:13 ("Return, O LORD! How long?"). Both verses employ the verbal form of the root *(shuv)* from which *teshuvah* is derived, yet they are at cross purposes, since one speaks of God's calling on Israel to return and the other of Israel's calling on God to return. Herewith the reconciliation proposed in the midrash:

> You will not return by Yourself, nor shall we return by ourselves. Rather, the two of us shall return together, as it is said, "Make us return, O God of our salvation. . . . Will You not return and give us life?" (Ps 85:5, 7)[32]

> *(Midrash. Psalms* 85:3)[33]

III

The striking parallel between Romans 5:12-21 and *Leviticus Rabbah* 29:1 is productive of deeper insights into the fundamental nature of the Jewish-Christian relationship. For we are dealing here with two midrashim that employ the fate of Adam to propound a vision of how sin might be repaired. In the rabbinic text, no less than the Pauline, Adam is the first of many who will partake of his nature and reenact the central drama of his life. Against the liberal Jewish apologetic mentioned earlier, it must be stressed that neither text presents an optimistic view of human nature, but both extend the possibility of a happy conclusion to a relationship defaced by human evildoing. In each case, we read of a transition from the sinful to the innocent state, from condemnation to acquittal. For our purposes, the most notable difference between the two texts concerns the time at which the reversal becomes possible. For Paul, it is with Jesus — that is to say, in his own generation — that the reign of sin came to an end and God's grace was activated. Until then, if God is involved at all, he is the God familiar from the Christian anti-Jewish polemic with which we began our investigation, the wrathful, legalistic, judgmental Deity who is the enemy, not the agent, of redemption. In the rabbinic parallel, the op-

---

32. The translation departs from the New American Bible in order to bring out the point of the midrash.

33. See Schechter, *Aspects of Rabbinic Theology,* pp. 326-28.

posite obtains. The two modes — the mode of human rebellion and divine judgment and the mode of human repentance and divine forgiveness — have coexisted from literally the first day of human existence. God's grace is not new, it is not a messianic or eschatological exception to his characteristic behavior, and it does not require a sinless victim in order to be actualized. In the rabbinic vision that underlies this midrash on the trial of Adam, it does not take a messianic intermediary to reestablish the broken relationship with God, because God's nature is forgiving. No one has to die for anyone else's sin, because God's nature is forgiving. God does not have to see blood in order to shed his grace on those children of Adam who sin like their forefather (or worse than he), because, once again, God's nature is forgiving.

In Christianity, there is a long tradition (one deeply implicated in theological anti-Semitism) of portraying the Jews as rejecting God's offer of forgiveness and reconciliation.[34] But our investigation turns the tables and prompts the reverse question: Could Paul have accepted the gracious and forgiving God of rabbinic theology who has kept the gates of repentance open from Adam's time on? Could the apostle, in other words, have accepted a God who forgave Adam?[35] At a minimum, one has to concede that, had he done so, the wind would immediately have gone out of the sails of his evangelism. For it is hardly good news that God is acting as he always has, responding with disproportionate generosity to human attempts (however feeble) to reapproach him in the wake of our transgression and disobedience. To make the latter proclamation is to undercut fundamentally the key assumption of Paul and most other early Christian authors. This is the assumption (itself drawn from Jewish apocalyptic) that reality has altogether changed, or is about to, and a new era, radically discontinuous with the past, is dawning. On this point, when Christians reaffirm their continuity with their Jewish antecedents, they give away one of the most potent weapons in early evangelism, the claim that Jesus Christ alone offers a way out of the wrath and condemnation of the altogether just God of Israel. Where the latter message is preached, however, as it is in most churches throughout the world, the likelihood inevitably

---

34. E.g., Matt. 5:11-12 and John 1:11-13.

35. Some later Christian sources portray Adam as the first person rescued by Jesus from hell (thus retrojecting the new situation onto the beginnings of human life), but this is not the Pauline view.

rises that people will subscribe to the notion that Jews believe in an angry and unforgiving God. How this dilemma can be solved is a question that I cannot address here and is best left to Christian theologians in any case. At the least, however, those who believe that God did not forgive before Jesus need to specify that this is a Christian confessional claim and not in accordance with the Jewish view of the matter.

IV

One of the great dangers in the comparison of religions is that of overgeneralization. In the case at hand, it is imperative to remember that there is more to Christian theology than Paul and more to Jewish views of judgment on Adam than the texts we have examined. It is not just that most of the pertinent rabbinic texts show Adam condemned rather than acquitted in the end, as we have noted.[36] The parallels, rather, go much further. Here, it is instructive to recall that in rabbinic eschatology, the messianic advent and the resurrection of the dead are two central items. Their very conjunction parallels Paul's view that Jesus reversed the death sentence under which humanity had suffered since Adam's sin. Even more germane is the observation of Rabbi Shimon ben Laqish (early third century C.E., land of Israel) that "Adam was," as E. A. Urbach puts it, "both the first man and the last."[37] Another remark of the same rabbi in the same midrashic passage may clarify this and certainly reinforces the suspicion of a Jewish background to Paul's own midrash in Romans 5:12-21. "Said Rabbi Shimon ben Laqish: 'the spirit of God was sweeping over the surface of the waters (Gen 1:2)' — this is the spirit of King Messiah."[38] This makes the Messiah both a protological and an eschatological figure and probably indicates some commonality with Paul's presentation of Adam as a type of Jesus.

These and other parallels notwithstanding, the differing shapes of Judaism and Christianity on the issue of sin and forgiveness do define an opposition that must not be neglected, and certainly not in the name of

---

36. See n. 30.

37. Ephraim E. Urbach, *The Sages: Their Concepts and Beliefs* (Cambridge, MA, and London: Harvard University Press, 1975), p. 230.

38. *Gen. Rab.* 8:1.

interfaith comity. For the overwhelming tendency in the Christian tradition is to see Jesus as playing a critical role, indeed *the* critical role, in the drama of sin and forgiveness. The overwhelming tendency in the Jewish tradition, on the other hand, is to see repentance as effective in reconciling sinners to God — quite without a messianic intervention. And whereas Paul thought that "the law entered in so that transgression might increase" (Rom. 5:20), for the rabbis the Torah and its hundreds of commandments are a potent counter-force to the universal impulse to transgress. As one sage puts it in the Talmud, "The Holy One (blessed be He) created the Evil Inclination; he created Torah as its antidote."[39]

These fundamental, structural differences between Judaism and Christianity cast considerable doubt upon one of the mainstays of Jewish-Christian dialogue as it is conventionally conducted. This is the claim that the two communities agree about God and the Tanakh/Old Testament but disagree about Jesus and the New Testament. Consider the first two themes in the celebrated recent document "*Dabru Emet:* A Jewish Statement on Christians and Christianity" (2000): "Jews and Christians worship the same God" and "Jews and Christians seek authority from the same book — the Bible (what Jews call 'Tanakh' and Christians call the 'Old Testament')."[40] It is no mystery, of course, why some Jewish authorities once saw Christian worship as idolatrous. If Christians consider Jesus to be God in some important sense, as trinitarian theology requires, then the claim that "Jews and Christians worship the same God" is deeply problematic. It is no wonder that *Dabru Emet,* in its eagerness to stress the commonalities of Judaism and Christianity, never once mentions either the doctrine of the Trinity or that of the incarnation. Nor is it a surprise that one important ancient title of Mary — "Mother of God" — also goes unmentioned in this document.[41] But, apart from these considerations, if the God in question is known principally from the biblical

---

39. *b. B. Batra.* 16a.

40. *Dabru Emet,* see pp. 179, 180 below. See Jon D. Levenson, "How Not to Conduct Jewish-Christian Dialogue," *Commentary* 112, no. 5 (December 2001): 31-37.

41. The divinity of the human Jesus was so important to the fathers of the Third Ecumenical Council (431 C.E.) that they placed an anathema on anyone who failed to confess that "the Holy Virgin is the Mother of God." See Henry Denzinger, *The Sources of Catholic Dogma* (St. Louis and London: B. Herder Book Co., 1957), p. 50. If "Jews and Christians worship the same God," why is it that only the latter (and not all of them, of course) venerate his mother?

story, then confronting the differences in the two stories will force us to ask how far the two conceptions of God coincide. For a God who condemned Adam and all his descendants and who gave the Torah (if at all)[42] "so that transgression might increase" is surely not identical to the God who forgave Adam and forgives all who, like him, repent. Nor is it quite the same God who gave Torah in part as an antidote to human sinfulness. Likewise, this difference undermines the claim that Jews and Christians have a book in common. For in each case, the volume that *Dabru Emet* naively calls "the same book" is read through a lens that the other community lacks. The story of Adam read through the lens of Pauline Christianity is not the same as the story of Adam as it appears in Genesis, and neither of them is the same as the story of Adam as read in the Oral Torah of rabbinic Judaism.[43] This is not to deny the importance of reading the Tanakh/Old Testament[44] according to a plain sense that is at odds with both the New Testament and the rabbinic tradition, or Oral Torah. The reading that results, however, will always be rather abstract and academic in comparison with the readings of the flesh-and-blood communities that are the church and the people Israel. For as much as Judaism and Christianity are defined by their common book, they are also defined by mutually exclusive and opposing readings of it. Authentic Jewish-Christian dialogue seeks to do justice not only to the commonalities but also to the oppositions.

42. Note Paul's view in Galatians that the Torah was given through angels, rather than directly by God (Gal. 3:19).

43. See Michael Goldberg, "God, Action, and Narrative: Which Narrative, Action, God?" *Journal of Religion* 68, no. 1 (1988): 39-56.

44. There are, of course, other senses in which the Tanakh and the Old Testament are not the same collection — for example, the order of the books and the presence of Jewish books in the Old Testament of the Orthodox and Roman Catholic Churches that are not canonical in rabbinic Judaism (and, in some cases, may never have been part of any Jewish canon).

Birds Never Sing in This Forest

REIDAR DITTMANN

As a backdrop for these remarks I'd like to remind you of a portion of Psalm 102:

> Hear my prayer, O Lord,
> let my cry come unto thee!
> Do not hide thy face from me
> in the days of my distress!
> For my days shall pass away like smoke,
> and my bones burn like a furnace. . . .
> All the day my enemies taunt me,
> those who deride me use my name like a curse.

In recent years you have heard it proclaimed, seen it written: "There was no Holocaust . . . the idea of such a horrendous act of humanity is a vicious figment of the imagination of International Zionism, created exclusively for the purpose of establishing a Jewish homeland." This pronouncement, issued by a Canadian educator, was seconded and elaborated upon by the executive director of the Red Crescent Society — the Arab equivalent of the Red Cross — who said, "The historical and political importance of the gas chambers for the Jews was the advantage that comes from the benefit of propaganda and international politics. Though the alleged crime is a great historical lie . . . the reparations the Jews received [from it] was a real fact."

The Holocaust as a fictitious product of propaganda is a view advanced by clusters of extremists, here in North America, in the Middle East, and increasingly in contemporary, post-reunification Germany. This unfounded yet carefully calculated claim of hate groups is inspired by well-established, age-old anti-Semitic sentiments, which in the course of time have generated similarly meaningless, precipitously disastrous, although not as overtly monstrous acts of brutality against a group of people with no political power, hence no such base to fall back on. We need only recall the malicious invectives of Martin Luther, the equally church-inspired Spanish inquisition, and in more recent history the imperial Russian pogroms quickly followed by Soviet persecutions. On the everyday level are the thoughtless linguistic invectives and metaphors ("those who deride me use my name as a curse") and the neighborhood vandalism of synagogues and cemeteries, carried out sometimes by individuals acting on their own behalf, but more often by groups advancing a program of self-serving extremist movements. In creative and more sophisticated circles, a sometimes veiled yet often outspoken anti-Semitism is found disturbingly often in English literature, from Shakespeare to Dickens to Agatha Christie and Dorothy Sayers.

A curious, somewhat peripheral, and now historically remote testimony to the same pervasive spirit is found in remote Norway, where members of the National Assembly of 1814, adopting an otherwise exemplary democratic constitution, included this paragraph: "Jews and Jesuits may not enter the kingdom." Shortly thereafter, however, due to the singular effort of Henrik Wergeland, Norway's most distinguished poet, whose clergyman father had authored the paragraph, it was amended, resulting in the entry of small groups of Jews, all but a few of their descendants becoming victims of the Holocaust. (Incidentally, the anti-Jesuit portion of the paragraph, forgotten by the populace, was not eliminated until the 1950s!)

Today such tendencies are further fueled by extremist political parties in Europe. Only two years ago, and with lingering effects to the present, these sentiments were brought out into the open political arena when self-righteous Austria, a nation in its days more thoroughly nazified than even Germany herself, rallied around a neo-Nazi, whose election campaign promised a positive reevaluation of the contribution of the SS.

Of course, the ongoing, unhappy, and ever more problematic situation in the Middle East, where the Israeli presence in a Jewish ethnic homeland long held by an Arab population has led to a precarious and, in its present territorial division, no doubt ultimately untenable status quo, has made the issue even more acute. Yet the Holocaust, the single most dire travesty and tragedy in modern history, does not relate to the current Israeli-Arab conflict, nor is the commemoration of its devastation a matter of interest and meaning to Jews only. It is in fact an observation of singular significance to gentiles as well, reminding all of us, as it does, of our total human frailty, of the limitless potential of our own humanity, threatening each one of us not as a possible victim of anything approaching the horror of that sequence of acts, but clearly demonstrating to us how low we are capable of sinking when determined to further our own misguided patriotic goals — as when, not long ago, we allowed our bombs to fall on the guilty and, as inherent in any massive military action, far more so on the innocent. We and our allies, even in the aftermath of a totally terminated Cold War, unhesitatingly continue to spend billions of our funds on the most sinister tools of destruction ever devised, while refusing, mostly on the grounds of supposed budgetary deficiencies, to lift our hands to alleviate the lot of starving millions.

If you had talked with a German, any German — *die Frau* or *der Mann in der Strasse* — in the early 1930s and had suggested that within a few years the group she or he had so enthusiastically elected to power would take a particular ethnic group of the European population and systematically kill them in proportions far beyond human experience and comprehension, you would, quite understandably, be met with the most emphatic denial and disbelief, rationally based on the premise that one simply does not do such things. Yet it was done, and I was a witness. I saw it done, not by an uninformed, ignorant populace, but by a population like ours, one of the best and most broadly educated nations in the world, a nation of scholars, creative geniuses, religious reformers and philosophers, scientists and humanists, poets and towering musical giants. It was a nation of this spiritual and intellectual quality that built the concentration camps and developed the gases to facilitate the genocide — a nation, so very much like ours, that carried out the Holocaust. So let us not rest on our fading laurels and claim that it could not have happened here.

Strange to say — strange only in view of what would happen in that particular part of Europe — one of the most impressive cultural regions of Germany was the state called Saxe-Weimar, ruled back in the seventeenth and eighteenth centuries by a culturally progressive, benevolent dynasty that opened the doors of its capital city, Weimar, to philosophers, artists, poets, and musicians. Among them were Bach, who came as organist and choir conductor; Goethe, the uncrowned king and leading spirit of modern German culture; and his contemporary Schiller, whose dramas earned him the title "The German Shakespeare." In the history books Weimar was called "The Athens of the North." Following World War I it again became a center of progressive activities, when a broken and defeated Reich, determined to rise from the ashes, wanted to draw up a democratic constitution freed from the shackles of Prussian militarism. Weimar, with its gleaming cultural slate, was chosen as the site of the negotiations and inspired the name of the new realm, the Weimar Republic, the Second Reich.

This revered city is also the gateway to beautiful Ettersbergwald, a tranquil forest region. Here Goethe found peace and inspiration as he wandered in the sylvan woods that reached from his doorstep high up into the Thuringian highlands. Yet in the mid-1930s, the western section of that wanderer's paradise, that cultural reserve, was mercilessly ravaged by the onslaught of another new age, the Third Reich, its ideals quite the opposite of those of the Weimar Republic. Bulldozers mowed down the pines and beeches and stripped the ground of its mossy verdure to make room for a village of gray concrete barracks fanning down the hillside. Built to accommodate those in opposition to the new system, the camp was planned for 3,000 inmates. Yet when I arrived, I entered as number 32,232, and by the time the last captives walked through its gates the number had reached 272,000 — although our population from one day to the next had never exceeded 40,000.

In the deep darkness of a wintry night, at the pre-Stalingrad time in World War II when the Germans were winning on all fronts, I tumbled with hundreds of others, all bewildered and frightened, out of a boxcar after days and nights of confinement. We were herded by pistol-swinging guards and snarling dogs along a broad avenue into the gate area, the narthex, of this temple dedicated to the new German spirit. I saw in the active play of the intersecting beacons of searchlights the camp's motto emblazoned in brass lettering above the towered gateway, *Recht oder Unrecht, mein Vaterland,* a sentiment that struck me then as viciously German, entirely in tune with the spirit that had brought me and thousands of others before me to that ravenously gaping port of entry. It was only much, much later that I learned of its origin. I was astonished to find that it wasn't German at all but American! Stephen Decatur, a naval hero, once lifting his glass to fellow officers, saluted them with this toast: "My country, may she always be right, but right or wrong, my country." In a language as guttural as German, it may sound more belligerent and threatening, *"Recht oder Unrecht, mein Vaterland,"* but let us not forget that we Americans said it the first time, that we suffer from a widespread disease of ultra-patriotism that blunts moral consciousness. Let us not forget that such patriotism gone astray was considered a most fitting apologia for a system, a cause we all abhor, a cause that ultimately brought an entire nation not only to its knees — from which it subsequently and quickly rose again — but to the pits of human depravity.

In the heart of Buchenwald rose a gigantic, then and now entirely naked tree. Having been spared from the devastation necessary to provide space for the building of the camp's iniquitous facilities, the tree in my days was no more than a petrified memento of its former grandeur. Its uniqueness and the cause for its singular survival were spelled out on a bronze plaque placed on its huge gray trunk: *"Hier ruhte Goethe auf seine Wanderungen in diesem Walde"* ("Here Goethe rested on his wanderings in these woods"). While it was nearly impossible in the prevailing surroundings to imagine Goethe as part of such a setting, I succeeded now and then, if only for a fleeting moment, to erase from view my actual day-to-day experience and to envision the great poet, his walking stick placed against the tree and he himself seated in the cool shadow of its generously spreading branches, contemplating the tranquil pastoral landscape cascading down the hillside toward the fertile farmland to the west. Perhaps in that very spot he may have conjured up the transcendental vision expressed in his single most famous short poem, *"Wanderers Nachtlied"*:

Über allen Gipfeln ist Ruh',
In allen Wipfeln spürest du
Kaum einen Hauch.
Die Vöglein schweigen im Walde —
Warte nur, balde
Ruhest du auch.

Two images in this six-line poem speak to us in our present context. The first is this: *"Die Vöglein schweigen im Walde . . ."* ("the birds keep silent in the forest"). In my years in that setting, then only a barren slope carved out of this once-verdant deciduous forest and still surrounded by towering silvery beech trees, once and only once did I hear a bird sing, and then it was the distant plaintive call of the nightingale, a faint elegy as though nature herself was voicing her dismay. And the other is this: *"Warte nur, balde ruhest du auch . . ."* ("Just wait, you too will soon be at rest"). Yes, a certain rest lay ahead, but not the pleasurable unwinding after a day's wandering on the mossy paths in the shelter of a cool, green forest, nor the deserved rest at the end of a working day, but the only rest available to a Buchenwald inmate: death. And not a soothing repose approached in dignity and hope but a deliberate or lingering death that was the inescapable consequence of the most gasping despair and deprivation.

I was there in a seemingly endless sequence of bleak Novembers. There must have been Octobers and Decembers and even Aprils and Mays, winter, spring, and summer, but with all that grayness without and within and no anticipation of a regenerative season, the months and years have floated together into the memory of a perpetual, vacuous, bone-chilling, deathly pale November.

In this community of the doomed, slightly larger than an average prairie town and surrounded by electric fences and beyond them menacing machine gun towers, where hosts of gaunt, emaciated people — a daily average of 40,000 — stalked around like skeletons and where hundreds, sometimes thousands died in a single day, there were rows of gray concrete blocks flanked by gray gravelly lanes extending in regimental order from the roll-call area with its gallows and sooty crematorium chimney down the hillside, past the Goethe Oak, to the grayest place of all, Niederlager, the lower camp, which served as a transit station on each group's way to the gas chambers.

It is one of these relentless, chilly November mornings. Lingering, shivering outside my barracks following the 5:30 reveille, I become aware of a distant grating, rasping dissonance: thousands of clogs shuffling against the frozen gravel, a familiar gray sound entirely in tune with the grim surroundings, only this time more compact, more massive, more threatening than on ordinary days. Masses of inmates, five abreast, begin to pass by on the lane by my barracks. And soon a new, even more ominous sound registers in my ears: the massive mechanical grinding of engines signifying the arrival at the roll-call area of the impatiently waiting mobile gas chambers.

And out there on the frozen lane, passing before me in a mute trance, are these thousands of male members of humanity — the females having been shipped elsewhere. They are the very old, the middle-aged, some in their best years; there are youths of my own age back then, and there are the children, yes, the children, too. Among the aged some are so frail they can no longer walk and need the support of stronger legs and arms, and among the children are the unsteady toddlers holding hands with each other and their elders, and there are many so young they have not yet learned to walk and are carried by fathers or brothers or grandfathers — all in a slow, relentless trek past me and the Goethe Oak, on their way to the waiting vehicles, the mobile gas chambers, near the crematorium.

More than 10,000 took part in that mournful march in the November dawn, all Jews, of course, this time from Hungary, having arrived the night before after a prolonged and tortuous transport from their homeland. And as those morning hours passed and the smoke, dense and never-ending, billowed forth from the crematorium chimney, daylight totally failed to break through — as indeed was proper, because what I witnessed was an act belonging only to the deepest, darkest part of the human condition. In retrospect, the importance of the event for me personally, then and now, is that I did witness this one manifestation of a ritual slaying that was occurring with horrendous and devastating frequency throughout occupied Europe, to the extent that, once it was all over, the continent had been deprived not only of a mass of people greater than the population of many of our American states but also of a major and irreplaceable portion of its productive, creative, and intellectual treasure.

Some years ago in Israel, I walked through a low concrete structure brooding on a hillside beyond the city of Jerusalem, the Yad Vashem, Holocaust Memorial Monument, where eternal flames flicker beside certain names and numbers. The names are those of the concentration camps that were the setting for the genocides, and the numbers are the estimates of the victims in that particular place: Auschwitz and Birkenau, Treblinka and Thersesienstadt, with numbers of incomprehensible magnitude, Ravensbrück and Neuengamme, Dachau and Bergen-Belsen. Even I, a victim and a witness, could not relate to the depth of the tragedy inherent in these dimly lit numbers — until I saw the name of my place, Buchenwald. And as I paused and contemplated that familiar name — in itself so innocuous and innocent, signifying nothing more than the topological nature of its setting, the Beechwoods, once a place of inspiring and poetic silence — and the number next to it, I felt suddenly as though the figures took shape and were transformed into human beings I had once known, if only for a brief hour of a bleak dawn, the young and the mature, the infants and the aged, all rising toward me through the ritual flame and in a massive but mute plea asking to be remembered. And I promised myself then, as I had vowed that very first morning and then over and over again in years to follow, to dedicate and constantly rededicate myself to such remembrance, not a difficult decision to make, for never, never in this life, where I have been so generously showered with blessings and benevolences, will I forget that November dawn on the barren slope below the skeletal forest, where the birds no longer sang and the poet's ancient oak tree had turned to stone. *"Warte nur, balde ruhest du auch. . . ."*

Dabru Emet: *A Jewish Statement on Christians and Christianity*

In recent years, there has been a dramatic and unprecedented shift in Jewish and Christian relations. Throughout the nearly two millennia of Jewish exile, Christians have tended to characterize Judaism as a failed religion or, at best, a religion that prepared the way for, and is completed in, Christianity. In the decades since the Holocaust, however, Christianity has changed dramatically. An increasing number of official Church bodies, both Roman Catholic and Protestant, have made public statements of their remorse about Christian mistreatment of Jews and Judaism. These statements have declared, furthermore, that Christian teaching and preaching can and must be reformed so that they acknowledge God's enduring covenant with the Jewish people and celebrate the contribution of Judaism to world civilization and to Christian faith itself.

We believe these changes merit a thoughtful Jewish response. Speaking only for ourselves — an interdenominational group of Jewish scholars — we believe it is time for Jews to learn about the efforts of Christians to honor Judaism. We believe it is time for Jews to reflect on what Judaism may now say about Christianity. As a first step, we offer eight brief statements about how Jews and Christians may relate to one another.

Jews and Christians worship the same God. Before the rise of Christianity, Jews were the only worshippers of the God of Israel. But Christians also worship the God of Abraham, Isaac, and Jacob; creator of heaven and earth. While Christian worship is not a viable religious choice

179

for Jews, as Jewish theologians we rejoice that, through Christianity, hundreds of millions of people have entered into relationship with the God of Israel.

Jews and Christians seek authority from the same book — the Bible (what Jews call "Tanakh" and Christians call the "Old Testament"). Turning to it for religious orientation, spiritual enrichment, and communal education, we each take away similar lessons: God created and sustains the universe; God established a covenant with the people Israel; God's revealed word guides Israel to a life of righteousness; and God will ultimately redeem Israel and the whole world. Yet, Jews and Christians interpret the Bible differently on many points. Such differences must always be respected.

Christians can respect the claim of the Jewish people upon the land of Israel. The most important event for Jews since the Holocaust has been the reestablishment of a Jewish state in the Promised Land. As members of a biblically based religion, Christians appreciate that Israel was promised — and given — to Jews as the physical center of the covenant between them and God. Many Christians support the State of Israel for reasons far more profound than mere politics. As Jews, we applaud this support. We also recognize that Jewish tradition mandates justice for all non-Jews who reside in a Jewish state.

Jews and Christians accept the moral principles of Torah. Central to the moral principles of Torah is the inalienable sanctity and dignity of every human being. All of us were created in the image of God. This shared moral emphasis can be the basis of an improved relationship between our two communities. It can also be the basis of a powerful witness to all humanity for improving the lives of our fellow human beings and for standing against the immoralities and idolatries that harm and degrade us. Such witness is especially needed after the unprecedented horrors of the past century.

Nazism was not a Christian phenomenon. Without the long history of Christian anti-Judaism and Christian violence against Jews, Nazi ideology could not have taken hold nor could it have been carried out. Too many Christians participated in, or were sympathetic to, Nazi atrocities against Jews. Other Christians did not protest sufficiently against these atrocities. But Nazism itself was not an inevitable outcome of Christianity. If the Nazi extermination of the Jews had been fully successful, it would have turned its murderous rage more directly to Christians. We recognize with gratitude those Christians who risked or sacrificed their lives to save Jews during the Nazi regime. With that in mind, we encourage the continuation of recent efforts in Christian theology to repudiate unequivocally contempt of Judaism and the Jewish people. We applaud those Christians who reject this teaching of contempt, and we do not blame them for the sins committed by their ancestors.

The humanly irreconcilable difference between Jews and Christians will not be settled until God redeems the entire world as promised in Scripture. Christians know and serve God through Jesus Christ and the Christian tradition. Jews know and serve God through Torah and the Jewish tradition. That difference will not be settled by one community insisting that it has interpreted Scripture more accurately than the other, nor by exercising political power over the other. Jews can respect Christians' faithfulness to their revelation just as we expect Christians to respect our faithfulness to our revelation. Neither Jew nor Christian should be pressed into affirming the teaching of the other community.

A new relationship between Jews and Christians will not weaken Jewish practice. An improved relationship will not accelerate the cultural and religious assimilation that Jews rightly fear. It will not change traditional Jewish forms of worship, nor increase intermarriage between Jews and non-Jews, nor persuade more Jews to convert to Christianity, nor create a false blending of Judaism and Christianity. We respect Christianity as a faith that originated within Judaism and that still has significant contacts with it. We do not see it as an extension of Judaism. Only if we cherish our own traditions can we pursue this relationship with integrity.

Jews and Christians must work together for justice and peace. Jews and Christians, each in their own way, recognize the unredeemed state of the world as reflected in the persistence of persecution, poverty, and human degradation and misery. Although justice and peace are finally God's, our joint efforts, together with those of other faith communities, will help bring the kingdom of God for which we hope and long. Separately and together, we must work to bring justice and peace to our world. In this enterprise, we are guided by the vision of the prophets of Israel:

> It shall come to pass in the end of days that the mountain of the Lord's house shall be established at the top of the mountains and be exalted above the hills, and the nations shall flow unto it . . . and many peoples shall go and say, "Come ye and let us go up to the mountain of the

Lord to the house of the God of Jacob and He will teach us of His ways and we will walk in his paths" (Isaiah 2:2-3).

Tikva Frymer-Kensky, University of Chicago
David Novak, University of Toronto
Peter Ochs, University of Virginia
Michael Signer, University of Notre Dame

A *Symposium on* Dabru Emet

WOLFHART PANNENBERG

The Jewish statement on Christianity marks important progress in Jewish-Christian dialogue. The most important of the eight theses is the first one, that "Jews and Christians worship the same God." The implication of this thesis is that the Christian trinitarian doctrine of God is no longer considered a violation of biblical monotheism. The God whom Jesus worshiped and proclaimed was, of course, the one God of Israel, and the trinitarian doctrine of the church does not "associate" something else to this one God, but claims that the one God is one with his revelation in Jesus, as the Hebrew Bible taught that the transcendent God is present in the world through his name, his glory *(kabod),* and his wisdom.

Closely connected with the fundamental acknowledgment that Jews and Christians worship the same God is the second thesis, that both Jews and Christians honor the authority of the Hebrew Bible, though they interpret the words of this book differently. The God whom the Hebrew Bible witnesses, the God of Israel, is also the God to whom Christians pray. Perhaps it should have been mentioned that this is so because the one whom Christians believe to be the Savior of the world was a Jew. That explains the unique relationship between the Christian faith and Judaism in spite of all the quarrels and antagonism between Christians and Jews in the course of history.

Christians, unfortunately, have not always cherished this close relationship with Judaism. There have been tendencies to emancipate the Christian faith from its Jewish origins. At least twice in the course of history those tendencies were connected with the attempt to get rid of the Old Testament, most recently in modern liberal Protestantism. Those tendencies were also connected with playing down the Jewish identity of Jesus and his proclamation of the kingdom of God. Though not directly responsible for Nazism, as thesis five correctly states, the liberal tendency to "dejudaize" the New Testament contributed to the dissemination of anti-Semitic sentiments among Christians.

The history of Christian persecution of Jews was also an effect of the intolerance of Christian dogmatism rooted in a wrong perception of the eschatological finality of God's revelation in Jesus Christ, forgetful of the difference between the present reality and the completion of God's creation in the eschatological future as expressed in the word of the apostle Paul that "now I know in part, then I shall understand fully" (1 Cor. 13:12). If this word had always been duly taken to heart, neither Christian dogmatism nor the lack of toleration regarding Jews and others could have developed.

Thesis four emphasizes correctly that "Jews and Christians accept the moral principles of Torah," though the gentile Christians since Paul no longer observed the other parts of Torah. The reason for preserving the moral principles of Torah was the teaching of Jesus, though he provided a new foundation for those principles by his eschatological proclamation of God's kingdom. Adherence to those principles is also the reason why "Jews and Christians must work together for justice and peace," as the last thesis states. The cautioning note in that thesis, however, is important in that "the unredeemed state of the world" will not finally be overcome except by God himself, and the quote from Isaiah 2:2-3 says explicitly that worship of the one God will be the source of the definitive attainment of justice and (consequently) peace. This is quite different from the secular mentality of our time that expects to bring about justice and peace without God, by merely human efforts.

Given their respect for the promises of the Hebrew Bible, Christians can indeed "respect the claim of the Jewish people upon the land of Israel," as the third thesis affirms. That this does not necessarily entail support for all actions of the Israeli government goes without saying. The relationship with the Arab population of Palestine should not be considered exempt from "the moral principles of Torah" that the next thesis emphasizes as a common concern of Christians and Jews. Particularly, Christians owe solidarity and sympathy to the Christian Arabs who get crushed between the Islamic majority of their own people, on the one hand, and the Israeli government, on the other.

One of the new developments made possible by the reestablishment of a Jewish state in Palestine has been the emergence of groups of "messianic Jews" within Israel, Jews who confess their faith in Jesus the Messiah without leaving the Jewish community and a Jewish way of life. Since the end of the Jewish congregation at Jerusalem in the first century, this is the first time that a Jewish-Christian church reemerges so that a Jew need not turn to a gentile church when he or she comes to believe in Jesus the Christ. The "messianic Jews" intend to remain Jews while professing Jesus to be the Messiah. Sooner or later Christian-Jewish dialogue will have to take notice of this fact, though in general it may remain true that the "difference between Jews and Christians will not be settled until God redeems the entire world," as thesis six affirms. The communities of "messianic Jews" in their own way give testimony to the next thesis, that the "new relationship between Jews and Christians will not weaken Jewish practice." Gentile Christians, in any event, have every reason to rejoice in the continuation and flowering of Jewish practice, because it strengthens and confirms their own sense and appreciation of the Jewish origin of their faith.

DAVID BENTLEY HART

Dabru Emet is a document of such potent terseness that it seems at once to defy analysis and to demand exhaustive commentary; it represents, moreover, so gracious a gesture on the part of its authors that one is little inclined — if one is on the "receiving end" of that gesture — to respond with anything more elaborate than heartfelt thanks. Even so, I shall make a handful of editorial remarks (which it really is not my place to do), because it allows me at least to raise a few questions of what I take to be genuine substance.

As a Christian reader of *Dabru Emet,* I am of course pleased, and even moved, by the contents of the paragraphs that follow most of the document's theses. I might wish that, in the fifth thesis, the clause "Nazism was not an inevitable outcome of Christianity" either had lacked the "inevitable" or, in place of "Christianity," had employed a phrase like "Christian history"; but that is perhaps a cavil. A similar, utterly semantic scruple makes me wish that the preamble had not included the clause "Christianity has changed dramatically": certainly the attitudes of many Christians, and of Christian culture in general, have appreciably altered, but (speaking from the purely doctrinaire side of my nature) I, for one, am no more prepared to say that Christianity has changed than that God has changed. I suppose, as this document is not a statement of Christian belief, that my unease over the eighth paragraph's suggestion that "our joint efforts . . . will help bring the kingdom of God" is irrelevant; but I record it nonetheless. As for the sixth paragraph's rather generous abjuration of dispute over whose interpretations of Scripture are more accurate, I acknowledge its magnanimity, but doubt its practicality (or even propriety). And as an Eastern Orthodox reader, I should like to pretend that the observation in the document's preamble that "Church bodies, both Roman Catholic and Protestant, have made public statements of their remorse" neglects to mention the Orthodox through an oversight; but I must admit, with profoundest shame, that the oversight is entirely ours.

These are all, obviously, small matters. I am not certain that this is so, however, in regard to a phrase that appears in the preamble, to wit: "Christians have tended to characterize Judaism as . . . at best, a religion that prepared the way for, and is completed in, Christianity." Here I want to pause and ponder the implications of what has been said. For one thing, I must observe that, at least in dogmatic terms, this language is not quite precise: the category of *praeparatio* is one traditionally applied to pagan culture; but Judaism, no matter how prone particular Christians might have been to fail to appreciate the fact, was always seen as the unique bearer of God's salvific covenant, into which gentiles had been grafted by the unmerited grace of Christ. It is cold comfort perhaps, but even the coarsest of traditional Christian language regarding the "synagogue's blindness" or the departure of the Angel of the Presence from the temple tended to maintain, if only implicitly, this distinction; and it is a distinction that (in a morally repristinated form) must be kept in mind when considering the issue of whether Christianity "completes" Judaism. After all, to say "completes" is not yet to say "supersedes"; and, more importantly, apart from their belief that in Christ the covenant with Israel is made complete, I very much doubt that Christians have the resources at

186

their disposal for intelligibly affirming that Judaism has not been — and can never be — superseded.

For Christians, to put it bluntly, Christ completes all things: in him lies the axis of the ages; he is the place where time emerges from eternity; he fulfills the act of God in creating, loving, and willing the salvation of the world; and this means, especially, that he completes the great movement of election by which God makes for himself a people. However — for such is the comprehensive and creative purpose of God — the sequence of election is not simply an evolution from more inchoate to more perfect realizations, but a constant pendulation between the most particular moments of God's loving action toward the world and the most universal scope of his intention for the world; or, rather, it is a simultaneous contraction upon and dilation from the unique center of God's election: Jesus of Nazareth. Scripture, after all, tells the story of a single will toward election on the part of God that — partly through the economy of God's inscrutable counsels and partly through the perversity of human hearts — must accommodate itself to an ever narrower set of arrangements. In a sense, creation is the first act of election, the vocation of all things from nonbeing to be the sphere of God's glory, of his indwelling *Shekhinah* — a truly universal call. With the fall of our first parents, however, the possibility of paradise withdraws, and the relation of creatures to God must now be lived out under more limited conditions: labor, discord, parturient pain, and death. From the time of Cain to that of Noah, each generation strays ever farther from God, until God must purge the world of sinful humanity and "begin again," under the conditions of a particular covenant and of certain precise laws. Then, when Babel's tower is built, the still universal accommodation of the Noachide covenant proves insufficient; so God scatters the nations and, after a time, forges a special covenant with one particular people, in the person of Abram. Here, at last, a very limited and guarded space is made for the difficult and even tempestuous working out of that relation between God and humanity that was the original purpose of creation: God clings to this his people, Israel — at times called his bride, his special portion, his son — reveals to them even his secret name, and "fences" them in by giving them, at last, the law, by whose grammar they can learn to respond to his gracious and mighty acts of love toward them. Yet even here the story does not draw to a close: through a long history marked by many estrangements and reconciliations, divisions and apostasies, divine gifts and divine chastisements, dereliction and rescue, God's favor and Israel's fidelity are often strained to the point of nearly breaking, and the figure of the saving remnant takes shape, and of the suffering servant, and of the Messiah (even as, in prophetic and apocalyptic literature, an eschatological horizon of universal redemption is ever more clearly descried). For Christians, obviously, this ever narrower (or perhaps one should say ever more intimate) movement of God toward Israel and Israel toward God culminates in a moment of the most fragile particularity, but also of the purest fidelity: the moment when, at once, the Mother of God's *fiat* perfectly realizes Israel's faith — Israel's nuptial vocation, to be the bride of God, the flesh and temple and people in whom the divine *Shekhinah* comes to dwell — and when the conception within her of the true vessel of that glory, of that glory made flesh, perfectly realizes Israel's eternal election, Israel's vocation, to be the Son of God.

How does all of this stand, though, in relation to the splendid and marmorean paragraphs of *Dabru Emet?* The answer may lie in the document's sixth thesis.

Jon Levenson somewhere remarks that Christianity nowhere so proclaims its Jewish filiation as in its supersessionism. There is some very penetrating — and poignant — truth in this. The constant biblical trope of the firstborn child's displacement, of the favor that belongs by right to the firstborn being passed to another (the most obvious example is that of Esau and Jacob), like Jeremiah's language of a "new covenant," is far more than an incidental feature of scriptural narrative; it testifies to a profound understanding of the oddly elliptical course of God's saving acts. For even within the very particular movement of election, which is the way by which a loving and personal God must act, a delay or divagation seems always to occur, which somehow "sweeps out" to gather in the excluded. Moreover (again, taking Esau and Jacob as our exemplars, but also the two brothers in the parable of the prodigal son), this very act of justice diverted turns out to be — when reconciliation is brought about — only justice delayed, which redounds to the benefit of the proper heir as well. This, at any rate, is how I understand Paul's reflections on church and Israel in the eleventh chapter of Romans (or of the author of Ephesians, in that book's first chapter): that were Israel as a whole to confess Jesus as the Christ, the entire course of God's action as creator and savior would reach its worldly conclusion; the wedding feast would be celebrated, the Kingdom would arrive, and the peace of God would radiate from Zion; but, so that God's love might reach out to embrace also the excluded, the gentiles who have no "natural" claim on God's favor, God has brought about a hardening of hearts, and so yet another delay or divagation occurs, a period of indefinite eschatological suspense, during which the nations have time to enter into the grace of the covenant, before the end arrives, so that when God comes at last to claim his own — the Jews — the gentiles too may be enfolded in his mercy. If this reading of Pauline theology is correct, then *Dabru Emet*'s claim that the "humanly irreconcilable difference between Jews and Christians will not be settled until God redeems the entire world" is merely a tautology.

Which yields, perhaps, a singular ambiguity — or, rather, to resort again to the word I employed above, a pendulation — between two kinds of causal priority. From the divine side, the completion of all things will come in the fullness of time, according to what has been hidden in God from before the ages; but, from the human side, it seems that the privilege belongs to Israel, the unique bearer of God's redeeming promise for the world, to speak the final word — the final *fiat* or *hosanna* — that confirms for all humanity that the covenant is fulfilled, that salvation has appeared, that God is faithful. This is even, perhaps, how one should interpret Christ telling Jerusalem that she will not see him again until she says, "Blessed is he who comes in the name of the Lord!" We tend to read these lines as condemnation, but perhaps, given the ever elliptical and often inverse course of election, we should really read them as promise. Israel abides as the undying witness, the first heir, the bride of youth; and if Paul believed that the end had drawn nigh because the nations were worshiping, through Christ, the God of Israel, he seems also perhaps to have believed that the end will only truly have come when Israel judges that in Christ the hope of the nations has been realized.

I cannot say whether these reflections draw me nearer to or farther away from the spirit of *Dabru Emet;* but I can reiterate that it is only because Christian thought sees in Christ the completion of Judaism that it must see in Judaism the final consummation of creation and the true vessel of Christ's saving acts. And this is not all: Christian dogma interprets the long history of election not simply as a series of actions indifferently related or extrinsic to the divine nature, but as the historical unfolding of the revelation of God's triune identity: Israel, as the bearer of God's glory, law, and name, is his Son; Israel, anointed by and made alive with God's breath, even raised up again from the valley of dry bones by that breath, is the flesh upon which his Spirit comes to rest; in Israel, God draws creation into his own being's eternal circle of love, and graciously makes of creation a place where this eternal love can reach out — "beyond" itself — to draw what would otherwise be excluded into his everlasting "election" of himself. I know that faithful Jews cannot simply adopt this language, but I hope that it makes clear to Jews and Christians alike that, for the church, it is necessary to say not only that God's covenant with Israel endures as long as creation endures, but also that his love of Israel is as eternal as is the Father's love for the Son and Spirit. That is, for faithful trinitarian Christians it is necessary to say that the election of Israel is, in some very real sense, who God is.

DAVID B. BURRELL, C.S.C.

Since the mid-1970s I have been reflecting on the internal relation of Christianity to Judaism, beginning with my work as chair of theology at Notre Dame, where we responded to the gift of a faculty position in Judaica by recasting our doctoral programs in Hebrew Scriptures, apostolic writings (New Testament), and early church to form a collaborative program called "Judaism and Christianity in Antiquity," allowing us to invite the new person in Judaica to enter into our theological inquiry and to learn from one another. Concurrently, a summer program at the Tantur Ecumenical Institute in Jerusalem with Jews, Christians, and Muslims allowed us to explore the meaning of the land while learning how we attempt to live our respective faith commitments. Later, two years in Jerusalem, first at Tantur and then in Beit Yesheyahu (Maison Ste Isaïe), facilitated work at Ratisbonne Center, where I discovered the sharp differences and abiding connections between our respective faith commitments, while tasting the gift of our shared prayer in the Psalms. The message of *Nostra Aetate* proved most startling in the way it underscored Paul's insistence that "God does not take back His gifts nor renege on his promises," when the Christian community had so long relied on other New Testament statements about the new replacing the old (Heb. 8:13), reinforced by pregnant patristic metaphors of shadow/substance or flesh/spirit. Living my way into a Christian faith more consciously shaped by the Hebrew Scriptures, and challenged by experience of the *shabbat*, I found that this encounter could only enrich that faith and renew it from within. So *Dabru Emet* comes as a welcome echo from the other side, as it were, and the more welcome given its origins in three persons whom I have come to know and respect from my heart. The statement itself aptly reflects the appreciation I had come to realize, as a Christian, of Judaism and the faith of my Jewish friends.

Yet there is one discordant note, and I suspect that particular article gave its authors the most trouble as well, for its key words are fatefully ambiguous, beginning with the opening sentence: "The most important event for Jews since the Holocaust has been the reestablishment of a Jewish state in the Promised Land." "Important" is studiedly neutral: one could as well say that the most important event in the history of America was the introduction of the first slaves in the South, for that event presaged a racist society and a bloody civil conflict. Moreover, that "Christians appreciate that Israel was promised — and given — to Jews as the physical center of the covenant between them and God" is celebrated, yet with no mention of the conditions attending that promise and gift. Christians are then applauded for "support[ing] the state of Israel for reasons far more profound than mere politics," but "support" can be mindless unless it be critical, and there is no mention of the central fact that any state — and notably one that assumes a religious adjective — is up for criticism. The opening for such criticism is acknowledged, however: "We also recognize that Jewish tradition mandates justice for all non-Jews who reside in a Jewish state." Yet what happens when that mandate is trampled by the same state? Who can enforce it against the power of that state, and perhaps even more, in the face of the conviction that the very existence of this state is "the most important event for Jews since the Holocaust"? What keeps Jews (and many Christians) from critically assessing injustice committed by this state as they would any other? Are not those voices which feared that the nationalistic dynamic inherent to Zionism would eclipse Torah now sounding prophetic (see Deut. 20:19)? What impelled Yesheyahu Leibowitz to shout "Give it back!" in the wake of the euphoria of 1967, turning from professor to prophet? Having long contended with protagonists as formidable as Judah Magnes and Martin Buber, in arguing for the idea and prospect of a Jewish state, he saw clearly that Israel could not be Jewish (in any normative sense) were it to rule over people whom it could never admit to citizenship, so that failing to return the land taken would sentence the Jewish state to be an occupying power *sine die*. Why have excuses prevailed for more than thirty years? What fears have paralyzed this state, keeping it from being normatively Jewish by forcing it into an atavistic nationalism that leaves this section's final sentence a dead letter? What contortions and betrayal of tradition is "support for Israel" forcing upon the Judaism that this prescient statement wishes to renew in response to the renewal they witness in Christianity?

BARRY CYTRON

The ancient rabbis say, *adam karov etzel atzmo* — "we humans are preoccupied by that closest to us." Though that Hebrew phrase originally applied to a legal setting, a warning to the courts that people may not offer testimony in their own behalf, over time the phrase has taken on a life of its own. In current usage, it speaks to a subtle but manifest truth — that what we say, and frequently do, is shaped by our perch, by who we are and which community we nest within.

Dabru Emet, and especially the book *Christianity in Jewish Terms,* which accompanied release of the statement, seem to contend with but finally accede to that judgment about ourselves. Both declaration and book represent sustained efforts by Jewish thinkers to confront Christian thought with empathy, *on its own terms.* In the end, though, it seems clear that authentic responses require acquiescence to the reality imbedded in that rabbinic adage: we are restrained by the separate worlds, and worldviews, we inhabit.

That seems quite evident in the responses *Dabru Emet* has elicited. For example, in the responses by Messrs. Pannenberg, Burrell, and Hart, with the exception of one substantive mention, none dwelt on what was the most controversial section of the statement for many members of the Jewish community. In fact, some Jews deeply committed to Jewish-Christian dialogue chose not to sign the document because of the wording of paragraph five. Its bold opening assertion that "Nazism was not a Christian phenomenon," and the accompanying thesis, was seen by some Jews (and at least two Christian theologians who have written on it) as an attempt to lift away, perhaps prematurely, the burden of a two-thousand-year history of anti-Judaism. Prof. Pannenberg, alone of the three Christian writers here, addresses that question directly, and Dr. Hart makes a touching brief reference. Both observations are ones that Jews can deeply appreciate.

In Prof. Pannenberg's response, he correctly stresses the importance of the first thesis, that "Jews and Christians worship the same God." To many, this assertion sounds quite uncontroversial, even obvious. Yet the relationship between our two faiths has foundered, in part, on Jewish misunderstandings and confusions about the Trinity and claims for the divinity of Jesus. That we Jews have reached a stage in the rapprochement that such a statement can sustain approval, not only by the authors of *Dabru Emet* but also by the hundreds of rabbis and academics who were co-signers, represents a milestone, a determination on our part to seek understanding of Christian religious categories in a profoundly new way.

In his remarks on "messianic Jews," Prof. Pannenberg touches on a sensitive, hurtful area in interfaith relationships. To many in the Jewish community, the tactics employed by "messianic Jews" to spread their beliefs are often unseemly. Several recent books have documented these efforts at conversion and the ill-will that lingers from such attempts. The guidelines of the Evangelical Lutheran Church in America on Jewish-Christian relationships forthrightly address this issue: "Groups such as 'Jews for Jesus' or 'Messianic Jews' consist of persons from a Jewish background who have converted to Christianity and who wish to retain their Jewish heritage and identity. Lutherans should be aware that most Jews regard such persons as having forsaken Judaism, and consider efforts to maintain otherwise to be deceptive."

It is impossible, therefore, to take any comfort, as does Prof. Pannenberg, that "messianic Jews," as he says, "give testimony to [thesis 7], that the 'new relationship between Jews and Christians will not weaken Jewish practice.'" On one level, that of outward ritual practice, that might seem true. But most Jews would say that groups like "messianic Judaism" and "Jews for Jesus" deeply threaten the Jewish people and its faith.

Dr. Hart has offered an eloquent, theologically sophisticated response, to which I offer but two brief comments. Halfway through his essay, he makes the following observation: "Jon Levenson somewhere remarks that Christianity nowhere so proclaims its Jewish filiation as in its supersessionism." As it turns out, that is not exactly how Prof. Levenson states it in his book *The Death and Resurrection of the Beloved Son.* Here are his words: "Nowhere does Christianity betray its indebtedness to Judaism more than in its supersessionism."

There is a world of difference in meaning between that quoted line and its remembered sense. I fully imagine that Dr. Hart's faith might well have shaped how he read Levenson's actual words. But for this particular Jew, as for Levenson, and for many other Jews devoted to the world of interfaith relations, the original words are the more precise. Any teaching of supersessionism is a betrayal, and history teaches how that breach of faith has had ghastly consequences.

That brings me to a related point. Throughout the last section of his response, Dr. Hart dwells on the issue of divine election. He addresses the question with subtlety and care, appropriately recalling the nuanced way in which Paul speaks of Israel in the book of Romans. As it turned out, I received his essay just a few days before September 11, 2001. In light of all that has unfolded since then, words like "chosen" and "election," the classic terminology of supersessionism and religious triumphalism, seem to ring hollow.

The world appears different, and our religious communities must deal with how religious teachings, for better or worse, matter profoundly in this new time. Some eighty years ago, M. M. Kaplan, a major theologian of American Judaism, urged his co-religionists to eschew the teaching of "election." He did so for many reasons, some wise, others less so. Now, after September 11, his warnings about the dangers of belief in divine election bear a second look, by any and everyone who claims that their tradition has a franchise on the truth.

In addressing the third responder, David Burrell, I write of, and to, a colleague and house guest. There is thus anguish in my heart that his remarks demand serious words of criticism on my part. And not only because he fails to tackle what I hoped he would have done in this assignment. I was truly looking forward to reading his views about *Dabru Emet*. But having read and reread his essay, I still don't know what he makes of the main thrust of the document. He limits his vision to only one issue!

And on that one, about Israel, he spills out the harshest of words. I'll leave it to the wordsmiths to discern the meaning of the word "important." Its use by the authors, when they write "The most important event for Jews since the Holocaust has been the reestablishment of a Jewish state in the Promised Land," seems straightforward enough.

Maybe this might help someone puzzled by the meaning of Israel for today's Jew. As Elie Wiesel has noted, Israel is no answer to the Holocaust, but it seems a response. And as Irving Greenberg has so eloquently written, the Holocaust tragically demonstrated the immorality of being powerless. No longer are the Jews who live in Israel powerless. The Holocaust, says Greenberg, teaches us that no people — none — should ever permit themselves to be so bereft.

To be sure, power is burdensome, oft-times corrupting. As the medieval church demonstrated, those in power often beget moral failure. So too, the Israeli government has sometimes failed to discharge its use of power in the way many of us Jews would have hoped.

But for Prof. Burrell to wrap up his brief against the current intolerable situation by a studied comment on the word "important" and then employ an offensive analogy about "a racist society and bloody civil conflict" is more than a reasonable conversation should expect. Does he not read the very sentence he wrote and hear echoes of the notorious "Zionism is Racism" canard?

More than that, I am confounded by his reference to Martin Buber and Judah Magnes. Is a reader of his response to conclude that those two figures didn't give one whit about the Arab population of that land, and that only Yesheyahu Leibowitz did? I gave Prof. Burrell's essay to a Christian colleague and asked him how he understood what was being said. He surmised that Burrell was implying precisely that: that only Leibowitz was concerned about the Jewish character of a Jewish state, and that Buber and Magnes were oblivious to such concerns, as well as to the plight of the Arab population.

Yet it was Buber and Magnes who risked their political capital to urge a bi-national state upon their fellow citizens of pre-state Israel. They fought tirelessly until their deaths to make Israel a home for two peoples. (See *A Land of Two Peoples: Martin Buber on Jews and Arabs,* ed. Paul R. Mendes-Flohr.) Buber contended, in dozens of letters, speeches, and addresses, with both his fellow Jews in the country and eminent gentile foes outside of it, arguing his belief that Israel could be both a state for Jews as well as a Jewish state, that is, one suffused with the preeminent Jewish values of *Hesed* (compassion) and *Tzedaka* (righteousness).

I still believe it can. So do most Jews I know. Its citizens live in a democracy in which some 60 percent say that there ought to be a Palestinian state. They wonder, as do I, if 6 percent, much less 60 percent, of Arabs in the Middle East are prepared to accept the reality of Israel. They search, as do I, for the Palestinian equivalents of Leibowitz, Buber, and Magnes. Where, they ask, are those voices in the Arab community, and where are those Arab democracies, in which Arabs will speak out for the justice of the Jewish cause, as those three Jews spoke out unswervingly for the justice of the Arab cause?

Rabbinic tradition takes note that Scripture says the following, as Jacob is about to meet his estranged brother Esau: "And Jacob was greatly frightened and distressed." "Why both emotions?" asks the midrash. "Because he was fearful his family might perish, as well as distraught that in defending his family, he might have to harm Esau."

In a world of conflicting responsibilities, this midrash speaks to a daunting demand. We are rightly anxious about the security of those closest to us. But we need to heed other voices, speaking in other rooms, who, out of the terror and history of their lives, yearn for that same security. That midrash offers, I believe, important guidance on two levels: for wrestling with the turmoil of the Middle East, as well as for healing the rift between our two faith communities.

Contributors

CARL E. BRAATEN, Director, Center for Catholic and Evangelical Theology, Sun City West, Arizona

DAVID B. BURRELL, C.S.C., Theodore M. Hesburgh Professor, Professor of Philosophy and Theology, University of Notre Dame, Notre Dame, Indiana

RABBI BARRY CYTRON, Director, Jay Phillips Center for Jewish-Christian Learning

REIDAR DITTMANN, Professor Emeritus of Art History and Norwegian, St. Olaf College, Northfield, Minnesota

DAVID BENTLEY HART, Fellow, Center of Theological Inquiry, Princeton, New Jersey

ROBERT W. JENSON, Senior Scholar for Research, Center of Theological Inquiry, Princeton, New Jersey

JON D. LEVENSON, Albert A. List Peofessor of Jewish Studies, The Divinity School, Harvard University, Cambridge, Massachusetts

GEORGE LINDBECK, Professor Emeritus of Historical Theology, The Divinity School, Yale University, New Haven, Connecticut

RICHARD JOHN NEUHAUS, Editor-in-Chief, *First Things;* President, The Institute on Religion and Public Life, New York, New York

DAVID NOVAK, Director of the Jewish Studies Program, University of Toronto, Toronto, Ontario, Canada

PETER OCHS, Department of Religious Studies, University of Virginia, Charlottesville, Virginia

WOLFHART PANNENBERG, Professor Emeritus of Systematic Theology, Protestant Faculty, University of Munich, Germany

R. KENDALL SOULEN, Professor of Systemic Theology, Wesley Theological Seminary, Washington, District of Columbia

MARVIN R. WILSON, Ockenga Professor of Bible and Theological Studies, Gordon College, Wenham, Massachusetts